Contemporary Issues in Economics and Econometrics

Contemporary Issues in Economics and Econometrics

Theory and Application

Edited by

Ralf Becker
Stan Hurn

School of Economics and Finance
Queensland University of Technology

Edward Elgar
Cheltenham, UK • Northampton, MA, USA

Published by
Edward Elgar Publishing Limited
Glensanda House
Montpellier Parade
Cheltenham
Glos GL50 1UA
UK

Edward Elgar Publishing, Inc.
136 West Street
Suite 202
Northampton
Massachusetts 01060
USA

A catalogue record for this book
is available from the British Library

Library of Congress Cataloguing in Publication Data

Econometric Society. Australasian Meeting (2002 : Brisbane, Qld.)
   Contemporary issues in economics and econometrics ; theory and application /
edited by Ralf Becker and Stan Hurn.
   p. cm.
   "Selected papers from the Australasian Meeting of the Econometric Society, July
2002, hosted by the Queensland University of Technology, Brisbane, Australia."
   1. Econometrics—Congresses. 2. Economics—Mathematical
models—Congresses. I.Hurn, Stan II. Becker. Ralf III. Queensland University of
Technology. IV. Title.

   HB139E2785 2004
   330'.01'5195—dc22

                                                                    2004047956
ISBN 1 84376 617 5

Printed and bound in Great Britain by MPG Books Ltd, Bodmin, Cornwall

Contents

Contributors

Heather Anderson, *Australian National University*
Gunnar Bårdsen, *Norwegian University of Science and Technology*
and Bank of Norway
Ralf Becker, *Queensland University of Technology*
Howard Doran, *University of New England*
Walter Enders, *University of Alabama*
William Griffiths, *University of Melbourne*
R. Carter Hill, *Louisiana State University*
David Hendry, *Nuffield College, Oxford University*
Stan Hurn, *Queensland University of Technology*
Paul Klemperer, *Nuffield College, Oxford University*
Hans-Martin Krolzig, *Nuffield College, Oxford University*
John Marriott, *Nottingham Trent University*
John Naylor, *Nottingham Clinical Research Limited*
Vlad Pavlov, *Queensland University of Technology*
Alicia Rambaldi, *University of Queensland*
Christophe Rault, *UniversityEvry-Val d'Essonne and Sorbonne University*
Pierre Siklos, *Wilfrid Laurier University*
Vladimir Smirnov, *University of Sydney*
Andy Tremayne, *University of Sydney*
Andrew Wait, *University of Sydney*

Foreword

The Australasian Meeting of the Econometric Society is a remarkable conference. The 2002 Meeting in Brisbane welcomed over 200 participants from 20 different countries. Virtually every econometrician from the continent attended, a level of participation that to my knowledge has no rival anywhere else in the world.

That remarkable participation rate is due to the exceptional collection of papers presented and forums for communicating new ideas and results. Although a heavy focus on econometric research and empirical investigations made it a must-attend event for econometricians, first-rate research on economic theory was also well represented at ESAM 2002.

This book, edited by Ralf Becker and Stan Hurn, collects 11 of the very best contributions from this exceptional conference. Reflecting the themes of the conference itself, two of these chapters fall into the category of economic theory, while the other nine are in the area of econometrics or applications. All of the chapters share a high level of practical relevance and usefulness that is sometimes missing in economic research. Indeed, the reader will find that very issue taken up as the theme of Paul Klemperer's delightful chapter, and all five chapters under the heading of 'econometric theory' will be extremely useful for most applied researchers. The volume includes contributions from two of the conference's keynote speakers.

I greatly valued my own opportunity to attend ESAM02 in Brisbane, and thank the conference Co-Chairs Stan Hurn and Allan Layton, in addition to many others on the staff of Queensland University of Technology, whose hard work and organizational efforts helped make this event such a success. I hope the reader will also share my feeling of gratitude toward Ralf Becker and Stan Hurn for putting together this outstanding permanent record of some of the conference's most important contributions.

James D. Hamilton
University of California, San Diego

PART I

Economic Theory

1. Using and Abusing Economic Theory

Paul Klemperer

Economic theory is often abused in practical policy-making. There is frequently excessive focus on sophisticated theory at the expense of elementary theory; too much economic knowledge can sometimes be a dangerous thing. Too little attention is paid to the wider economic context and to the dangers posed by political pressures. Superficially trivial distinctions between policy proposals may be economically significant, while economically irrelevant distinctions may be politically important. I illustrate with some disastrous government auctions, but also show the value of economic theory.

FOREWORD

This is the text of the *Colin Clark Lecture* of the Econometric Society, presented to its Annual Australasian Meeting. It is always an honour to give the *Colin Clark Lecture*, but it was a particular honour in 2002 when the meetings were held in Brisbane where he spent so much of his life, where much of his seminal work was published, and where he was very involved in practical economic policy-making for the Queensland government. Clark always stressed the importance of quantification of empirical facts which, I argue below, is often underemphasized by modern economic theorists.

Indeed in the foreword to his classic work *The Conditions of Economic Progress* (1939), written in Brisbane where this lecture was presented, he wrote:

> It would be laughable, were it not tragic, to watch the stream of books and articles, attempting to solve the exceptionally complex problems of present day economics by theoretical arguments, often without even a single reference to the observed facts ... Theory has a valuable, indeed an essential part to play in the development of economic science. But it must be theory which respects these facts, not tries to supersede them ...
>
> I have ... left my former colleagues in the English Universities ... with dismay at their continued preference for the theoretical ... approach to economic problems. Not one in a hundred ... seems to understand [the need for] the testing

of conclusions against ... observed facts ... The result is a vast output of literature of which it is safe to say, scarcely a syllable will be read in fifty years' time.

I hope he would be pleased that an academic from an English University travelled over 15,000 miles to quote his syllables, well over fifty years after he wrote them.

1. INTRODUCTION*

For half a century or more after the publication of his *Principles* (1890), it was routinely asserted of economic ideas that 'they're all in Marshall'. Of course, that is no longer true of the theory itself. But Marshall was also very concerned with applying economics, and when we think about how to use the theory, the example that Marshall set still remains a valuable guide. Today, therefore, I want to use some of Marshall's views, and my own experience in auction design, to discuss the use (and abuse) of economic theory. [1]

Although the most elegant mathematical theory is often the most influential, it may not be the most useful for practical problems. Marshall (1906) famously stated that 'a good mathematical theorem dealing with economic hypotheses [is] very unlikely to be good economics', and continued by asserting the rules '(1) Translate [mathematics] into English; (2) Then illustrate by examples that are important in real life; (3) Burn the mathematics; (4) If you can't succeed in 2, burn 1'! Certainly this view now seems extreme, but it is salutary to be reminded that good mathematics need not necessarily be good economics. To slightly update Marshall's rules, if we can't (1) offer credible intuition and (2) supply empirical (or perhaps case-study or experimental) evidence, we should (4) be cautious about applying the theory in practice.[2]

*Acknowledgements
I advised the UK Government on the design of its '3G' mobile phone auction and I am a Member of the UK Competition Commission, but the views expressed in this chapter are mine alone. I do not intend to suggest that any of the behaviour discussed violates any applicable rules or laws. This chapter has been improved by an enormous number of helpful comments from Tony Atkinson, Sushil Bikhchandani, Erik Eyster, Nils-Henrik von der Fehr, Tim Harford, Michael Landsberger, Kristen Mertz, Meg Meyer, Paul Milgrom, David Myatt, Marco Pagnozzi, Rob Porter, Kevin Roberts, Mike Rothschild, Peter Temin, Chris Wallace, Mike Waterson and many others.

Furthermore, when economics is applied to policy, proposals need to be robust to the political context in which they are intended to operate. Too many economists excuse their practical failure by saying 'the politicians (or bureaucrats) didn't do exactly what I recommended'. Just as medical practitioners must allow for the fact that their patients may not take all the pills they prescribe, or follow all the advice they are given, so economics practitioners need to foresee political and administrative pressures and make their plans robust to changes that politicians, bureaucrats, and lobbyists are likely to impose. And in framing proposals, economists must recognize that policies that seem identical, or almost identical, to them may seem very different to politicians, and vice versa.

Some academics also need to widen the scope of their analyses beyond the confines of their models which, while elegant, are often short on real-world detail. Marshall always emphasized the importance of a deep 'historical knowledge of any area being investigated and referred again and again to the complexity of economic problems and the naivety of simple hypotheses'.[3] Employing 'know it all' consultants with narrowly focused theories instead of experienced people with a good knowledge of the wider context can sometimes lead to disaster.

One might think these lessons scarcely needed stating – and Marshall certainly understood them very well – but the sorry history of 'expert' advice in some recent auctions shows that they bear repetition. So although the lessons are general ones, I will illustrate them using auctions and auction theory: Auction theory is often held up as a triumph of the application of economic theory to economic practice, but it has not, in truth, been an unalloyed success. For example, while the European and Asian 3G spectrum auctions famously raised over 100 billion euros in total revenues, Hong Kong's, Austria's, the Netherlands', and Switzerland's auctions, among others, were catastrophically badly run yielding only a quarter or less of the per capita revenues earned elsewhere – and economic theorists deserve some of the blame.[4,5] Hong Kong's auction, for example, was superficially well-designed, but not robust to relatively slight political interference that should perhaps have been anticipated. Several countries' academic advisors failed to recognize the importance of the interaction between different countries' auction processes, and bidders advised by experts in auction theory who ignored (or were ignorant of) their clients' histories pursued strategies that cost them billions of euros. Many of these failures could have been avoided if the lessons had been learned to: pay more attention to elementary theory, to the wider context of the auctions, and to political pressures – and pay less attention to sophisticated mathematical theory.[6]

Of course, mathematical theory, even when it has no direct practical application, is not merely beautiful. It can clarify the central features of a problem, provide useful benchmarks and starting points for analysis and – especially – show the deep relationships between problems that are superficially unconnected. Thus, for example, the sophisticated tools of auction theory that have sometimes been abused in practical contexts turn out to have valuable applications to problems that, at first blush, do not look like auctions.

Section 2 briefly discusses what is often taken to be the 'standard auction theory', before discussing its real relevance. Sections 3 to 5 illustrate its abuse using examples from the Asian and European 3G auctions, and discuss the broader lessons that can be drawn from these misapplications. Section 3 is in large part based on Klemperer (2000b, 2002a–d) where many additional details can be found – and this section may be skipped by readers familiar with that material – but the other sections make different points using additional examples. Section 6 illustrates how the same concepts that are abused can have surprisingly valuable uses in different contexts. Section 7 concludes.

2. THE RECEIVED AUCTION THEORY

The core result that everyone who studies auction theory learns is the remarkable *Revenue Equivalence Theorem* (RET).[7] This tells us, subject to some reasonable sounding conditions, that all the standard (and many non-standard) auction mechanisms are equally profitable for the seller, and that buyers are also indifferent between all these mechanisms.

If that were all there was to it, auction design would be of no interest. But of course the RET rests on a number of assumptions. Probably the most influential piece of auction theory apart from those associated with the RET is Milgrom and Weber's remarkable (1982) paper – it is surely no coincidence that this is also perhaps the most elegant piece of auction theory apart from the RET. Milgrom and Weber's seminal analysis relaxes the assumption that bidders have independent private information about the value of the object for sale, and instead assumes bidders' private information is *affiliated*. This is similar to assuming positive correlation,[8] and under this assumption they show that ordinary ascending auctions are more profitable than standard (first-price) sealed-bid auctions, in expectation.

Milgrom and Weber's beautiful work is undoubtedly an important piece of economic theory and it has been enormously influential.[9] As a result, many economists leave graduate school 'knowing' two things about auctions. First, that if bidders' information is independent then all auctions are equally good, and second, that if information is affiliated (which is generally the plausible case) then the ascending auction maximizes the seller's revenue.[10]

But is this correct?

Relevance of the Received Theory

Marshall's (updated) tests are a good place to start. The value of empirical evidence needs no defence, while examining the plausibility of an intuition helps check whether an economic model provides a useful caricature of the real world, or misleads us by absurdly exaggerating particular features of it.[11]

The intuition behind the exact RET result cannot, to my knowledge, be explained in words that are both accurate and comprehensible to lay people. Anyone with the technical skill to understand any verbal explanation would probably do so by translating the words back into the mathematical argument. But it is easier to defend the weaker claim that it is ambiguous which of the two most common auction forms is superior: it *is* easy to explain that participants in a sealed-bid auction shade their bids below their values (unlike in an ascending auction), but that the winner determines the price (unlike in an ascending auction), so it is not hard to be convincing that there is no clear reason why either auction should be more profitable than the other. This is not quite the same as arguing that the standard auction forms are approximately similarly profitable, but the approximate validity of the RET (under its key assumptions) in fact seems consistent with the available evidence. (Some would say that the mere fact that both the ascending auction and the sealed-bid auction are commonly observed in practice is evidence that neither is always superior.) So the 'approximate RET' seems a reasonable claim in practice, and it then follows that issues assumed away by the RET's assumptions should be looked at to choose between the standard auction forms. These issues should include not just those made explicitly in the statement of the theorem, for example bidders are symmetric and risk-neutral, but also those that are implicit, for example bidders share common priors and play non-cooperative Nash equilibrium, or semi-implicit, for instance the numbers and types of bidders are independent of the auction form.

However, as already noted, much attention has focused on just one of the RET's assumptions, namely independence of the bidders' information, and the theoretical result that if information is non-independent (affiliated) then ascending auctions are more profitable than first-price sealed-bid auctions. There is no very compelling intuition for this result. The verbal explanations that are given are unconvincing and/or misleading, or worse. The most commonly given 'explanation' is that ascending auctions allow bidders to be more aggressive, because their 'winner's curses' are reduced,[12] but this argument is plain wrong: the winner's curse is only a feature of common-value auctions, but common values are neither necessary nor sufficient for the result.[13]

A better explanation of the theoretical result is that bidders' profits derive from their private information, and the auctioneer can profit by reducing that private information.[14] An ascending auction reveals the information of bidders who drop out early, so partially reveals the winner's information (if bidders' information is correlated), and uses that information to set the price (through the runner-up's bid), whereas the price paid in a sealed-bid auction cannot use that information. Since the ascending and sealed-bid auctions are revenue-equivalent absent any correlation (that is with independent signals), and provided the runner-up's bid responds to the additional information that an ascending auction reveals in the appropriate way (which it does when information is affiliated), this effect makes the ascending auction the more profitable. Of course, this argument is obviously still incomplete,[15,16] and even if it were fully convincing, it would depend on the *exact* RET applying – which seems a very strong claim.

Furthermore, before relying on any theory mattering in practice, we need to ask: what is the likely order of magnitude of the effect? In fact, numerical analysis suggests the effects of affiliation are often tiny, even when bidders who exactly fit the assumptions of the theory compute their bids exactly using the theory. Riley and Li (1997) analyse equilibrium in a natural class of examples and show that the revenue difference between ascending and first-price auctions is very small unless the information is very strongly affiliated: when bidders' values are jointly normally distributed, bidders' expected rents are about 10 per cent (20 per cent) higher in a sealed-bid auction than in an ascending auction even for correlation coefficients as high as 0.3 (0.5). So these results suggest affiliation could explain why a 3G spectrum auction earned, for example, 640 rather than 650 euros per capita when bidders' valuations were 700 euros per capita. But the actual range was from just 20 (*twenty*) to 650 euros per capita! Riley and Li also find that even with very strong affiliation, other effects, such as those of asymmetry, are more important and often reverse the effects of affiliation, even taking the numbers of bidders, non-cooperative behaviour, common priors, and so on, as given.[17] This kind of quantitative analysis surely deserves more attention than economists often give it.

Finally, all the previous discussion is in the context of single-unit auctions. Perry and Reny (1999) show that the result about affiliation does not hold – even in theory – in multi-unit auctions.[18]

Given all this, it is unsurprising that there is no empirical evidence (that I am aware of) that argues the affiliation effect is important.[19,20]

So there seems no strong argument to expect affiliation to matter much in most practical applications; independence is not the assumption of the RET that most needs relaxing.

The theory that really matters most for auction design is just the very elementary undergraduate economics of relaxing the implicit and semi-implicit assumptions of the RET about (fixed) entry and (lack of) collusion.[21] The intuitions are (as Marshall says they should be) easy to explain – we will see that it is clear that bidders are likely to understand and therefore to follow the undergraduate theory. By contrast the intuition for affiliation gives no sense of how bidders should compute their bids, and the calculations required to do so optimally require considerable mathematical sophistication and are sensitive to the precise assumptions bidders make about the 'prior' distributions from which their and others' private information is drawn. Of course this does not mean agents cannot intuitively make approximately optimal decisions (Machlup, 1946; Friedman, 1953), and individual agents need not understand the intuitions behind equilibrium group outcomes. But we can be more confident in predicting that agents will make decisions whose logic is very clear, especially in one-off events such as many auctions are.

Not surprisingly, practical examples of the undergraduate theory are easy to give (as Marshall also insists). But there is no elegant theory applying to the specific context of auctions; such theory is unnecessary since the basic point is that the main concerns in auctions are just the same as in other economic markets, so much of the same theory applies (see below). Furthermore, some of the key concerns are especially prominent when the assumption of symmetry is dropped, and models with asymmetries are often inelegant.

So graduate students are taught the elegant mathematics of affiliation and whenever, and wherever, I give a seminar about auctions in practice,[22] I am asked a question along the lines of 'Haven't Milgrom and Weber shown that ascending auctions raise most revenue, so why consider other alternatives?' This is true of seminars to academics. It is even more true of seminars to policy-makers. Thus, although a little knowledge of economic theory is a good thing, too much knowledge can sometimes be a dangerous thing. Moreover, the extraordinary influence of the concept of affiliation is only the most important example of this. I give a further illustration, involving over-attention to some of my own work, in the next subsection. In short, a little graduate education in auction theory can often distract attention from the straightforward 'undergraduate' issues that really matter.[23]

3. THE ELEMENTARY ECONOMIC THEORY THAT MATTERS

What really matters in practical auction design is robustness against collusion and attractiveness to entry – just as in ordinary industrial markets.[24] Since I have repeatedly argued this, much of the material of this section is drawn from Klemperer (2000b, 2002a, 2002b) and any reader familiar with these papers may wish to skip to Section 4.

Entry

The received theory described above takes the number of bidders as given. But the profitability of an auction depends crucially on the number of bidders who participate, and different auctions vary enormously in their attractiveness to entry; participating in an auction can be a costly exercise that bidders will only undertake if they feel they have realistic chances of winning. In an ascending auction a stronger bidder can always top any bid that a weaker bidder makes, and knowing this the weaker bidder may not enter the auction in the first place – which may then allow the stronger bidder to win at a very low price. In a first-price sealed-bid auction, by contrast, a weaker bidder may win at a price that the stronger bidder could have beaten, but didn't because the stronger bidder may risk trying to win at a lower price and can't change his bid later. So more bidders may enter a first-price sealed-bid auction.[25]

The intuition is very clear, and there is little need for sophisticated theory. Perhaps because of this, or because the argument depends on asymmetries between bidders so any theory is likely to be inelegant, theory has largely ignored the point. Vickrey's (1961) classic paper contains an example (relegated to an Appendix, and often overlooked) which illustrates the basic point that the player who actually has the lower value may win a first-price sealed-bid auction in Nash equilibrium, but that this cannot happen in an ascending auction (with private values). But little has been said since.

In fact, some of what has been written about the issue of attracting entry provides a further illustration of the potentially perverse impact of sophisticated theory. Although the point that weaker bidders are unlikely to win ascending auctions, and may therefore not enter them, is very general, some work – including Klemperer (1998)[26] – has emphasized that the argument is especially compelling for 'almost-common-value' auctions, and this work may have had the unintended side-effect of linking the entry concern to common values in some people's minds;[27] I have heard economists who know the latter work all too well say that because an auction does not involve common values, therefore there is no entry problem![28] To the extent that the almost-common values theory (which is both of more limited application, and also assumes quite sophisticated reasoning by bidders) has distracted attention from the more general point, this is another example of excessive focus on sophisticated theory at the expense of more elementary, but more crucial, theory.

There is an additional important reason why a first-price sealed-bid auction may be more attractive to entrants: bidders in a sealed-bid auction may be much less certain about opponents' strategies, and the advantage of stronger players may therefore be less pronounced, than standard equilibrium theory predicts. The reason is that in practice, players are not likely to share common priors about distributions of valuations and, even if they do, they may not play Nash equilibrium strategies (that is, a sealed-bid auction induces 'strategic uncertainty'). So even if players were in fact ex-ante symmetric (that is, their private information is drawn from identical distributions) the lower-value player might win a first-price sealed-bid auction, but would never win an ascending auction (in which bidders' strategies are very straightforward and predictable). When players are not symmetric, Nash equilibrium theory predicts that a weaker player will sometimes beat a stronger player in a sealed-bid auction, but I conjecture strategic uncertainty and the absence of common priors make this outcome even more likely than Nash equilibrium predicts. Since this point is very hard for standard economic theory to capture, it has largely been passed over. But it reinforces the point that a sealed-bid auction is in many circumstances more likely than an ascending auction to attract entry, and this will often have a substantial effect on the relative profitabilities of the auctions.

The 3G auctions provide good examples of over-sensitivity to the significance of information revelation and affiliation at the expense of insensitivity to the more important issue of entry. For example, the Netherlands sold five 3G licences in a context in which there were also exactly five incumbent mobile-phone operators who were the natural winners, leaving no room for any entrant. (For competition-policy reasons, bidders were permitted to win no more than one licence each.) The problem of attracting enough entry to have a competitive auction should therefore have been uppermost in planners' minds. But the planners seem instead to have been seduced by the fact that ascending auctions raise (a little) extra revenue because of affiliation and also increase the likelihood of an efficient allocation to those with the highest valuations.[29] The planners were probably also influenced by the fact that previous spectrum auctions in the US and UK had used ascending designs,[30] even though they had usually done so in contexts in which entry was less of a concern, and even though some US auctions did suffer from entry problems. The result of the Netherlands auction was both predictable, and predicted (see, for example, Maasland, 2000, and

Klemperer, 2000b, quoted in the Dutch press prior to the auction). There was no serious entrant.[31] Revenue was less than a third of what had been predicted and barely a quarter of the per capita amounts raised in the immediately preceding and immediately subsequent 3G auctions (in the UK and Germany respectively). The resulting furore in the press led to a Parliamentary Inquiry.

By contrast, when Denmark faced a very similar situation in its 3G auctions in late 2001 – four licences for sale and four incumbents – its primary concern was to encourage entry.[32] (The designers had both observed the Netherlands fiasco, and also read Klemperer, 2000b.) It chose a sealed-bid design (a '4th price' auction) and had a resounding success. A serious entrant bid, and revenue far exceeded expectations and was more than twice the levels achieved by any of the other three European 3G auctions (Switzerland, Belgium and Greece) that had taken place since late 2000.

The academics who designed the UK sale (which was held prior to the Netherlands and Danish auctions) also thought much harder about entry into their 3G auction.[33] The UK had four incumbent operators, and when design work began it was unclear how many licences it would be possible to offer given the technological constraints. We realized that if there were just four licences available it would be hard to persuade a non-incumbent to enter, so we planned in that case to use a design including a sealed-bid component (an 'Anglo-Dutch' design) to encourage entry. In the event, five licences were available so, given the UK context, we switched to an ascending auction, since there was considerable uncertainty about who the fifth strongest bidder would be (we ran the world's first 3G auction in part to ensure this – see Section 5).[34] Thirteen bidders entered, ensuring a highly competitive auction which resulted in the highest per capita revenue among all the European and Asian 3G auctions.

Collusion

The received auction theory also assumes bidders play non-cooperatively in Nash equilibrium. We have already discussed how Nash equilibrium may be a poor prediction because of 'strategic uncertainty' and the failure of the common priors assumption, but a more fundamental problem is that players may behave collusively rather than non-cooperatively. In particular, a standard ascending auction – especially a multi-unit ascending auction – often satisfies *all* the conditions that elementary economic theory tells us are important for facilitating collusion, even without any possibility of interaction or discussion among bidders beyond the information communicated in their bids.

For example, Waterson's (1984) standard industrial organization textbook lists five questions that must be answered affirmatively for firms to be able to support collusion in an ordinary industrial market: (1) can firms easily identify efficient divisions of the market? (2) can firms easily agree on a division? (3) can firms easily detect defection from any agreement? (4) can firms credibly punish any observed defection? (5) can firms deter non-participants in the agreement from entering the industry? In a multi-unit ascending auction: (1) the objects for sale are well-defined, so firms can see how to share the collusive 'pie' among them (by contrast with the problem of sharing an industrial market whose definition may not be obvious), (2) bids can be used to signal proposals about how the division should be made and to signal agreement, (3) firms' pricing (that is, bidding) is immediately and perfectly observable, so defection from any collusive agreement is immediately detected, (4) the threat of punishment for defection from the agreement is highly credible, since punishment is quick and easy and often costless to the punisher in a multi-object auction in which a player has the ability to raise the price only on objects that the defector will win,[35] and (5) we have already argued that entry in an ascending auction may be hard.

So collusion in an ascending auction seems much easier to sustain than in an 'ordinary' industrial market, and it should therefore be no surprise that ascending auctions provide some particularly clear examples of collusion, as we illustrate below.

By contrast, a first-price sealed-bid auction is usually much more robust to collusion: bidders cannot 'exchange views' through their bids, or observe opponents' bids until after the auction is over, or punish defection from any agreement during the course of the auction, or easily deter entry. But, perhaps because auction theorists have little that is new or exciting to say about collusion, too little attention has been given to this elementary issue in practical applications.

In the Austrian 3G auction, for example, twelve identical blocks of spectrum were sold to six bidders in a simultaneous ascending auction (bidders were allowed to win multiple blocks each). No one was in the least surprised when the bidding stopped just above the low reserve price with each bidder winning two blocks, at perhaps one third the price that bidders valued them at.[36] Clearly the effect of 'collusion' (whether explicit and illegal, or tacit and possibly legal) on revenues is first-order.

Another elegant example of bidders' ability to 'collude' is provided by the 1999 German DCS-1800 auction in which ten blocks of spectrum were sold by ascending auction, with the rule that any new bid on a block had to exceed the previous high bid by at least 10 per cent.[37] There were just two credible bidders, the two largest German mobile-phone companies T-Mobil and Mannesmann, and Mannesmann's first bids were 18.18 million deutschmarks per megahertz on blocks 1–5 and 20 million deutschmarks per MHz on blocks 6–10. T-Mobil – who bid even less in the first round – later said

'There were no agreements with Mannesmann. But [we] interpreted Mannesmann's first bid as an offer' (Stuewe, 1999, p.13). The point is that 18.18 plus a 10 per cent raise equals 20.00. It seems T-Mobil understood that if it bid 20 million deutschmarks per MHz on blocks 1–5, but did not bid again on blocks 6–10, the two companies would then live and let live with neither company challenging the other on the other's half. Exactly that happened. So the auction closed after just two rounds with each of the bidders acquiring half the blocks for the same low price, which was a small fraction of the valuations that the bidders actually placed on the blocks.[38]

This example makes another important point. The elementary theory that tells us that 'collusion' is easy in this context is important. The reader may think it obvious that bidders can 'collude' in the setting described, but that is because the reader has been exposed to elementary undergraduate economic theory. This point was beautifully illustrated by the behaviour of the subjects in an experiment that was specifically designed to advise one of the bidders in this auction by mimicking its setting and rules: the experimental subjects completely failed to achieve the low-price 'collusive' outcome that was achieved in practice. Instead '... in [all] the [experimental] sessions the bidding was very competitive. Subjects went for all ten units in the beginning, and typically reduced their bidding rights only when the budget limit forced them to do so' (Abbink et al., 2002). So the elementary economic theory of collusion which makes it plain, by contrast, that the 'collusive' outcome that actually arose was to be expected from more sophisticated players does matter – and I feel confident that the very distinguished economists who ran the experiments advised their bidder more on the basis of the elementary theory than on the basis of the experiments.[39]

Both the UK's and Denmark's academic advisors gave considerable thought to preventing collusion. Denmark, for example, not only ran a sealed-bid auction, but also allowed bidders to submit multiple bids at multiple locations with the rule that only the highest bid made by any bidder would count, and also arranged for phoney bids to be submitted – the idea was that bidders could not (illegally) agree to observe each other's bids without fear that their partners in collusion would double-cross them, and nor could bidders observe who had made bids, or how many had been made.[40]

4. ROBUSTNESS TO POLITICAL PRESSURES

To be effective, economic advice must also be sensitive to the organizational and political context; it is important to be realistic about how advice will be acted on. Economic advisors commonly explain a policy failure with the excuse that 'it would have been okay if they had followed our advice'. But medical practitioners are expected to take account of the fact that patients will not follow their every instruction.[41] Why should economic practitioners be different? Maybe it should be regarded as economic malpractice to give advice that will actually make matters worse if it is not followed exactly.

For example, the economic theorists advising the Swiss government on its 3G auction favoured a multi-unit ascending auction, apparently arguing along the standard received auction-theory lines that this was best for both efficiency and revenue. But they recognized the dangers of such an auction encouraging 'collusive' behaviour and deterring entry, and the advisors therefore also proposed setting a high reserve price. This would not only directly limit the potential revenue losses from collusion and/or inadequate entry but, importantly, also reduce the likelihood of collusion. (With a high reserve price, bidders are relatively more likely to prefer to raise the price to attempt to drive their rivals out altogether, than to collude with them at the reserve price – see Klemperer, 2002b, and Brusco and Lopomo, 2002b.)

But serious reserve prices are often unpopular with politicians and bureaucrats who – even if they have the information to set them sensibly – are often reluctant to run even a tiny risk of not selling the objects, which outcome they fear would be seen as 'a failure'.

The upshot was that no serious reserve was set. Through exit, joint-venture, and possibly – it was rumoured – collusion,[42] the number of bidders shrank to equal the number of licences available, so the remaining bidders had to pay only the trivial reserve price that had been fixed. (Firms were allowed to win just a single licence each.) The outcome was met with jubilation by the bidders and their shareholders; per capita revenues were easily the lowest of any of the nine western European 3G auctions, and less than one-thirtieth of what the government had been hoping for. [43] Perhaps an ascending auction together with a carefully chosen reserve price was a reasonable choice. But an ascending auction with only a trivial reserve price was a disaster, and the economic-theorist advisors should have been more realistic that this was a likely outcome of their advice.[44]

Economic Similarity ≠ Political Similarity

Hong Kong's auction was another case where designers should perhaps have anticipated the political response to their advice. The Hong Kong auction's designers, like Denmark's, had observed the Netherlands fiasco (and had also read Klemperer, 2000b). So they were keen to use a sealed-bid design, given Hong Kong's situation.[45] Specifically, they favoured a 'fourth-price' sealed-bid design so that all four winners (there were four licences and firms could win at most one licence each) would pay the same fourth-highest bid – charging winners different amounts for identical properties might both be awkward and lead to cautious bidding by managements who did not want to risk the embarrassment of paying more than their rivals.[46]

However, the designers were also afraid that if the public could observe the top three bids after the auction, then if these were very different from the price that the firms actually paid (the fourth highest bid), the government would be criticized for selling the licences for less than the firms had shown themselves willing to pay. Of course, such criticism would be ill-informed, but it could still be damaging, because even well-intentioned commentators find it hard to explain to the general public that requiring firms to pay their own bids would result in firms bidding differently. Thus far, nothing was different from the situation in Denmark. However, whereas the Danish government simply followed the advice it was given to keep all the bids secret and reveal only the price paid, the Hong Kong government felt it could not do this.

Openness and transparency of government was a big political issue in the wake of Hong Kong's return to Chinese rule, and it was feared that secrecy would be impossible to maintain. The advisors therefore proposed to run an auction that was *strategically equivalent* (that is, has an identical game-theoretic structure and therefore should induce identical behaviour) to a fourth-price auction, but that did not reveal the three high bids to *anyone*.[47] To achieve this, an ascending auction would be run for the four identical licences, but dropouts would be kept secret and the price would continue to rise until the point at which the number of players remaining dropped from four to *three*. At this point the last four (including the firm that had just 'dropped out') would pay the last price at which four players remained in the bidding. Since nothing was revealed to any player until the auction was over, no player had any decision to make except to choose a single dropout price, in the knowledge that if its price was among the top four then it would pay the fourth-highest dropout price; that is, the situation was identical from the firm's viewpoint of choosing a single bid in a fourth-price sealed-bid auction. But, unlike in Denmark, no one would ever see the 'bids' planned by the top three winners (and since these bids would never even have been placed, very little credibility would have attached to reports of them).

However, although the proposed auction was mathematically (that is strategically) equivalent to a sealed-bid auction, its verbal description was very different. The stronger incumbents lobbied vigorously for a 'small change' to the design – that the price be determined when the numbers dropped from five to four, rather than from four to three.

This is the 'standard' way of running an ascending auction, and it recreates the standard problem that entry is deterred because strong players can bid aggressively in the knowledge that the winners will only pay a loser's bid (the fifth bid) and not have to pay one of the winners' bids.

Revealingly, one of the strong players that, it is said, lobbied so strongly for changing the proposal was at the same time a weaker player (a potential entrant) in the Danish market and, it is said, professed itself entirely happy with the fourth-price sealed-bid rules for *that* market.

The lobbyists' arguments that their suggested change was 'small' and made the auction more 'standard', and also that it was 'unfair' to have the bidders continue to 'bid against themselves' when there were just four left, were politically salient points, even though they are irrelevant or meaningless from a strictly game-theoretic viewpoint.[48] Since the academic consultants who proposed the original design had very little influence at the higher political levels at which the final decision was taken, and since perhaps not all the ultimate decision-makers understood – or wanted to understand – the full significance of the change, the government gave way and made it.[49]

The result? Just the four strongest bidders entered and paid the reserve price – a major disappointment for the government, and yielding perhaps one third to one half the revenue that had been anticipated (allowing for market conditions). Whether other potential bidders gave up altogether, or whether they made collusive agreements with stronger bidders not to enter (as was rumoured in the press), is unknown. But what is certain is that the design finally chosen made entry much harder and collusion much easier.

It is not clear what the economic theorists advising should have recommended. Perhaps they should have stuck to a (fourth-price) sealed-bid auction run in the standard way, but used computer technology that could determine the price to be paid while making it impossible for anyone other than the bidders to know the other bids made.

The moral, however, is clear. Auction designs that seem similar to economic theorists may seem very different to politicians, bureaucrats and the public, and vice versa. And political and lobbying pressures need to be predicted and planned for in advance.

When the designers of the UK 3G auction proposed a design – the Anglo-Dutch – that was very unattractive to the incumbent operators, it probably helped that two alternative versions of the design were initially offered. While the incumbent operators hated the overall design and lobbied furiously against it,[50] they also had strong preferences between its two versions, and much of their lobbying efforts therefore focused on the choice between them. When the government selected the version the operators preferred (the designers actually preferred this version too) the operators felt they had got a part of what they had asked for, and it proved politically possible for the government to stick to the Anglo-Dutch design until the circumstances changed radically.[51]

Another notorious 'political failure' was the design of the 1998 Netherlands 2G spectrum auction. The EU Commission objected to the

Netherlands government's rules for the auction shortly before the (EU imposed) deadline for the allocation of the licences. The rules were therefore quickly rewritten by a high-ranking civil servant on a Friday afternoon. The result was an auction that sold similar properties at prices that differed by a factor of about two, and almost certainly allocated the licences inefficiently.[52]

Economists are now waking up to the importance of these issues: Wilson (2002) addresses political constraints in the design of auction markets for electricity, and Roth (2002) also discusses political aspects of market design. But the politics of design remains understudied by economic theorists, and underappreciated by them in their role as practitioners.

5. UNDERSTANDING THE WIDER CONTEXT

Any consultant new to a situation must beware of overlooking issues that are well understood by those with more experience of the environment. The danger is perhaps particularly acute for economic theorists who are used to seeing the world through models that, while very elegant, are often lacking in real-world detail and context.

The German 3G auction illustrates the importance of the wider context. As we described in Section 3, in Germany's 1999 DCS-1800 auction Mannesmann used its bids to signal to T-Mobil how the two firms should divide the blocks between them and end the auction at a comparatively low price. T-Mobil then cut back its demand in exactly the way Mannesmann suggested, and Mannesmann followed through with its half of the 'bargain' by also cutting back its demand, so the auction ended with the two firms winning similar amounts of spectrum very cheaply.

It seems that Mannesmann used the same advisors in the 3G auction that it had used in the GSM auction. Although the rules for the 3G auction were not identical, it was another simultaneous ascending auction in which individual bidders were permitted to win multiple blocks. After the number of bidders had fallen to six competing for a total of twelve blocks, and when it was clear that the other four bidders would be content with two blocks each, Mannesmann apparently signalled to T-Mobil to cut back its demand to just two blocks.[53] If T-Mobil and Mannesmann had both done this the auction would have ended at modest prices. Instead T-Mobil seemingly ignored Mannesmann's signals, and drove up the total price 15 billion euros before cutting back demand. Once T-Mobil did cut back its demand, Mannesmann followed, so the auction ended with the allocation that Mannesmann had originally signalled but with each of the six firms paying an additional 2.5 billion euros!

It seems that Mannesmann's advisors saw the GSM auction as a template for the 3G auction; they took the view that, following previous practice, Mannesmann would signal when to reduce demand, T-Mobil would acquiesce, and Mannesmann would then follow through on its half of the bargain.[54] The bargain would be enforced by firms not wishing to jeopardize their cooperation in subsequent auctions (including 3G auctions in other countries) and in negotiating with regulators, and so on (and the short-run advantage that could be gained by failing to cooperate was anyway probably small; see Klemperer, 2002c). But given their expectation that T-Mobil would cut back demand first, Mannesmann's advisors were unwilling to reduce demand when T-Mobil did not.

Clearly, T-Mobil's advisors saw things differently. It seems that their main advisors had not been involved in the GSM auction and the example of the previous auction was certainly not in the forefront of their minds. Instead they mistrusted Mannesmann's intentions, and were very unwilling to cut back demand without proof that Mannesmann had already done so. True the 3G auction was a much more complicated game than the GSM auction because of the other parties involved, and Klemperer (2002c) discusses other factors that may have contributed to the firms' failure to reduce demand.[55] But T-Mobil's refusal to cut back demand very likely stemmed partly from viewing the 3G auction in a different, and narrower, context than Mannesmann did.

Just as previous auctions within any country might have been an important part of the wider context, auctions in other countries are also relevant parts of the broader environment: the sequencing of the 3G auctions across countries was crucial. Countries that auctioned earlier had more entrants, because weaker bidders had not yet worked out that they were weaker and quit the auctions, because stronger bidders had not yet worked out how and with whom to do joint-ventures, and because complementarities between the values of licences in different countries reinforced these effects – the number of entrants in the nine western European auctions were (in order) 13, 6, 7, 6, 6, 4, 3, 3, and 5 respectively.[56] Countries that auctioned earlier also suffered less from 'collusive' behaviour, because bidders had had less practice in learning how best to play the game. For example, when the Austrian 3G auction followed the German 3G auction that we have just described, using almost the same design, all the bidders very quickly saw the mutual advantage of coordinating a demand reduction (see Section 3).[57]

The UK government's advisors anticipated this pattern of declining competition, and chose to run its auction first; indeed we persisted in the policy of running the first auction even when others were advising us to delay (see Binmore and Klemperer, 2002). Yet in more than one country auction theorists advising on 3G auction design seemed either unaware of (!), or at least unaffected in their thinking, by the fact that there was to be a sequence of auctions across Europe. Clearly these designers had far too narrow a view of the problem.[58]

Of course, other auctions are only the most obvious aspects of the wider context that auction designers need to consider. There are many other ways in which designers showed themselves very poor at thinking about the wider game. For example, many of the 3G auction designers had a very limited understanding of how the auction process affected, and was affected by, the series of telecom mergers and alliances that the advent of 3G engendered – in the UK alone, there were no fewer than *five* mergers involving the four incumbent 2G operators, in less than a year around the auction.[59]

6. USING ECONOMIC THEORY

I have argued that while a good understanding of elementary undergraduate economic theory is essential to successful auction design, advanced graduate auction theory is often less important. It is important to emphasize, therefore, the crucially important role that advanced formal theory plays in developing our economic understanding. In particular, advanced theory often develops deeper connections between apparently distinct economic questions than are superficially apparent.

For example, Klemperer (2003a) demonstrates that auction-theoretic tools provide useful arguments in a broad range of mainstream economic contexts. As a further illustration, I will discuss how a part of the received auction theory – the effect of affiliation – that was, I have argued, not central to the auctions of 3G licences, can help develop useful insights about the economics of the 'M-Commerce' industry that 3G will create.[60]

Do e-Commerce and M-Commerce Raise Consumer Prices?

Some commentators and regulators have expressed concern that e-commerce and M-commerce ('mobile commerce' in which people purchase through their mobile phones, and which is predicted to expand rapidly as a result of 3G technology) allow firms to easily identify and collect information about their customers which they can use to 'rip them off'.[61]

A simple analysis reveals that each consumer is analogous to an auctioneer, while firms are bidders competing to sell to that consumer. As we discussed in Section 2, bidders' expected profits derive from their private information, and the auctioneer generally gains by reducing the amount of bidders' private information. So if all firms learn the same piece of information about a given consumer, this (weakly) reduces the private information that any bidder has relative to the other bidders, and so often benefits the auctioneer, that is, lowers the consumer's expected transaction price.

Although this result is a good start, it is neither very novel,[62] nor does it address the bigger concern that e-and M-commerce allow different firms to learn different information about any given consumer. However, Bulow and Klemperer (forthcoming) show how to use the mathematics of affiliation to address this issue too; in our model, even if firms learn different information about the consumers, this makes the market more competitive. In other words, a quick application of Milgrom and Weber's (1982) analysis suggests that the 'loss of privacy' caused by 3G and the internet is actually *good* for consumers.

Of course, having been cautious about the practical significance of affiliation in auction design, we should also be cautious about asserting that Bulow and Klemperer's argument shows that 3G is not as valuable to firms as some people once thought.[63] However, our model suggests a possibility which needs further study – including considering any empirical evidence and the plausibility of the intuitions – to confirm or disconfirm. Moreover, it certainly demonstrates that just because firms learn more about consumers, it does not follow that they can exploit them better – just as the RET refutes any simple presumption that one form of auction is always the most profitable. Our analysis therefore shows that firms' learning has other effects in addition to the very obvious one that firms can price-discriminate more effectively, and it helps us to see what these effects are[64] – we can then consider further whether these effects are plausibly significant. It also provides a structure which suggests what other factors not in the simplest model might in fact be important, and might perhaps yield the originally hypothesized result.[65] And it very quickly and efficiently yields results that provide a good starting point for such further analysis.

Bulow and Klemperer pursue these issues in the context of this specific application. Klemperer (2003a) considers a range of other applications, including some that at first glance seem quite distant from auctions. The moral is that the 'received auction theory' *is* of great value in developing our understanding of practical issues. But it needs to be used in conjunction with developing intuition and gathering empirical evidence to check its applicability to specific situations.

7. CONCLUSION

This chapter is *not* attacking the value of economic theory. I have argued that elementary economic theory is essential to successful economic policy. Furthermore, the methods of thinking that undergraduate economics teaches are very valuable, for example, in understanding the important distinction between Hong Kong's two superficially similar auction designs (the one proposed and the one actually implemented). I have focused on examples from auctions, but the more I have been involved in public policy (for example, as a UK Competition Commissioner), the more I have been impressed by the importance of elementary undergraduate economics.

Nor is this lecture intended as an attack on modern, or sophisticated, or graduate economics. True, the emphasis of some graduate courses is misleading, and the relative importance of different parts of the theory is not always well-understood, but almost all of it is useful when appropriately applied; it is *not* true that all economic problems can be tackled using undergraduate economics alone.[66]

Policy errors are also less likely when expertise is not too narrowly focused in one subdiscipline – for example, auction designers should remember their industrial economics and political economy (at least) in addition to pure auction theory.

While advanced theory can be misapplied, the correct answer is not to shy away from it, but rather to develop it further to bring in the important issues that have been omitted. It may sometimes be true that 'a little bit too much economics is a dangerous thing', but it is surely also true that a great deal of economic knowledge is best of all. Moreover auction theory also illustrates that when a subdiscipline of economics becomes more widely used in practical policy-making, its development becomes more heavily influenced by the practical problems that really matter. Like a rapidly growing bush, theory may sometimes sprout and develop in unhelpful directions, but when pruned with the shears of practical experience it will quickly bear fruit!

Furthermore, advanced economic theory is of practical importance in developing our economic understanding of the world, even when it cannot be directly applied to an immediate practical problem. To recapitulate only the incomplete list of its merits that was illustrated by our example in Section 6, it refutes over-simple arguments, makes precise and quantifies other arguments, allows us to see the relationship between superficially unconnected problems, organizes our ideas, brings out the important features of problems, shows possibilities, and quickly develops general results which, even when they are not final answers, provide good starting points for further analysis.

Nevertheless, the main lesson of this chapter is that the blinkered use of economic theory can be dangerous. Policy advisors need to learn from Marshall's example to beware of the wider context, anticipate political pressures and, above all, remember that the most sophisticated theory may not be the most relevant.

NOTES

1. This is also the text of the 2002 *Alfred Marshall Lecture* of the European Economic Association, given at its Annual Congress, in Venice and published in the *Journal of the European Economic Association* (Klemperer, 2003c). It is reproduced here with the kind permission of the European Economic Association and the MIT Press. Marshall and Clark both spent much of their careers in Oxford and Cambridge, and were both very involved in practical economic policy-making. Similar material also formed the core of the biennial 2002 *Lim Tay Boh Lecture* in Singapore. Lim was another very distinguished economist (and Vice-Chancellor of the National University of Singapore), who also made significant contributions to policy as an advisor to the Singapore government. Finally, some of these ideas were presented in the Keynote Address to the 2002 Portuguese Economic Association's 2002 meetings. I am very grateful to all those audiences for helpful comments.
2. I *mean* cautious about the theory. Not dismissive of it. And (3) seems a self-evident mistake, if only because of the need for efficient communication among, and education of, economists, let alone the possibilities for further useful development of the mathematics.
3. Sills (1968, p.28). An attractively written appreciation of Marshall and his work is in Keynes (1933).
4. We take the governments' desire for high revenue as given, and ask how well the auctions met this objective. While an efficient allocation of licences was most governments' first priority, there is no clear evidence of any differences between the efficiencies of different countries' allocations, so revenues were seen as the measure of success. (Binmore and Klemperer (2002, Section 2) argue governments were correct to make revenue a priority because of the substantial deadweight losses of raising government funds by alternative means, and because the revenues were one-time sunk costs for firms so should be expected to have only limited effects on firms' subsequent investment and pricing behaviour.)
5. The six European auctions in year 2000 yielded 100 (Austria), 615 (Germany), 240 (Italy), 170 (Netherlands), 20 (Switzerland), and 650 (UK) euros per capita for very similar properties. True, valuations fell during the year as the stockmarkets also fell, but Klemperer (2002a) details a variety of evidence that valuations ranged from 300 to 700 euros per capita in all of these auctions. Klemperer (2002a) gives a full description of all nine west European 3G auctions.
6. Another topical example of overemphasis on sophisticated theory at the expense of elementary theory is European merger policy's heavy focus on the 'coordinated' effects that may be facilitated by a merger (and about which we have learned from repeated game theory) and, at the time of writing, relative lack of concern about the more straightforward 'unilateral' effects of mergers (which can be understood using much simpler static game theory). (As a UK Competition Commissioner, I stress that this criticism does not apply to UK policy!)
7. The RET is due in an early form to Vickrey (1961), and in its full glory to Myerson (1981), Riley and Samuelson (1981), and others. A typical statement is 'Assume each of a given number of risk-neutral potential buyers has a privately-known signal about the value of an object, independently drawn from a common, strictly increasing, atomless distribution. Then any auction mechanism in which (i) the object always goes to the buyer with the highest signal, and (ii) any bidder with the lowest feasible signal expects zero surplus, yields the same expected revenue (and results in each bidder making the same expected payment as a function of her signal)'.
    Klemperer (1999a) gives an elementary introduction to auction theory, including a simple exposition, and further discussion, of the RET. See also Klemperer (2003b).
8. Affiliation is actually a stronger assumption, but it is probably typically approximately satisfied.
9. Not only is the concept of affiliation important in applications well beyond auction theory (see Section 6) but this paper was also critical to the development of auction theory, in that

it introduced and analysed a general model including both private and common value components.

10. Or, to take just one very typical example from a current academic article 'The one useful thing that our single unit auction theory can tell us is that when bidders' [signals] are affiliated ... the English [i.e. ascending] auction should be expected to raise the most revenue'.

11. Whether the intuition need be non-mathematical, or even comprehensible to lay people, depends on the context, but we can surely have greater confidence in predicting agents' actions when the agents concerned understand the logic behind them, especially when there are few opportunities for learning.

12. The 'winner's curse' reflects the fact that winning an auction suggests one's opponents have pessimistic views about the value of the prize, and bidders must take this into account by bidding more conservatively than otherwise.

13. The result applies with affiliated private values, in which bidders' values are unaffected by others' information, so there is no winner's curse, and the result does not apply to independent-signal common-value auctions which do suffer from the winner's curse. (Where there is a winner's curse, the 'theory' behind the argument is that bidders' private information can be inferred from the points at which they drop out of an ascending auction, so less 'bad news' is discovered at the moment of winning than is discovered in winning a sealed-bid auction, so bidders can bid more aggressively in an ascending auction. But this assumes that bidders' more aggressive bidding more than compensates for the reduced winner's curse in an ascending auction − in independent-signal common-value auctions it exactly compensates, which is why there is no net effect, as the RET proves.) In fact, many experimental and empirical studies suggest bidders fail to fully account for winner's curse effects, so these effects may in practice make sealed-bid auctions more profitable than ascending auctions!

14. Absent private information, the auctioneer would sell to the bidder with the highest expected valuation, and bidders would earn no rents. The more general result that, on average, the selling price is increased by having it depend on as much information as possible about the value of the good is Milgrom and Weber's (1982, 2000) Linkage Principle. However, in more recent work, Perry and Reny (1999) show that the Principle applies less generally (even in theory) than was thought.

15. Revealing more information clearly need not necessarily reduce bidders' profits (if bidders' information is negatively correlated, the contrary is typically true), the conditions that make the ascending price respond correctly to the additional information revealed are quite subtle, and nor does the argument say anything about how affiliation affects sealed bids. Indeed there are simple and not unnatural examples with the 'wrong kind' of *positive* correlation in which the ranking of auctions' revenues is reversed (see Bulow and Klemperer, forthcoming), and Perry and Reny (1999) also show the trickiness of the argument by demonstrating that the result only holds for single-unit auctions. A more complete verbal argument for the theoretical result is given in Klemperer (1999a, Appendix C), but it is very hard (certainly for the layman).

16. Another loose intuition is that in an ascending auction each bidder acts as if he is competing against an opponent with the same valuation. But in a sealed-bid auction a bidder must outbid those with lower valuations. With independent valuations, the RET applies. But if valuations are affiliated, a lower valuation bidder has a more conservative estimate of his opponent's valuation and therefore bids more conservatively. So a bidder in a sealed-bid auction attempting to outbid lower-valuation bidders will bid more conservatively as well. But this argument also rests on the RET applying exactly, and even so several steps are either far from compelling (for example, the optimal bid against a more conservative opponent is not always to be more conservative), or very non-transparent.

17. An easier numerical example than Riley and Li's assumes bidder i's value is $v_i = \theta + t_i$, in which θ and the t_i's are independent and uniform on $[0,1]$, and i knows only v_i. With two bidders, expected revenue is 14/18 in a first-price sealed-bid auction and 15/18 in an ascending auction, so bidder rents are 7/18 and 6/18 respectively (though with n bidders of

whom $n/2$ each win a single object, as $n \to \infty$ bidder rents are 42 per cent higher in the sealed-bid auction).

With very extreme affiliation, an auctioneer's profits may be more sensitive to the auction form. Modifying the previous example so that there are two bidders who have completely diffuse priors for θ, bidder rents are 50 per cent higher in a first-price sealed-bid auction than in an ascending auction (see Klemperer, 1999a, Appendix D), and Riley and Li's example yields a similar result for correlation coefficients around 0.9 (when bidder rents are anyway small). These examples assume private-values. Auctioneers' profits may also be more sensitive to auction form with common-values and, in the previous extreme-affiliation model with diffuse priors on θ, if bidders' signals are v_i and the true common value is θ, bidders' rents are twice as high in the sealed-bid auction as in the ascending auction. But, with common values, small asymmetries between bidders are *very* much more important than affiliation (see Klemperer, 1998 and Bulow and Klemperer, 2002). Moreover, we will see that other effects also seem to have been quantitatively much more important in practice than is affiliation even in any of these theoretical examples.

18. The RET, also, only generalizes to a limited extent to multi-unit auctions.

19. For example, empirical evidence about timber sales suggests rough revenue equivalence, or even that the sealed-bid auction raises more revenue given the number of bidders (Hansen, 1986; Mead and Schneipp, 1989; Paarsch, 1991; Rothkopf and Engelbrecht-Wiggans, 1993; Haile, 1996) though information is probably affiliated. The experimental evidence (see Kagel and Roth, 1995 and Levin, Kagel and Richard, 1996) is also inconclusive about whether affiliation causes any difference between the revenues from ascending and sealed-bid auctions.

20. Like Marshall, Colin Clark (1939) emphasized the importance of quantification and real-world facts (see Foreword to this chapter).

21. See Klemperer (2002b). Risk-aversion and asymmetries (even absent entry issues) also arguably matter more than affiliation (and usually have the opposite effect). It is striking that Maskin and Riley's (1984, 2000) important papers on these topics (see also Matthews, 1983, 1984) failed to have the same broad impact as Milgrom and Weber's work on affiliation.

22. I have done this in over twenty countries in five continents.

23. True, the generally accepted notion of the 'received auction theory' is changing and so is the auction theory that is emphasized in graduate programmes. And recent auctions' research has been heavily influenced by practical problems. But it will probably remain true that the elegance of a theory will remain an important determinant of its practical influence.

24. Of course, auction theorists have not altogether ignored these issues – but the emphasis on them has been far less. The literature on collusion includes Robinson (1985), Cramton, Gibbons and Klemperer (1987), Graham and Marshall (1987), Milgrom (1987), Hendricks and Porter (1989), Graham, Marshall and Richard (1990), Mailath and Zemsky (1991), McAfee and McMillan (1992), Menezes (1996), Weber (1997), Engelbrecht-Wiggans and Kahn (1998), Ausubel and Schwartz (1999), Brusco and Lopomo (2002a), Hendricks, Porter and Tan (1999) and Cramton and Schwartz (2000). That on entry includes Matthews (1984), Engelbrecht-Wiggans (1987), McAfee and McMillan (1987, 1988), Harstad (1990), Engelbrecht-Wiggans (1993), Levin and Smith (1994), Bulow and Klemperer (1996), Menezes and Monteiro (1997), Persico (1997), Klemperer (1998) and Gilbert and Klemperer (2000). See also Klemperer (1999a, 2000a, 2003b).

25. The point is similar to the industrial-organization point that because a Bertrand market is more competitive than a Cournot market for any given number of firms, the Bertrand market may attract less entry, so the Cournot market may be more competitive if the number of firms is endogenous.

26. See also Bikhchandani (1988), Bulow, Huang and Klemperer (1999), Bulow and Klemperer (2002), and Klemperer and Pagnozzi (2003).

27. In spite of the fact that I have made the point that the argument applies more broadly in, for example, Klemperer (1999b, 2002b). See also Gilbert and Klemperer (2000).

28. Similarly others have asserted that the reason the UK planned to include a sealed-bid component in its 3G design if only four licences were available for sale (see later), was because the auction designers (who included me) thought the auction was almost-common values – but publicly-available government documents show that we did not think that this was likely.

29. It seems unlikely that the efficiency of the Netherlands auction was much improved by the ascending design.

30. We discuss the UK design below. The design of the US auctions, according to McMillan (1994, pp.151–2) who was a consultant to the US government, was largely determined by faith in the linkage principle and hence in the revenue advantages of an ascending auction in the presence of affiliation; the economic theorists advising the government judged other potential problems with the ascending design 'to be outweighed by the bidders' ability to learn from other bids in the auction' (McMillan, 1994). (See also Perry and Reny, 1999.) Efficiency was also a concern in the design of the US auctions.

31. There was one entrant who probably did not seriously expect to win a licence in an ascending auction – indeed it argued strongly prior to the auction that an ascending auction gave it very little chance and, more generally, reduced the likelihood of entry into the auction. Perhaps it competed in the hope of being bought off by an incumbent by, for example, gaining access rights to an incumbent's network, in return for its quitting the auction early. The Netherlands government should be very grateful that this entrant competed for as long as it did! See Klemperer (2002a) and van Damme (2002) for details.

32. Attracting entry was an even more severe problem in late 2001 than in early summer 2000 when the Netherlands auction was held. The dotcom boom was over, European telecoms stock prices at the time of the Danish auction were just one third the levels they were at in the Dutch auction, and the prospects for 3G were much dimmer than they had seemed previously.

33. I was the principal auction theorist advising the Radiocommunications Agency which designed and ran the UK auction. Ken Binmore had a leading role, including also supervising experiments testing the proposed designs. Other academic advisors included Tilman Borgers, Jeremy Bulow, Philippe Jehiel and Joe Swierzbinksi. Ken Binmore subsequently advised the Danish government on its very successful auction. The views expressed in this chapter are mine alone.

34. With five licences, the licences would be of unequal size, which argued for an ascending design. Note that in some contexts an ascending design may promote entry. For example, when Peter Cramton, Eric Maskin and I advised the UK government on the design of its March 2002 auction of reductions in greenhouse gas emissions, we recommended an ascending design to encourage the entry of small bidders for whom working out how to bid sensibly in a discriminatory sealed-bid auction might have been prohibitively costly. (Strictly speaking the auction was a descending one since the auction was a reverse auction in which firms were bidding to sell emissions reductions to the government. But this is equivalent to an ascending design for a standard auction to sell permits.) (Larry Ausubel and Jeremy Bulow were also involved in the implementation of this design.). See Klemperer et al. (forthcoming).

35. For example, in a multi-licence US spectrum auction in 1996–97, U.S. West was competing vigorously with McLeod for lot number 378 – a licence in Rochester, Minnesota. Although most bids in the auction had been in exact thousands of dollars, U.S. West bid \$313,378 and \$62,378 for two licences in Iowa in which it had earlier shown no interest, overbidding McLeod, who had seemed to be the uncontested high-bidder for these licences. McLeod got the point that it was being punished for competing in Rochester, and dropped out of that market. Since McLeod made subsequent higher bids on the Iowa licences, the 'punishment' bids cost U.S. West nothing (Cramton and Schwartz, 2000).

36. Although it did not require rocket science to determine the obvious way to divide twelve among six, the largest incumbent, Telekom Austria probably assisted the coordination when it announced in advance of the auction that it 'would be satisfied with just two of the 12 blocks of frequency on offer' and 'if the [five other bidders] behaved similarly it should

be possible to get the frequencies on sensible terms', but 'it would bid for a third frequency block if one of its rivals did' (Crossland, 2000).

37. Unlike my other examples this was not a 3G auction; however, it is highly relevant to the German 3G auction which we will discuss.

38. See Jehiel and Moldovanu, 2001, and Grimm, Riedel and Wolfstetter, 2001. Grimm et al. argue that this outcome was a non-cooperative Nash equilibrium of the fully specified game. This is similar to the familiar industrial organization point that oligopolistic outcomes that we call 'collusive' may be Nash equilibria of repeated oligopoly games. But our focus is on whether outcomes look like competitive, non-cooperative, behaviour in the simple analyses that are often made, not on whether or not they can be justified as Nash equilibria in more sophisticated models.

39. Abbink et al. write: 'The lessons learnt from the experiments are complemented by theoretical strategic considerations'. Indeed, auctions-policy advice should always, if possible, be informed by both theory and experiments.

40. In the UK's ascending auction, the fact that bidders were each restricted to winning at most a single object, out of just five objects, ruled out tacit collusion to divide the spoils (provided that there were more than five bidders). More important, the large number of bidders expected (because the UK ran Europe's first 3G auction – see Section 5) also made explicit (illegal) collusion much less likely (see Klemperer, 2002a), and the fact that the UK retained the right to cancel the auction in some circumstances also reduced bidders' incentive to collude.

41. Doctors are trained to recognize that some types of patients may not take all prescribed medicines or return for follow-up treatment. Pharmaceutical companies have developed one-dose regimens that are often more expensive or less effective than multiple-dose treatments, but that overcome these specific problems. For example, the treatment of chlamydial infection by a single dose of azithromycin is much more expensive and no more effective than a seven day course of doxycycline; there is a short (two month) course of preventive therapy for tuberculosis that is both more expensive, and seems to have more problems with side-effects, than the longer six month course; and the abridged regimen for HIV positive women who are pregnant (to prevent perinatal transmission) is less effective than the longer, more extensive treatment.

42. Two bidders merged the day before the auction was to begin, and a total of five bidders quit in the last four days before the auction. At least one bidder had quit earlier after hearing from its bidding consultants that because it was a weaker bidder it had very little chance of winning an ascending auction. Furthermore, the regulator investigated rumours that Deutsche Telekom agreed not to participate in the auction in return for subsequently being able to buy into one of the winners.

43. In fact, when the denouement of the auction had become clear, the Swiss government tried to cancel it and re-run it with different rules. But in contrast to the UK auction (see Note 40), the designers had omitted to allow themselves that possibility.

The final revenues were 20 euros per capita, compared to analysts' estimates of 400–600 euros per capita in the week before the auction was due to begin. Meeks (2001) shows the jumps in Swisscom's share price around the auction are highly statistically-significant and, controlling for general market movements, correspond to the market believing that bidders paid several hundred euros per capita less in the auction than was earlier anticipated.

44. I am not arguing that an ascending auction plus reserve price is always bad advice, or even that it was necessarily poor advice here. But advisors must make it very clear if success depends on a whole package being adopted, and should think carefully about the likely implementation of their proposals.

Greece and Belgium did set reserve prices that seem to have been carefully thought out, but they were perhaps encouraged to do so by the example of the Swiss auction, and also of the Italian and Austrian auctions which also had reserve prices that were clearly too low, even if not as low as Switzerland's.

45. In Hong Kong, unlike in the Netherlands and Denmark, there were actually more incumbents than licences. But not all Hong Kong's incumbents were thought strong. Furthermore, it is much more attractive for strong firms to form joint ventures or collude

with their closest rivals prior to a standard ascending auction (when the strengthened combined bidder discourages entry) than prior to a standard sealed-bid auction (when reducing two strong bidders to one may attract entry). So even though the difference in strength between the likely winners and the also-rans seemed less dramatic in Hong Kong than in the Netherlands and Denmark, a standard ascending auction still seemed problematic. So there was a very serious concern – well-justified as it turned out – that a standard ascending auction would yield no more bidders than licences.

46. In a simple model, if a winning bidder suffers 'embarrassment costs' which are an increasing function of the difference between his payment and the lowest winning payment, then bidders are no worse off in expectation than in an auction which induces no embarrassment costs, but the auctioneer suffers. This is a consequence of the Revenue Equivalence Theorem: under its assumptions, mechanisms that induce embarrassment costs cannot affect bidders' utilities (it is irrelevant to the bidders whether the 'embarrassment costs' are received by the auctioneer or are social waste), so in equilibrium winning bidders' expected payments are lower by the expected embarrassment costs they suffer. See Klemperer (2003b, Part I).

47. I had no direct involvement with this auction but, embarrassingly, I am told this 'solution' was found in a footnote to Klemperer (2000b) that pointed out this method of running a strategically equivalent auction to the uniform fourth-price auction, and that it might (sometimes) be more politically acceptable. See also Binmore and Klemperer (2002).

48. The lobbyists also successfully ridiculed the original design, calling it the 'dark auction', arguing that it 'perversely' hid information when 'everyone knows that transparent markets are more efficient', and claiming it was an 'unfair tax' since bidders 'paid more than if they had all the information'.

49. The highly sophisticated security arrangements that had been made to ensure secrecy of the dropouts (removal of bidding teams to separate top-secret locations in army camps, and so on) were not altered even though they had become much less relevant; there was no need to lobby against these.

50. It is rumoured that a single bidder's budget for economic advice for lobbying against the design exceeded the UK government's expenditure on economic advice during the entire three-year design process; the lobbying effort included hiring two Nobel prize winners in the hope of finding arguments against the design. See Binmore and Klemperer (2002) for details of the two versions of the design.

51. When it became possible to offer an additional fifth licence in the UK the design changed – as had been planned for this circumstance – to a pure ascending one; see Section 3.

52. See van Damme (1999). This auction also illustrates the potential importance of bidders' errors: although high stakes were involved (the revenues were over 800 million euros) it seems that the outcome, and perhaps also the efficiency of the licence allocation, was critically affected by a bidder unintentionally losing its eligibility to bid on additional properties later in the auction; it has been suggested that the bidder's behaviour can only be explained by the fact that it happened on 'Carnival Monday', a day of celebrations and drinking in the south of the Netherlands where the bidder is based (van Damme, 1999)! (The German 3G auction described below provides another example of the large role that bidder error can play.)

53. According to the *Financial Times*, 'One operator has privately admitted to altering the last digit of its bid ... to signal to other participants that it was willing to accept a small licence' (3/11/2000, p. 21).

54. It seems that another reason why Mannesmann expected the firms to coordinate by T-Mobil reducing demand first in response to Mannesmann's signals was that Mannesmann saw itself as the leading firm in the market. However, T-Mobil may not have seen Mannesmann as the leading firm – the two firms were closely matched – and this seems to have contributed to the problem.

55. In particular, the firms might have been concerned about their relative performances. See also Grimm, Riedel and Wolfstetter (2002), Jehiel and Moldovanu (2002), and Ewerhart and Moldovanu (2002).

56. Furthermore, the number (6) achieved in the second auction (Netherlands) was perhaps lowered by the peculiarly incompetent design; the number (5) achieved in the last auction (Denmark) was raised by its design, which was very skilful except in its timing – see Section 3.

    Of course, other factors, in particular the fall in the telecoms stock price index, might have contributed to the fall in the number of entrants.

57. Klemperer (2002a) develops the arguments in this paragraph in much more detail.

58. Some of the incumbent bidders, by contrast, might possibly have had a clearer understanding. In an interesting example of the importance of political pressures, the Dutch operators successfully lobbied to delay the Netherlands auction and the clear gap that was thereby created between the UK and Dutch auctions might have been a contributory factor to the Dutch fiasco.

59. Klemperer (2002d) gives another illustration of how real-world context that was non-obvious to outsiders was important to the UK 3G auction.

60. Klemperer (2003a) uses the other main piece of the received auction theory – the Revenue Equivalence Theorem – to solve a war of attrition between several technologies competing to become an industry standard in, for example, 3G (see also Bulow and Klemperer, 1999) and to compute the value of new customers to firms when consumers have switching costs as they do for 3G phones for example (see also Bulow and Klemperer, 1998). Klemperer (2003a) also uses auction theory to address how e-commerce (and likewise M-commerce) affects pricing.

61. The US Federal Trade Commission has held hearings on this issue, and the European Commission is currently studying it. Amazon has admitted charging different prices to different consumers.

62. Thisse and Vives (1988), Ulph and Vulkan (2001), and Esteves (forthcoming), for example, have developed similar results.

63. Of course, there are more important reasons why 3G is no longer thought as valuable as it once was (see Klemperer, 2002c).

64. In this case, while a firm may raise prices against consumers who particularly value its product, in a competitive environment it will also lower prices to other consumers who like it less – and other firms will then have to respond.

65. For example, the analysis shows that even though it may be no bad thing for consumers if different firms learn different pieces of information about them, the result depends on firms learning the same amount of information about any given consumer. It probably is costly for a consumer to 'lose his privacy' to only one firm, just as having asymmetrically informed bidders may be a bad thing for an auctioneer. Furthermore, even when firms learn the same amount of information about consumers' tastes, this information may sometimes lead to inefficient price-discrimination which reduces total welfare, in which case consumers may be made worse off even though firms' profits are lowered, just as inefficient auctions may be had for both auctioneers and bidders. Learning information may also affect firms' abilities to collude, and the ease of new entry.

66. Furthermore, it is often only the process of thinking through the sophisticated graduate theory that puts the elementary undergraduate theory in proper perspective.

REFERENCES

Abbink, K., B. Irlenbusch, B. Rockenbach, A. Sadrieh and R. Selten (2002), 'The Behavioural Approach to the Strategic Analysis of Spectrum Auctions: The Case of the German DCS-1800 Auction', Working Paper, Universities of Nottingham, Erfurt, Tilburg, and Bonn.

Ausubel, L. and J. Schwartz (1999), 'The Ascending Auction Paradox', Working Paper, University of Maryland.

Bikhchandani, S. (1988), 'Reputation in Repeated Second-price Auctions', *Journal of Economic Theory,* **46**, 97–119.

Binmore, K. and P. Klemperer (2002), 'The Biggest Auction Ever: The Sale of the British 3G Telecom Licences', *Economic Journal*, **112**(478), C74–C96.

Brusco, S. and G. Lopomo (2002a), 'Collusion via Signalling in Simultaneous Ascending Bid Auctions with Heterogeneous Objects, with and without Complementarities', *Review of Economic Studies*, **69**, 407–436.

Brusco, S. and G. Lopomo (2002b), 'Simultaneous Ascending Auctions with Budget Constraints', Working Paper, Stern School of Business, New York University.

Bulow, J., M. Huang and P. Klemperer (1999), 'Toeholds and Takeovers', *Journal of Political Economy*, **107**, 427–454, reprinted in B. Biais and M. Pagano (eds.) (2002), *New Research in Corporate Finance and Banking*, Oxford: Oxford University Press, pp. 91–116.

Bulow, J. and P. Klemperer (1996), 'Auctions vs. Negotiations', *American Economic Review*, **86**(1), 180–194.

Bulow, J. and P. Klemperer (1998), 'The Tobacco Deal', *Brookings Papers on Economic Activity: Microeconomics*, 323–394.

Bulow, J. and P. Klemperer (1999), 'The Generalized War of Attrition', *American Economic Review*, **89**, 175–189.

Bulow, J. and P. Klemperer (2002), 'Prices and the Winner's Curse', *Rand Journal of Economics*, **33**(1), 1–21.

Bulow, J. and P. Klemperer (forthcoming), 'Privacy and Pricing', Discussion Paper, Nuffield College, Oxford University.

Clark, C. (1939), *The Conditions of Economic Progress*, Brisbane, Australia.

Cramton, P., R. Gibbons and P. Klemperer (1987), 'Dissolving a Partnership Efficiently', *Econometrica*, **55**, 615–632.

Cramton, P. and J. Schwartz (2000), 'Collusive Bidding: Lessons from the FCC Spectrum Auctions', *Journal of Regulatory Economics*, **17**(3), 229–252.

Crossland, D. (2000), 'Austrian UMTS Auction Unlikely to Scale Peaks', *Reuters*, 31 October, Available at www.totaltele.com.

Engelbrecht-Wiggans, R. (1987), 'Optimal Reservation Prices in Auctions', *Management Science*, **33**, 763–770.

Engelbrecht-Wiggans, R. (1993), 'Optimal Auctions Revisited', *Games and Economic Behaviour*, **5**, 227–239.

Engelbrecht-Wiggans, R. and C. Khan (1998), 'Low Revenue Equilibria in Simultaneous Auctions', Working Paper, University of Illinois.

Esteves, R. (forthcoming), 'Targeted Advertising and Price Discrimination in the New Media', DPhil Thesis, Oxford University.

Ewerhart, C. and B. Moldovanu (2002), 'The German UMTS Design: Insights from Multi-object Auction Theory', *ifo Studien*, **48**(1), 158–174.

Friedman, M. (1953), *Essays in Positive Economics*, Chicago: University of Chicago Press.

Gilbert, R. and P. Klemperer (2000), 'An Equilibrium Theory of Rationing', *Rand Journal of Economics*, **31**(1), 1–21.

Graham, D. and R. Marshall (1987), 'Collusive Bidder Behaviour at Single-object Second-price and English Auctions', *Journal of Political Economy*, **95**, 1217–1239.

Graham, D., R. Marshall and J. Richard (1990), 'Differential Payments within a Bidder Coalition and the Shapley Value', *American Economic Review*, **80**, 493–510.

Grimm, V., F. Riedel and E. Wolfstetter (2001), 'Low Price Equilibrium in Multi-unit Auctions: The GSM Spectrum Auction in Germany', Working Paper, Humboldt Universität zu Berlin.

Grimm, V., F. Riedel and E. Wolfstetter (2002), 'The Third Generation (UMTS) Spectrum Auction in Germany', *ifo Studien*, **48**(1), 123–143.

Haile, P. (1996), 'Auctions with Resale Markets', PhD Dissertation, Northwestern University.

Hansen, R. (1986), 'Sealed Bids versus Open Auctions: The Evidence', *Economic Inquiry*, **24**, 125–142.

Harstad, R. (1990), 'Alternative Common Values Auction Procedures: Revenue Comparisons with Free Entry', *Journal of Political Economy*, **98**, 421–429.

Hendricks, K. and R. Porter (1989), 'Collusion in Auctions', *Annales D'Économie et de Statistique*, **15–16**, 217–230.

Hendricks, K., R. Porter and G. Tan (1999), 'Joint Bidding in Federal Offshore Oil and Gas Lease Auctions', Working Paper, University of British Columbia.

Jehiel, P. and B. Moldovanu (2001), 'The UMTS/IMT-2000 License Auctions', Working Paper, University College London, and University of Mannheim.

Jehiel, P. and B. Moldovanu (2002), 'An Economic Perspective on Auctions', Working Paper, University College London, and University of Mannheim.

Kagel, J. and A. Roth (eds.) (1995), *The Handbook of Experimental Economics*, Princeton, NJ: Princeton University.

Keynes, J. (1933), *Essays in Biography*, London: Macmillan and Co. Ltd.

Klemperer, P. (1998), 'Auctions with Almost Common Values', *European Economic Review*, **42**(3–5), 757–769.

Klemperer, P. (1999a), 'Auction Theory: A Guide to the Literature', *Journal of Economic Surveys*, **13**(3), 227–286, reprinted in S. Dahiya (ed.) (1999), *The Current State of Economic Science*, **2**, pp. 711–766.

Klemperer, P. (1999b), 'Applying Auction Theory to Economics', Invited Lecture to Eighth World Congress of the Econometric Society, at www.paulklemperer.org.

Klemperer, P. (ed.) (2000a), *The Economic Theory of Auctions*, Cheltenham, UK and Northampton, MA, USA: Edward Elgar.

Klemperer, P. (2000b), *What Really Matters in Auction Design*, May 2000 version, at www.paulklemperer.org.

Klemperer, P. (2002a), 'How (Not) to Run Auctions: The European 3G Telecom Auction's', *European Economic Review*, **46** (4–5), 829–845.

Klemperer, P. (2002b), 'What Really Matters in Auction Design', *Journal of Economic Perspectives*, **16**(1), 169–189.

Klemperer, P. (2002c), 'Some Observations on the German 3G Telecom Auction', *ifo Studien*, **48**(1), 145–156, and at www.paulklemperer.org.

Klemperer, P. (2002d), 'Some Observations on the British 3G Telecom Auction', *ifo Studien*, **48**(1), 115–120, and at www.paulklemperer.org.

Klemperer, P. (2003a), 'Why Every Economist Should Learn Some Auction Theory', in M. Dewatripont, L. Hansen and S. Turnovsky (eds.), *Advances in Economics*

and Econometrics, Invited Lectures to Eighth World Congress of the Econometric
Society, Cambridge, UK: Cambridge University Press, 1, pp. 25–55.

Klemperer, P. (2003b), Auctions: Theory and Practice, Book manuscript available at
www.paulklemperer.org.

Klemperer, P. (2003c), 'Using and Abusing Economic Theory', Journal of the
European Economic Association, 1, 272–300.

Klemperer, P. and M. Pagnozzi (2003), Advantaged Bidders and Spectrum Prices: An
Empirical Analysis, forthcoming at www.paulklemperer.org.

Levin, D., J. Kagel and J. Richard (1996), 'Revenue Effects and Information
Processing in English Common Value Actions', American Economic Review,
86(3), 442–460.

Levin, D. and J. Smith (1994), 'Equilibrium in Auctions with Entry', American
Economic Review, 84, 585–599.

Maasland, E. (2000), 'Veilingmiljarden Zijn een Fictie (Billions from Auctions:
Wishful Thinking)', ESB, 9 June, 479, and translation available at
www.paulklemperer.org.

Machlup, F. (1946), 'Marginal Analysis and Empirical Research', American
Economic Review, 36, 519–554.

Mailath, G. and P. Zemsky (1991), 'Collusion in Second Price Auctions with
Heterogeneous Bidders', Games and Economic Behaviour, 3, 467–486.

Marshall, A. (1890), Principles of Economics, London: Macmillan & Co. Ltd.

Marshall, A. (1906), Letter to A. L. Bowley, February 27, 1906, in A. Pigou (ed.)
(1925), Memorials of Alfred Marshall, London: Macmillan, pp. 427–428.

Maskin, E. and J. Riley (1984), 'Optimal Auctions with Risk Averse Buyers',
Econometrica, 52, 1473–1518.

Maskin, E. and J. Riley (2000), 'Asymmetric Auctions', Review of Economic Studies,
67, 413–439.

Matthews, S. (1983), 'Selling to Risk Averse Buyers with Unobservable Tastes',
Journal of Economic Theory, 3, 370–400.

Matthews, S. (1984), 'Information Acquisition in Discriminatory Auctions', in
M. Boyer and R. Kihlstrom (eds.), Bayesian Models in Economic Theory, New
York: North-Holland, pp. 181–207.

McAfee, R. and J. McMillan (1987), 'Auctions with Entry', Economics Letters, 23,
343–347.

McAfee, R. and J. McMillan (1988), 'Search Mechanisms', Journal of Economic
Theory, 44, 99–123.

McAfee, R. and J. McMillan (1992), 'Bidding Rings', American Economic Review,
82, 579–599.

McMillan, J. (1994), 'Selling Spectrum Rights', Journal of Economic Perspectives, 8,
145–162.

Mead, W. and M. Schneipp (1989), Competitive Bidding for Federal Timber in
Region 6, An Update: 1983–1988, Community and Organization Research
Institute, University of California, Santa Barbara.

Meeks, R. (2001), 'An Event Study of the Swiss UMTS Auction', Research Note,
Nuffield College, Oxford University.

Menezes, F. (1996), 'Multiple Unit English Auctions', European Journal of Political
Economy, 12, 671–684.

Menezes, F. and P. Monteiro (1997), 'Auctions with Endogenous Participation',
Mimeo, Australian National University and IMPA.

Milgrom, P. (1987), 'Auction Theory', in T. Bewley (ed.), Advances in Economic
Theory: Fifth World Congress, Cambridge, UK: Cambridge University Press.

Milgrom, P. and R. Weber (1982), 'A Theory of Auctions and Competitive Bidding', *Econometrica*, **50**, 1089–1122.

Milgrom, P. and R. Weber (2000), 'A Theory of Auctions and Competitive Bidding, II', in P. Klemperer (ed.), *The Economic Theory of Auctions*, Cheltenham, UK and Northampton, MA, USA: Edward Elgar.

Myerson, R. (1981), 'Optimal Auction Design', *Mathematics of Operations Research*, **6**, 58–73.

Paarsch, H. (1991), 'Empirical Models of Auctions and an Application to British Columbian Timber Sales', Discussion Paper, University of British Columbia.

Perry, M. and J. Reny (1999), 'The Failure of the Linkage Principle in Multi-Unit Auctions', *Econometrica*, **67**(4), 895–900.

Persico, N. (1997), 'Information Acquisition in Auctions', Working Paper, UCLA.

Riley, J. and H. Li (1997), 'Auction Choice: A Numerical Analysis', Mimeo, UCLA.

Riley, J. and W. Samuelson (1981), 'Optimal Auctions', *American Economic Review*, **71**, 381–392.

Robinson, M. (1985), 'Collusion and the Choice of Auction', *Rand Journal of Economics*, **16**, 141–145.

Roth, A. (2002), 'The Economist as Engineer: Game Theory, Experimentations, and Computation as Tools for Design Economics', *Econometrica*, **70**(4), 1341–1378.

Rothkopf, M. and R. Engelbrecht-Wiggans (1993), 'Misapplications Reviews: Getting the Model Right – The Case of Competitive Bidding', *Interfaces*, **23**, 99–106.

Sills, D. (ed.) (1968), *International Encyclopedia of the Social Sciences*, Macmillan Company and The Free Press, vol. 10.

Stuewe, H. (1999), *'Auktion von Telefonfrequenzen: Spannung bis zur letzten Minute'*, *Frankfurter Allgemeine Zeitung*, 29 October.

Thisse, J., and X. Vives (1988), 'On the Strategic Choice of Spatial Price Policy', *American Economic Review*, **78**, 122–137.

Ulph, D. and N. Vulkan (2001), 'e-Commerce, Mass Customisation and Price Discrimination', Mimeo, UCL and University of Bristol.

van Damme, E. (1999), 'The Dutch DCS-1800 Auction', in F. Patrone, I. Garcia-Jurado and S. Tijs (eds.), *Game Practise: Contributions from Applied Game Theory*, Kluwer Academic Publishers, pp. 53–73.

van Damme, E. (2002), 'The European UMTS Auctions', *European Economic Review*, **45**(4–5), 846–858.

Vickrey, W. (1961), 'Counterspeculation, Auctions, and Competitive Sealed Tenders', *Journal of Finance*, **16**, 8–37.

Waterson, M. (1984), *Economic Theory of the Industry*, Cambridge, UK: Cambridge University Press.

Weber, R. (1997), 'Making More from Less: Strategic Demand Reduction in the FCC Spectrum Auctions', *Journal of Economics and Management Strategy*, **6**(3), 529–548.

Wilson, R. (2002), 'Architecture of Power Markets', *Econometrica*, **70**(4), 1299–1340.

2. Industry Sunk Cost and Entry Dynamics

Vladimir Smirnov and Andrew Wait

---

1. INTRODUCTION

The development of a new market often involves sunk costs. For example, a firm may need to invest heavily in advertising in order to generate knowledge and stimulate interest in a new product. Importantly, it can be the case that a significant component of these costs are industry sunk costs, as opposed to firm-specific sunk costs. Similarly, investment in research and development can aid potential competitors when intellectual property rights are poorly protected (possibly internationally).[1] This chapter incorporates industry sunk costs into a strategic model of investing as a leader or as a follower.

The basics of the model are as follows. Before any firm can exploit a new profitable market opportunity, a certain amount of resources needs to be expended on either advertising, to inform the public of the new product, or on non-patented research. This cost is borne by firms that initially enter the market, but this expenditure is a public good for all potential entrants in that, once the investment has been sunk, all firms can benefit from this investment if they choose to enter the market. The question then arises for each firm as to when they should enter the market: early entry allows them to benefit from fewer competitors but may mean they incur some of the industry set-up costs; delayed entry may allow a firm to avoid the set-up costs but they also forgo some benefits by not participating in the market.

Several interesting results arise out of the model. First, consider the case when there are two potential entry periods. This means a firm can enter immediately or it can sit out of the market for one period and enter in the next period. A firm cannot enter the market if it decides not to enter in either of the first two periods. If sunk costs are sufficiently high, each firm has a dominant strategy to wait and not enter the market until the second potential investment period. This result is a type of prisoners' dilemma: welfare is reduced by the delay in entry but no firm has an incentive to deviate.

Second, as the number of potential investment periods are increased (from two periods), the benefit of waiting until the last opportunity to enter the market, evaluated at the start of the game, is reduced as future returns are discounted. When the potential investment horizon is sufficiently long, firms will adopt a mixed strategy between investing and not investing in this period: this is a coordination game.[2]

Third, interesting dynamics can arise as the potential investment horizon is further extended, in which it is possible for the outcome of the game to switch between a prisoners' dilemma and a coordination game and back again. For example, consider the case when the firms play a mixed strategy (coordination game) when there are k potential investment periods. With an additional potential investment period, in the first of the $k + 1$ periods each firm will consider the benefit of not investing immediately: this is the outcome of the k-period coordination game, appropriately discounted. This outcome may be sufficiently large to provide an incentive for the firms to wait; the game has reverted to a prisoners' dilemma.

Fourth, in the infinite-horizon game firms play a mixed strategy in the unique symmetric equilibrium. Of course, other non-symmetric equilibria also exist.

Last, once one player has entered the market, all other potential suppliers enter as soon as possible. This creates an entry cascade. A similar result was generated by Zhang (1997) when firms have differing private information regarding an investment opportunity. In Zhang's model, after a strategic delay, the best-informed firm enters the market. Following this all other firms enter immediately in an investment cascade. The result in the model presented here is significant as it generates an investment cascade without private information.

In addition, it is worth mentioning the model of Fudenberg and Tirole (1985) that potentially generated an investment cascade. In their model each firm has a cost of adopting a new technology that decreases over time. The advantage of investing sooner, however, is to preempt investment by the rival firm. If, given certain parameter values, any investment would induce immediate investment in response by the rival, the value of preemption is greatly diminished. In this case, Fudenberg and Tirole show that equilibrium exists where there is no investment for a period, then both firms invest virtually simultaneously, as in an investment cascade. The difference between their paper and ours is that in their paper late adoption is optimal whereas here, any delay in investment reduces surplus.

2. N-PLAYER INVESTMENT GAME

Consider the following set-up. There are $n \geq 2$ firms that are potential
entrants to some new market. The net benefit from entering is B per period, to
be shared amongst all firms that have entered.[3]

Once entry has occurred there are an infinite number of production
periods; all parties discount future returns by δ per period. There are some
costs C that are incurred in the first period in which entry occurs, where C is
shared among all the firms that enter in that initial period. Entry (by at least
one firm) is efficient in that $B/(1 - \delta) > C$.[4]

First, consider the situation where there are only two potential entry
periods, so that a firm can enter in the first period, enter in the second period,
or decide not to enter the market at all.[5] Let us show that it is always
profitable for a firm to enter the market in the second period if it has not
already done so. Consider the case where no firms enter the market in the first
period. If m firms enter in the second period, the payoff to any individual firm
from entering, evaluated at the start of the game, is $\delta B/m(1 - \delta) - \delta C/m$. As
$B/(1 - \delta) > C$ entry is profitable for every firm. If at least one firm entered in
the first period the payoff to a firm from entering in the second period, again
evaluated at the start of the two potential investment periods, is $\delta B/m(1 - \delta)$ if
a total of m firms entered over both periods. Clearly entry is profitable in this
case. As a consequence, if a firm has not already done so it will enter the
market in the final potential investment period.

Second, using the result above, now consider a firm's decision as to
whether or not to enter the market in the first period. To examine this issue
we consider: the payoffs from entry when (a) the firm is the only entrant; and
(b) when they share entry in the first period.

If $n - 1$ firms decide to wait, the benefit to the other firm from entering in
the first period is:

$$\frac{B}{n(1-\delta)} + \left(1 - \frac{1}{n}\right) B - C \qquad (2.1)$$

If the firm does not enter in the first period, all of the other firms will enter in
the second period, so the payoff to this firm is just the payoff of all firms
entering, discounted by one period:

$$\frac{\delta B}{n(1-\delta)} - \frac{\delta C}{n} \qquad (2.2)$$

As a result, the payoff of waiting (not investing in the first period) is bigger if:

$$\left(1 - \frac{\delta}{n}\right)C > B \tag{2.3}$$

Conversely, the firm will enter in the first period, given that no other firms enter, if $B > (1 - \delta / n)C$.

Now consider the entry decision of one firm when $k > 0$ of the other firms decide to enter in the first potential investment period and $n - k - 1$ decide to wait. If the firm enters in the first period it will get the following benefit:

$$\frac{B}{n(1-\delta)} + \left(\frac{1}{k+1} - \frac{1}{n}\right)B - \frac{C}{k+1} \tag{2.4}$$

On the other hand, if it does not enter it will enter in the second period and receive a surplus of:

$$\frac{\delta B}{n(1-\delta)} \tag{2.5}$$

Comparing these two equations one can infer that the benefit of waiting is bigger if and only if:

$$C > B \tag{2.6}$$

From both these cases, the firm has a dominant strategy to invest immediately if $B > C$. When $C > B > C(1 - \delta / n)$, the firm prefers to wait if k other firms enter but invest if no other firms invest, where $n \geq k > 0$. Consequently, the firm will adopt a mixed strategy. Finally, if $B < C(1 - \delta / n)$, the firm has a dominant strategy to wait and not invest in the first period. This discussion is summarized in Proposition 1.

Proposition 1. *Consider the entry game with two potential investment (entry) periods. If $B > C$ all firms invest immediately in the first period in any subgame perfect equilibrium (SPE). If $C > B > (1 - \delta / n)C$ each firm will have a mixed strategy regarding entering immediately and waiting to enter in the second period in the SPE. Finally, if $B < C(1 - \delta / n)$, in the SPE, all firms will wait and only enter the market in the second period.*

If $B < C(1 - \delta / n)$ the firms are in a prisoners' dilemma: the welfare of every firm would be improved if they could all commit to invest immediately but each firm has a dominant strategy to wait, reducing total surplus.

Assume that $B < C(1 - \delta / n)$, so that the players are in a prisoners' dilemma in the two-period investment game. Now consider the optimal strategies of the firms when there are three potential investment periods. In this case, the payoff from waiting for a firm if no one invests in the first period is the two-period payoff discounted by an additional δ – the extra period of delay reduces the benefit of waiting. Reducing the benefit from waiting makes immediate entry more attractive. If this reduction in the benefit from waiting is sufficient, a firm will no longer have a dominant strategy to wait. Instead they will adopt a mixed strategy between investing and waiting. This point is illustrated in the following example.

Example 1. *This example shows that when $B < C(1 - \delta / n)$ for two investment periods, as the potential investment horizon is extended, the optimal strategy switches from a prisoners' dilemma game to a coordination game when there are a sufficient number of potential investment periods.*

Let $C = 5$, $B = 3$, $\delta = 0.9$. Further, assume that there are three potential investors. Figure 2.1 shows the normal form game when there are two potential investment periods. In the figure, I refers to the strategy to invest immediately and W indicates that the investor does not invest in that period. The left-hand payoff matrix refers to when player 3 invests immediately and the right-hand panel relates to when she does not invest in that immediate period (she plays W).

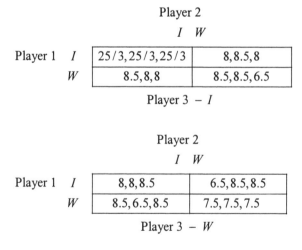

Figure 2.1   A prisoners' dilemma game for three players and two potential investment periods

As there are two periods, the choice for each player is to invest immediately or invest in the second and final investment period. Each player has a dominant strategy to wait and only invest in the second period, as in a prisoners' dilemma game. This follows because $B < C(1 - \delta/n)$ when there are two potential investment periods.

If the potential investment horizon is extended so that there are three possible investment periods, the only payoff that is changed from the above figure is when all three parties opt to wait (W) in the first period. In this case, the game proceeds to the next period; given that there are just two potential investment periods left, the game exactly resembles the two-period game. As a result, the payoff to each player when they all decide to wait in the first period is the payoff from the two-period game (7.5) discounted by the additional period, which in this case is 6.75. The payoffs for the three-period game are illustrated in Figure 2.2.

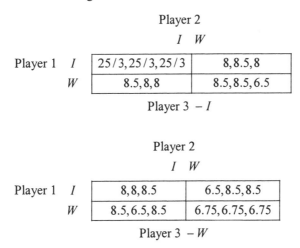

Figure 2.2 A prisoners' dilemma game for three players in a three-period investment game

Again, each player has a dominant strategy to wait in this game.

Finally, if the horizon is extended to four potential investment periods the payoff to each player if they all opt to wait in the first investment period is the three-period game payoff, discounted by the additional period. This is illustrated below in Figure 2.3.

Here, due to the additional discounting, the payoff from waiting is not as great as the payoff from investing for a player if the other two parties do not invest immediately (6.5 > 6.075). Each player no longer has a dominant strategy to wait and will adopt a mixed strategy.

Note, the mixed strategy equilibrium is a coordination game similar in structure to what Binmore (1992) described as the Australian Battle of the Sexes. In this coordination game, players wish to coordinate to undertake the activity that the other players do not do. Alternatively, of course, the reduction in the benefit from waiting will not be sufficient, and the players will remain in a prisoners' dilemma entry game.

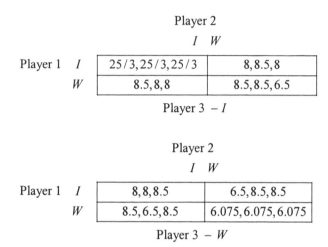

Player 2

I W

Player 1 I	$25/3,25/3,25/3$	$8,8.5,8$
W	$8.5,8,8$	$8.5,8.5,6.5$

Player 3 $- I$

Player 2

I W

Player 1 I	$8,8,8.5$	$6.5,8.5,8.5$
W	$8.5,6.5,8.5$	$6.075,6.075,6.075$

Player 3 $- W$

Figure 2.3 A coordination game for three players with four potential investment periods

3. SWITCHING BETWEEN PRISONERS' DILEMMA AND THE COORDINATION GAME

In the previous section we implicitly assumed that the joint payoff of all players in any state is always the same. If this is the case once the game switches from a prisoners' dilemma to a coordination game as the potential investment horizon is extended, the player's optimal strategies will continue to be those of a coordination game in every subsequent period as the number of potential investment periods is increased.[6] However, if we generalize this model to allow the joint payoff to be different across states then the equilibrium strategies of the players can switch between prisoners' dilemma and a coordination game as the number of potential investment periods is increased.

To further explore this point, consider the following generalization of the basic model. Let B_k be the payoff of a player if he invests in that period and C_k the payoff if he does not invest in that period; k indicates the number of players investing. We assume that:

$$C_{n-1} \geq \ldots \geq C_1 \geq B_n \geq \ldots \geq B_1 \geq C_0 \qquad (2.7)$$

This assumption means that benefits from investing second are higher when there are not many investors who invest second. The intuition is that if a party is to invest second, they wish to do so alone as they must share the spoils with firms that enter the market at the same time. On the other hand, the benefits from investing first are higher when there are many parties that invest first because all of these investors share the set-up costs. Note, with this assumption, total surplus depends on the sequence of entry, whereas in the previous section total surplus was invariant to the number of firms in the market, provided at least one firm had entered.

The following proposition presents the necessary conditions for the game to exhibit switching behaviour.

Proposition 2. *As the game is extended from k periods, to k + 1, k + 2 periods etc., the game in each subsequent initial period can alternate between a prisoners' dilemma and a coordination game if the following necessary conditions hold:*

$$B_2 - C_1 \geq B_n - C_{n-1}, B_3 - C_2 \geq B_n - C_{n-1}, \ldots \qquad (2.8)$$

Proof. *See the Appendix.* □

As an illustration of this switching result consider the following example for the three-player game.

Example 2. *This example shows the possibility of switching between a prisoners' dilemma and a coordination game when there are many potential investment periods.*

As above, let $\delta = 0.9$, $B = 3$ and $C = 5$. Figure 2.4 illustrates the 'normal form game' of the investment decision for three parties when there are $k = 2$ potential investment periods. The 'normal form game' on the left-hand side of the figure illustrates the payoffs to players 1, 2 and 3 respectively when player 3 chooses I. Similarly, the 'normal form game' on the right hand-side slows the payoffs to the players when player 3 chooses to wait (W).

One can see that for all players the dominant strategy is to wait. The same story happens when $k = 3$. When $k = 4$ the only difference arises with respect to the payoffs for (W,W,W) (instead of 7.5 it will be 6.075 due to discounting). Thus, for $k = 4$ there is no dominant strategy. The players will adopt mixed strategies.

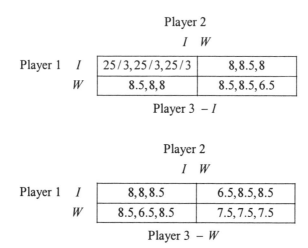

Player 2

I W

Player 1   I | 25/3, 25/3, 25/3 | 8, 8.5, 8 |
           W | 8.5, 8, 8 | 8.5, 8.5, 6.5 |

Player 3 – *I*

Player 2

I W

Player 1   I | 8, 8, 8.5 | 6.5, 8.5, 8.5 |
           W | 8.5, 6.5, 8.5 | 7.5, 7.5, 7.5 |

Player 3 – *W*

Figure 2.4   A three-player strategic game, in which player 3 chooses I or W.

Now extend the potential investment horizon further, so that $k = 5$. In this case, the expected payoff if all parties choose W is simply the mixed strategy payoff when $k = 4$, discounted for the extra period. This discounted mixed payoff is 6.534, which is higher than 6.5, the payoff from investing immediately, given that the other players choose W. Thus, when $k = 5$, the players again face the prisoners' dilemma.

This result is noteworthy for several reasons. First, there is no similar result in the literature that exhibits switching behaviour between a dominant strategy (prisoners' dilemma) to a mixed strategy equilibrium as the horizon of the game is extended. Second, the welfare implications of extending the time horizon are ambiguous. For example, welfare can fall if the addition of another potential investment period induces the parties to switch to a dominant strategy of not investing. There is an analogous result in the bargaining literature: Fudenberg and Tirole (1983) showed that in a bargaining model with asymmetric information, the addition of extra bargaining periods had an ambiguous effect on welfare. Last, entry behaviour depends in a non-monotonic manner on the perceived potential entry period. A similar point could be made for other decisions such as research and development.

3.1 Infinite-horizon Game

In the infinite-period case, the symmetric stationary SPE is unique. This SPE is a mixed strategy.

Proposition 3. *In the infinite-horizon investment game there always exists a unique symmetric mixed strategy SPE.*

Proof. *See the Appendix.*□

As noted above, other non-symmetric equilibria also exist.

4. CASCADING INVESTMENT

Finally, consider the observable entry behaviour of firms in either the finite or infinite-horizon game when firms adopt a mixed strategy between immediate entry and waiting. In this case there is a positive probability that no entry occurs for one or more periods. However, once at least one firm has entered, all firms enter at the next possible opportunity, as in an investment cascade. A similar dynamic could exist in the finite-horizon model where the optimal strategies of the firms switch between having a dominant strategy to wait (prisoners' dilemma) and mixing (the coordination game). Again, the industry may display no entry for several periods, but once entry has occurred all firms immediately enter. This is summarized in Proposition 4.

Proposition 4. *An investment cascade can result in an investment game when there are industry sunk costs.*

Also note, if the firms have a finite number of potential investment periods and they have a dominant strategy to wait until the last period to enter, the entry behaviour of the firms looks similar to the investment cascade: there is no entry for $n - 1$ periods, after which time all firms enter in the n-th period.

This result provides an explanation for the observation of entry cascades. Further, this proposition suggests that entry cascades are more likely to occur when there are industry sunk costs or when there is poor protection of intellectual property.

NOTES

1. For example, see Stegemann (2000), Ostergard (2000) and Levy (2000) for a discussion of international protection of intellectual property and copyright. In another context, Roberts (2000) argued that patents provided limited protection to internet companies and their technologies.
2. Note, this game differs from the usual coordination game somewhat: it is, instead, similar to what Binmore (1992) described as an Australian Battle of the Sexes.
3. B could represent profits in the industry that the firms share with perfect collusion, as assumed by Mankiw and Whinston (1986).
4. Note that, given that there are no firm-specific sunk costs, the welfare outcome in this model is the same regardless of the number of firms producing, provided at least one firm is in the market.
5. This two-period investment game has a similar structure to the bank-run game analysed by Gibbons (1992, pp. 73–75) and Diamond and Dybvig (1983) and Chamley's (2001) model of exchange rate speculation.
6. Note, this applies to the strategies at the start of the investment process. For example, assume that there are k potential investment periods, and each firm adopts a mixed strategy between mixing and entering. If the number of potential investment periods are extended to $k + 1$ periods, the players would also adopt a mixed strategy at the start of these $k + 1$ potential investment periods.

REFERENCES

Binmore, K. (1992), *Fun and Games: A Text on Game Theory*, Lexington: D.C. Heath and Company.

Diamond, D. and P. Dybvig (1983), 'Bank Runs, Bank Insurance, and Liquidity', *Journal of Political Economy*, **91**, 401–419.

Chamley, C. (2001), 'Dynamic Speculative Attacks', mimeo.

Fudenberg, D. and J. Tirole (1983), 'Sequential Bargaining with Incomplete Information', *Review of Economic Studies*, **50**, 221–247.

Fudenberg, D. and J. Tirole (1985), 'Preemption and Rent Equalization in the Adoption of New Technology', *Review of Economic Studies*, **52**, 383–401.

Gibbons, R. (1992), *A Primer in Game Theory*, Hertfordshire: Harvester Wheatsheaf.

Levy, C. (2000), 'Implementing TRIPS – A Test of Political Will', *Law and Policy in International Business*, **31**, 789–795.

Mankiw, N. and G. Whinston (1986), 'Free Entry and Social Inefficiency', *RAND Journal of Economics*, **17**, 48–58.

Ostergard, R. (2000), 'The Measurement of Intellectual Property Rights Protection', *Journal of International Business Studies*, **31**, 349–360.

Roberts, B. (2000), 'The Truth About Patents', *Internet World*, **6**, 72–79.

Stegemann, K. (2000), 'The Integration of Intellectual Property Rights into the WTO System', *World Economy*, **23**, 1237–1267.

Zhang, J. (1997), 'Strategic Delay and the Onset of Investment Cascades', *RAND Journal of Economics*, **28**, 188–205.

APPENDIX

Proposition 2. *As the game is extended from k periods, to k + 1, k + 2 periods etc., the game in each subsequent initial period can alternate between a prisoners' dilemma and a coordination game if the following necessary conditions hold:*

$$B_2 - C_1 \geq B_n - C_{n-1}, B_3 - C_2 \geq B_n - C_{n-1} \cdots \tag{2.9}$$

Proof. To prove the necessary condition we present a proof by contradiction. Let us first prove the proposition when there are only two players. Consider Figure 2.A.1.

Firm 2

I W

Firm 1 I | B_2, B_2 | B_1, C_1 |
W | C_1, B_1 | C_0, C_0 |

Figure 2.A.1 Normal form for k period game with two firms

If the firms face a prisoners' dilemma in period $k - 1$, while in period k they face a coordination game, it follows that

$$B_1 = C_0 d^{-\alpha} = B_2 d^{k-\alpha}, \alpha \in (0,1). \tag{2.10}$$

If in period $k + 1$ the game will again be a prisoners' dilemma, then the mixed strategy return is greater than B_1. This requires that

$$\frac{B_1 C_1 - B_2 C_0}{B_1 + C_1 - B_2 - C_0} d > B_1. \tag{2.11}$$

Using the fact that

$$C_0 = d^k B_2 \tag{2.12}$$

inequality (2.11) can be written as

$$\left(C_1 - B_2 d^{\alpha}\right) d > C_1 - B_2 + \left(d^{-\alpha} - 1\right) d^k B_2. \tag{2.13}$$

Now, let us assume that

$$B_1 + C_1 = 2B_2 \qquad (2.14)$$

This allows inequality (2.13) to be written as

$$\left(2 - d^\alpha\right)d - 1 > d^k \left(d^{1-\alpha} - 1\right) \qquad (2.15)$$

When $k = 0$, inequality (2.15) transforms to

$$2d > d^{1+\alpha} - d^{1-\alpha} \qquad (2.16)$$

which contradicts the fact that the geometrical average is always less than arithmetical one. To get a similar contradiction for $k > 0$, notice that the right-hand side is negative and increasing with k.

Thus, when $B_1 + C_1 = 2B_2$ there is no immediate jump to the prisoners' dilemma when there are only two players. It means that inequality (2.13) is satisfied when $B_1 + C_1 = 2B_2$. When $B_1 + C_1 = 2B_2$ the result holds because the derivative of inequality (2.13) with respect to C_1 is negative.

Now the question is whether there can be a jump that does not immediately occur. Let us show that this is not possible. From inequality (2.11) it follows that the mixed return is greater than $B_1 d$, that is

$$B_1 > \frac{\left(B_1 C_1 - B_2 C_0\right)}{\left(B_1 + C_1 - B_2 - C_0\right)d} > B_1 d \qquad (2.17)$$

which means that the mixed return can be written as $B_1 d^{-\alpha_2}$. This mixed return is actually C_0 for the next period. Thus, the same logic works for a non-immediate jump as well.

Now consider a game where there are n players. First, let B_k represent the payoff of a player if he invests and C_k the payoff if he does not invest; k indicates number of players investing. By assumption

$$C_{n-1} \geq \ldots \geq C_1 \geq B_n \geq \ldots \geq B_1 \geq C_0 \qquad (2.18)$$

In the mixed strategy equilibrium the probability of investing solves the following equation

$$\begin{aligned}
&\left(1-p\right)^{n-1} B_1 + C_{n-1}^1 p\left(1-p\right)^{n-2} B_2 + \ldots + p^{n-1} B_n \\
&= \left(1-p\right)^{n-1} C_0 + C_{n-1}^1 p\left(1-p\right)^{n-2} C_1 + \ldots + p^{n-1} B_{n-1}
\end{aligned} \qquad (2.19)$$

The payoff is either the left-hand side or the right-hand side of this equation. To demonstrate that $\delta \cdot payoff < B_1$, let us show when this payoff is less than the payoff from the two-player game with C_{n-1}, C_0, B_n and B_1. For the moment assume that

$$B_2 - C_1 = B_3 - C_2 = \ldots = B_n - C_{n-1} \qquad (2.20)$$

In this case the payoff is at the maximum when $C_1 = C_2 = \ldots = C_{n-1}$ and $B_2 = B_3 = \ldots = B_n$ and this maximum is equal to the payoff from the two-player game. Now equation (2.19) can be written as

$$\frac{(1-p)^{n-1}}{1-(1-p)^{n-1}} = \frac{B_n - C_{n-1}}{B_1 - C_0} \qquad (2.21)$$

Using equation (2.19), the payoff will be exactly the same as the payoff from a two-player game with C_{n-1}, C_0, B_n and B_1. Thus, when condition (2.20) holds, there is no return to the prisoners' dilemma as the potential investment horizon is extended once the game has reverted to a coordination game at a particular length of the investment time horizon.

Now consider a general case where condition (2.20) does not hold. Here we make use of a similar technique that we use when we prove Proposition 3 below. The left-hand side and the right-hand side of equation (2.19) are increasing functions with respect to p. From Figure 2.A.2 it is possible to see that when we decrease B_i, where $i = 2, \ldots, n - 1$, we move curve B_1B_n lower; as a result, this change decreases the player's payoff. This means that for values

$$B_2 - C_1 \leq B_n - C_{n-1}, B_3 - C_2 \leq B_n - C_{n-1}, \ldots \qquad (2.22)$$

there is no return to the prisoners' dilemma. This observation concludes the proof. □

Proposition 3 *In the infinite horizon investment game there always exists a unique symmetric mixed strategy SPE.*

Proof. First, let us prove that there is at least one symmetric mixed strategy SPE. The following condition is assumed:

$$C_{n-1} \geq \ldots \geq C_1 \geq B_n \geq \ldots \geq B_1 \geq C_0 \qquad (2.23)$$

Let us find the mixed strategy equilibrium. The probability of investing solves the following equation

$$(1-p)^{n-1} B_1 + C_{n-1}^1 p (1-p)^{n-2} B_2 + \ldots p^{n-1} B_n$$
$$= (1-p)^{n-1} C_0 + C_{n-1}^1 p (1-p)^{n-2} B_1 + \ldots p^{n-1} C_{n-1} \qquad (2.24)$$

The payoff is either the left-hand side or the right-hand side of this equation and this payoff satisfies the following condition

$$\delta \cdot payoff = C_0 \qquad (2.25)$$

Thus, our goal is to find such C_0 that all mentioned above conditions hold. Note that if we assume $C_0 = B_1$ then $p = 0$ and $payoff = B_1$, which means $\delta \cdot payoff < C_0$. On the other hand, when $C_0 = 0$ it follows that $\delta \cdot payoff > C_0$ because by definition $payoff \geq B_0$. Thus, always there is at least one value of C_0 that satisfies all the conditions.

Now, let us prove that this value is always unique. First, let us show that there is always only one p that solves equation (2.24). Really, if we divide this equation by $(1-p)^{n-1}$ and let $q = p/(1-p)$ then we get

$$C_{n-1}^1 (B_2 - C_1) q + \ldots + (B_n - C_{n-1}) q^{n-1} = B_1 - C_0 \qquad (2.26)$$

The value on the right-hand side of this equation is constant, while all the coefficients on the left-hand side are positive. It means that the left-hand side is increasing in q, which means that there is a unique solution for q that corresponds to a unique solution for p.

Second, we show that for a unique p there is a unique C_0. To do this, we prove that the payoff is decreasing in C_0. Then the uniqueness follows from equation (2.25). Really, from Figure 2.A.2 one can see that when we increase C_0 we move curve $C_0 C_{n-1}$ higher and this change decreases the payoff.

Here we have used the fact that both curves are increasing; this follows because the coefficients are positive and increasing. It is a simple exercise to take derivatives and show that the derivatives are positive. This fact concludes the proof. □

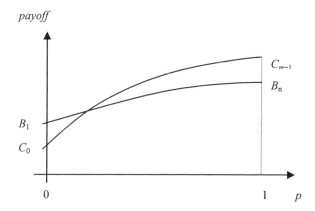

Figure 2.A.2 Graphical interpretation of why the payoff is decreasing in
C_o

PART II

Econometric Theory

3.   Sub-sample Model Selection Procedures in General-to-Specific Modelling

David Hendry and Hans-Martin Krolzig

1. INTRODUCTION

Despite the many difficulties intrinsic to model selection, viewed as searching for an unknown specification in a large class of models, recent automatic procedures have achieved high success rates in locating the data generation process (DGP) across a variety of simulation experiments such as Hoover and Perez (1999, 2000), Hendry and Krolzig (1999, 2002), Krolzig and Hendry (2001), Krolzig (2001, 2003), and Brüggemann, Krolzig and Lütkepohl (2002). Here we consider one of the selection strategies embodied in *PcGets*, namely its 'sub-sample significance evaluation' procedure. After a final model has been selected by the search process, its behaviour in overlapping sub-samples is evaluated, as a reliability check on the selected model.[1]

Hendry and Krolzig (2002) distinguish between the costs of inference, which are an inevitable consequence of non-zero significance levels and non-unit powers and apply even when the DGP is known, and the costs of search, which are additional to those faced when commencing from a model that is the DGP. In summarizing the Monte Carlo evidence on the performance of *PcGets* in a range of experiments, including those used to calibrate its settings, Hendry and Krolzig (2003) show that *PcGets* performs well – in the sense that the costs of search are low – but naturally varies across the (unknown) states of nature. Their simulation evidence also shows that the sub-sample assessment procedure substantially lowers the 'size' of the selection algorithm, defined as the average incorrect retention rate of irrelevant variables, with a small reduction in power. However, Lynch and Vital-Ahuja (1998) show that 'selecting variables that are significant on all three splits (the two sub-samples and overall)' delivers no gain over simply using a smaller nominal size. The Lynch and Vital-Ahuja (1998) argument applies to Hoover and Perez (1999, 2000) who retain variables at the selection stage only if they are significant in two overlapping sub-samples.

However, those approaches differ at first sight from selecting only on full sample evidence, followed by evaluation on sub-samples, which is the *PcGets* approach investigated here. Nevertheless, the simulation evidence alone does not establish the efficacy of sub-sample selection: as Lynch and Vital-Ahuja (1998) express the matter, the key issue is whether the power loss of the sub-sample 'significance evaluation' procedure is smaller – given the size reduction achieved – than that resulting from just setting a tighter initial significance level. Unfortunately, power depends on both the unknown state of nature (through a non-centrality parameter) and on the significance level set for the null, and varies in a highly non-linear manner as a function of these. For example, if the power were close to unity, little loss could occur for small changes in nominal significance levels (called size as a shorthand below), whereas for smaller values of the non-centrality parameter, a large reduction in power might ensue.

The structure of the chapter is as follows. Section 2 describes the various sub-sample selection procedures in Hoover and Perez (1999) and *PcGets*. Section 3 investigates, by simulation, the distributional properties and the implied power-size trade-off of the Hoover–Perez sub-sample selection method and the *PcGets* sub-sample reliability assessment; different states of nature and various choices of the percentage of overlap are considered. Section 4 concludes.

2. THE FORM OF SUB-SAMPLE SELECTION PROCEDURES

Hoover–Perez

Hoover and Perez (1999, 2000) select variables only if they are significant in two overlapping sub-samples. In the former paper, they graph the trade-off between size and power (defined as the average retention probability of relevant variables) as the percentage of overlap varies from 50% to 90%, and find that a split at about 70–80% performs best, in that the slope of the trade-off is steeper below and flatter above. At first sight, that evidence looks persuasive; but the non-linear relation between size and power for a *t*-test would also show a similar shape as the size varied from (say) 10% to 0.1% for values of the non-centrality parameter in the neighbourhood of 2. To see this, consider a normal random variable:

$$x \sim N\left(\mu, \sigma^2\right) \qquad (3.1)$$

where $\mu = 2$ and $\sigma^2 = 1$ so:

$$P\left(x \geq c_\alpha\right) = P\left(x - 2 \geq c_\alpha - 2\right) = \frac{1}{\sqrt{2\pi}} \int_{c_\alpha - 2}^{\infty} \exp\left(-\frac{1}{2}(x-2)^2\right) dx.$$

Figure 3.1 (left panel) plots the resulting power-size trade-off. The dashed line shows the evident slope change around 5%, suggesting that the trade-off 'worsens' sharply as the size falls, but that is simply the correct power cost of a smaller size, which should be determined by the relative losses on type 1 versus type 2 errors, not by the slope – which is an intrinsic feature of the test. To reinforce that point, the solid line shows a three-way division, with an intermediate slope in the region of 5%. Thus, to be of benefit, a split-sample evaluation would need to lose less power per reduction in size than the inherent trade-off.

There is a separate such trade-off line for each value of μ in (3.1), and in Figure 3.1 (right panel), the trade-off from Hoover and Perez (1999) is shown with the corresponding lines for $t = 3$ and $t = 3.3$, between which it lies. While it is difficult to judge the mean t-value in their simulation study, the evidence of a steeper fall to the left, and a shallower rise to the right, does not by itself suggest gains.

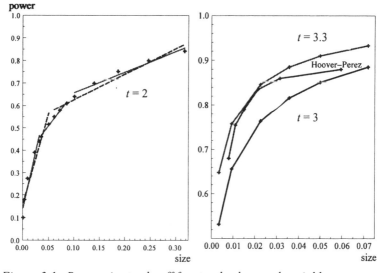

Figure 3.1 Power-size trade-off for standard normal variable

The *PcGets* Approach

After selection, the relevance of variables in the final model selected by *PcGets* is explored by post-selection reliability checks to ascertain whether 'significance' is substantive or adventitious. Post-selection evaluation is an attempt to mimic the role in an automatic procedure of recursive estimation, aiming to evaluate whether apparently significant effects are substantive or chance. It is not a check on constancy, which has already been tested for in the general unrestricted model (GUM), and checked by diagnostics at each potential reduction.

Under the null hypothesis H_0, using a two-sided test, a t-value will exceed (in absolute value) a critical value c_α on $\alpha\%$ of the occasions, where α is the significance level, so:

$$P\left(-c_\alpha \leq t \leq c_\alpha \mid H_0\right) = \alpha. \tag{3.2}$$

However, after selecting a model, the retained variables will have significant t-values by construction.[2] The selected set of variables in the final model thus comprises (on average) $\alpha\%$ of the initial set – which are significant by chance – and the remainder – which are significant by having non-central t-distributions. The issue is whether conditional on observing full-sample significance, there is a division of the sample into sub-samples that would help discriminate between these, exploiting the fact that non-central t-values diverge, whereas central t-values are only significant by a chance value falling outside the range $[-c_\alpha, c_\alpha]$ at the end of the sample.

Our proposed filter between variables that really matter (non-central t-distributions) and those that are adventitiously significant (central t-distributions that happen to take large end-of-period values) is to check sub-sample reliability. The idea is that the central t-tests should be low in at least one of the two sub-periods, so revealing the actual irrelevance of the associated variable. However, because the sample sizes are smaller, less stringent critical values must be used to ensure a coherent inference procedure. *PcGets* centres on the Hoover and Perez (1999) split of 75–25 (so 50% of observations are in common), and adjusts the sub-sample nominal significance levels as a function of those selected for the full-sample selection.

It is clear from all the Monte Carlo studies that we have conducted that the reliability check reduces the size, and perhaps more importantly, has helped stabilize performance over different states of nature. Nevertheless, that by itself does not resolve the key issue of whether an equivalent size reduction achieved by lowering the initial significance level of every test would result in higher or lower power, and if so, how that changes across different DGPs.

As noted above, the power-size trade-off is highly non-linear in both the significance level and the non-centrality parameters of the variables, and the analysis must be conditional on having retained each associated regressor at its observed t-value.

3. ASSESSING SUB-SAMPLE-BASED MODEL SELECTION PROCEDURES

It is important to distinguish the reliability assessment of a model (which has been selected based on the full-sample information) from selection rules that are formulated in terms of sub-sample evidence. We now provide some Monte Carlo evidence indicating that the latter procedure is dominated by the former.

The Curse of Sub-samples

Both sub-sample-based selection rules rely on information from sub-sample t-tests, so it is useful to start by analysing the properties of a simple sub-sample t-test (without conditioning on full-sample significance), and its relation to the full-sample t-test. Because of the difficulty induced by overlapping samples, we first consider when the sub-sample t-values are independent, so the sub-samples are non-overlapping, and then discuss overlapping sub-samples.

Non-overlapping sub-samples
We consider the following approximation of the t-statistic:

$$
t_0 = \frac{\hat{\beta}}{\hat{\sigma}_\beta} = \left(\frac{\hat{\sigma}_\varepsilon^2}{T} \left[\frac{1}{T} \sum_{t=1}^{T} x_t^2 \right]^{-1} \right)^{-1/2} \frac{1/T \sum_{t=1}^{T} x_t y_t}{1/T \sum_{t=1}^{T} x_t^2}
$$

$$
= \frac{\sqrt{T}}{\hat{\sigma}_\varepsilon} \frac{1/T \sum_{t=1}^{T} x_t y_t}{\sqrt{1/T \sum_{t=1}^{T} x_t^2}} \approx \frac{\sqrt{T}}{\sigma_\varepsilon \sigma_x} \left(\frac{1}{T} \sum_{t=1}^{T} x_t y_t \right). \tag{3.3}
$$

Under stationarity and ergodicity, sample moments are consistent for population, so replacing the sample second moments by their population counterparts will introduce an error, but should not bias the calculations. However, when the data second moments for the conditioning variables change substantially over the sample, different outcomes could be obtained. We also assume a small number of regressors in the selected model such that degree-of-freedom corrections can be neglected, and focus the analysis on the scalar problem to highlight the key issues.

If the sample is split into J non-overlapping partitions, the full-sample t-value is then given approximately by:

$$t_0 \simeq \frac{\sqrt{T}}{\sigma_\varepsilon \sigma_x} \left(\frac{1}{T} \sum_{j=1}^{J} \sum_{t \in T_j} x_t y_t \right), \tag{3.4}$$

where the jth sub-sample t-value is given by:

$$t_0 \simeq \frac{\sqrt{\tau_j T}}{\sigma_\varepsilon \sigma_x} \left(\frac{1}{\tau_j T} \sum_{t \in T_j} x_t y_t \right), \tag{3.5}$$

when τ_j is the fraction of observations belonging to the jth partition, with $\sum_j \tau_j = 1$. Hence:

$$t_0 = \sum_{j=1}^{J} \sqrt{\tau_j} t_j > \sum_{j=1}^{J} \tau_j t_j. \tag{3.6}$$

So the sum of sub-sample t-values is less than the full-sample t-value. If the partitions are of equal size, $\tau_j = 1/J$, we have that:

$$t_0 \simeq \frac{1}{\sqrt{J}} \sum_{t=1}^{J} t_j \tag{3.7}$$

and, hence, $E[t_0] \simeq \sqrt{J} E[t_j]$.

Furthermore, we have for non-overlapping sub-samples that the t_j-values are independently distributed. So we can derive the average squared t-value in the full sample from the sub-sample t_j^2-values as follows:

$$E[t_0^2] \simeq \sum_{j=1}^{J} \tau_j E[t_j^2] + \sum_{j=1}^{J} \sum_{i \neq j} \sqrt{\tau_i \tau_j} E[t_j] E[t_i]. \tag{3.8}$$

Assuming again equal-sized partitions:

$$E[t_0^2] \simeq E[t_j^2] + \left(1 - \frac{1}{J} \right) \psi^2 \tag{3.9}$$

for the given (full-sample) non-centrality parameter ψ, so we get the following relationship between the average squared t-value in the full sample and the sub-samples:

$$E[t_j^2] \simeq \frac{1}{J} \psi^2, \tag{3.10}$$

which is confirmed by a comparison of (3.4) and (3.5). The higher the non-centrality ψ, the stronger the shrinkage of the expected sub-sample $|t|$-value (compared to that of the full sample). This reduction in the information content of the sub-sample $|t|$-test might be referred to as the 'curse of sub-samples'. It indicates that sub-sample-based selection rules will find it harder to detect DGP variables (at a given size).

Overlapping sub-samples

Suppose, for the following, that $J = 2$. If the sub-samples are overlapping, i.e., $\tau \in (0.5, 1)$, their t-values are no longer independent. To overcome the correlation problem, we partition the sample into three independent partitions (say, a, b and c) and construct from these the two sub-samples and the full-sample t-values. The three generated t-distributed random variables are $t_i \sim t(\tau_i T, \sqrt{t_i}\psi)$ for $i = a$ and c and $t_b \sim t((2\tau-1)T, \sqrt{2\tau-1}\psi)$ such that $t_0 \sim t(T, \psi)$. It follows from (3.6) that the full-sample t-value is given by:

$$t_0 \cong \sqrt{1-\tau T} t_a + \sqrt{2\tau-1} t_b + \sqrt{1-\tau} t_c. \tag{3.11}$$

The two sub-sample t-values result as follows:

$$t_1 \cong \sqrt{\frac{1-\tau T}{\tau T}} t_a + \sqrt{\frac{2\tau-1}{\tau T}} t_b \tag{3.12}$$

$$t_2 \cong \sqrt{\frac{1-\tau T}{\tau T}} t_c + \sqrt{\frac{2\tau-1}{\tau T}} t_b. \tag{3.13}$$

It can be shown that the result in (3.6) holds: the sum of sub-sample t-values is again less than the full-sample t-value.

The advantage of this procedure is that t_0 as well as t_1 and t_2 can be generated as weighted sums of independently t-distributed random variables. Next we use the framework laid out here to investigate the Hoover–Perez sub-sample selection rule, which evaluates the minimum of the two sub-sample t-values. Then we examine the properties of the *PcGets* post-selection reliability check, which assesses the sub-sample evidence conditional on full-sample significance.

The Hoover–Perez Approach

Selection rule

We first consider the selection rule of Hoover and Perez, namely include a regressor if and only if its coefficient is significant in both sub-samples. In other words, the minimum of the two sub-sample $|t|$-values needs to be significant:

$$\min\left\{|t_1|,|t_2|\right\} > c_{\alpha,\tau T}^{\min} \tag{3.14}$$

where τ denotes the size of the sub-sample as a fraction of the (full) sample and α is the size of the test. For the simple framework considered here, we can define and control the size of the procedure as:

$$\alpha = \Pr\left(\min\left\{|t_1|,|t_2|\right\} > c_{\alpha,\tau T}^{\min}\,\middle|\,\psi = 0\right). \tag{3.15}$$

So α is the nominal and empirical size of the procedure, which implies that the power of the selection procedure is given by:

$$\pi\left(\alpha,\tau,\psi\right) = \Pr\left(\min\left\{|t_1|,|t_2|\right\} > c_{\alpha,\tau T}^{\min}\,\middle|\,\psi > 0\right) \tag{3.16}$$

where ψ is the full-sample population $|t|$-value of the DGP variable. The properties of the selection rule will ultimately depend on the distribution of $\min\{|t_1|,|t_2|\}$ for given ψ, which we will explore in the following.[3]

Deriving the distribution of $\min\{|t_1|,|t_2|\}$ by simulation
Design. We investigate the properties of the $\min\{|t_1|,|t_2|\}$ statistic by simulation. The Monte Carlo study consists of $M = 5{,}000{,}000$ replications of an experiment with $t\left(\tau T,\sqrt{\tau}\psi\right)$ distributed random variables with a (full-sample) non-centrality of $\psi \in \{0,2,3,4,5\}$ and a full-sample size of $T = 100$. The size of the sub-samples is $[\tau T]$, where $\tau \in [0.5,1]$, such that $\tau = 0.5$ denotes the case of non-overlapping sub-samples, $\tau \in (0.5,1)$ implies overlapping sub-samples and $\tau = 1$ is the borderline case with the sub-samples and the full sample coinciding.

In the case of non-overlapping sub-samples ($\tau = 0.5$), the experiment consists of two $t(v,(1/\sqrt{2})\psi)$ distributed random variables with $v = (T/2) = 50$ degrees of freedom and a (full-sample) non-centrality ψ. Let $\{t_1,t_2\}$ be $t(v)$ distributed random variables. Then, the full-sample t-value is given by:

$$t_0 = \frac{1}{\sqrt{2}}\left(t_1 + t_2\right).$$

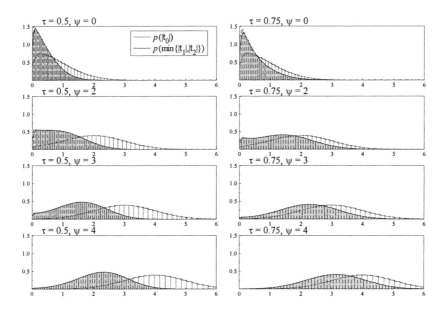

Figure 3.2   Density of the full-sample $|t|$ and $\min\{|t_1|,|t_2|\}$ for $T = 100$

For overlapping sub-samples we use the approach in equations (3.11) to (3.13).

Probability density function (pdf) of $\min\{|t_1|,|t_2|\}$. The probability density function of $\min\{|t_1|,|t_2|\}$ is illustrated in Figure 3.2 for the case of non-overlapping sub-samples (i.e., $\tau = 0.5$) and overlapping sub-samples ($\tau = 0.75$). Furthermore, Figure 3.2 compares the pdf of $\min\{|t_1|,|t_2|\}$ to the density of the simple full-sample t-value. It can be seen that the probability mass is shifted to the left. The shift is greater for the non-overlapping sub-samples and increases with a growing non-centrality. This indicates that the discrimination between DGP variables ($\psi > 0$) and nuisance variables ($\psi = 0$) is getting harder when the analysis is based on sub-sample information. This intuition will be confirmed in the analysis below. We now continue to evaluate the properties of the distribution of $\min\{|t_1|,|t_2|\}$.

Critical values. Table 3.1 reports the critical values $c_{\alpha,\tau T}^{\min}$ of the $\min\{|t_1|,|t_2|\}$ statistic for given size α:

$$c_{\alpha,\tau T}^{\min} = \left\{c \,\middle|\, \Pr\left(\min\left\{|t_1|,|t_2|\right\} > c \,\middle|\, \psi = 0\right) = \alpha\right\}.$$

When compared to the critical values of a full-sample t-test ($\tau = 1.0$), much lower critical values have to be chosen to reflect the shift of the probability mass to the left. The smaller τ, the stronger the shift. For $\alpha = 0.05$, the critical value $c_{0.05,100\tau}^{\min}$ drops from 1.984 for $\tau = 1.0$, to over 1.556 for $\tau = 0.75$, and 1.232 for $\tau = 0.5$.

Table 3.1 Critical values $c_{\alpha,\tau T}^{\min}$ for the sub-sample min $\{|t_1|,|t_2|\}$ test

τ	$\alpha = 1\%$	2.5%	5%	7.5%	10%
0.50	1.677	1.434	1.232	1.106	1.012
0.65	1.985	1.667	1.410	1.249	1.131
0.70	2.082	1.754	1.484	1.315	1.189
0.75	2.167	1.832	1.556	1.381	1.250
0.80	2.244	1.906	1.624	1.446	1.313
0.85	2.320	1.977	1.691	1.511	1.376
1.00	2.623	2.275	1.984	1.799	1.660

Table 3.2 Nominal t-probabilities $\eta(\alpha,\tau)$ for the critical values $c_{\eta,\tau T} = c_{\alpha,\tau T}^{\min}$

τ	$\alpha = 1\%$	2.5%	5%	7.5%	10%
0.50	0.0966	0.1546	0.2206	0.2712	0.3137
0.65	0.0498	0.0985	0.1616	0.2143	0.2604
0.70	0.0397	0.0823	0.1409	0.1914	0.2371
0.75	0.0325	0.0697	0.1227	0.1701	0.2140
0.80	0.0269	0.0594	0.1074	0.1512	0.1921
0.85	0.0223	0.0505	0.0937	0.1337	0.1718
1.00	0.0100	0.0249	0.0499	0.0749	0.0999

Also, Table 3.2 reports the corresponding nominal significance levels of a simple t-test (with $v = \tau T$). In the case of non-overlapping sub-samples ($\tau = 0.5$), sizes of 1%, 5% and 10% of the $\min\{|t_1|,|t_2|\}$ test would only require critical values associated with a significance level of a simple t-test at 9.7%, 22.1% and 31.4%. For $\tau = 0.75$, the required levels are reduced to 3.3%, 12.3% and 21.4%.

Table 3.3 Size α(η,τ) of the min {|t₁|,|t₂|}>c η,T test

τ	α = 1%	2.5%	5%	7.5%	10%
0.50	0.0001	0.0006	0.0025	0.0057	0.0100
0.65	0.0011	0.0038	0.0096	0.0168	0.0249
0.70	0.0017	0.0053	0.0129	0.0217	0.0315
0.75	0.0024	0.0071	0.0163	0.0268	0.0383
0.80	0.0031	0.0089	0.0201	0.0323	0.0455
0.85	0.0040	0.0111	0.0243	0.0385	0.0534
1.00	0.0099	0.0249	0.0500	0.0749	0.0999

In Table 3.3, we suppose that the critical values have been taken from the $t(\tau T)$ distribution. As the probability mass of the $\min\{|t_1|,|t_2|\}$ statistic is shifted to the left of the $|t_0|$-density, the test becomes dramatically undersized. For a nominal significance level of 1%, 5% and 10%, the resulting size of the $\min\{|t_1|,|t_2|\}$ test in non-overlapping sub-samples ($\tau = 0.5$) is 0.01%, 0.25% and 1%, respectively.

Power-size trade-off
We now derive the *power-size trade-off* of the $\min\{|t_1|,|t_2|\}$ test statistic for given size α with the sub-sample size being a fraction τ of the full sample:

$$\pi(\alpha,\tau,\psi) = \Pr\left(\min\{|t_1|,|t_2|\} > c_{\alpha,\tau T}^{\min}\,\middle|\,\psi > 0\right),$$

$$\text{where } \alpha = \Pr\left(\min\{|t_1|,|t_2|\} > c_{\alpha,\tau T}^{\min}\,\middle|\,\psi = 0\right).$$

Figure 3.3 reports the resulting power-size trade-off function $\pi(\alpha;\tau,\psi)$ for the given (full-sample) non-centrality parameter $\psi \in \{2,3,4,5\}$, sub-sample size $\tau \subset \{0.50,0.55,\ldots,1.00\}$ and, for greater numerical stability, $T = 1,000$. The $(\alpha,\pi(\tau,\psi))$ functional is derived by parametric variation of the critical value $c_{\alpha,\tau T}^{\min} = c_{\eta(\alpha,\tau),\tau T}$ according to its simple t-test significance level η, resulting in sequences of $\alpha(\eta,\tau)$ and $\pi(\alpha(\eta,\tau);\tau,\psi)$.

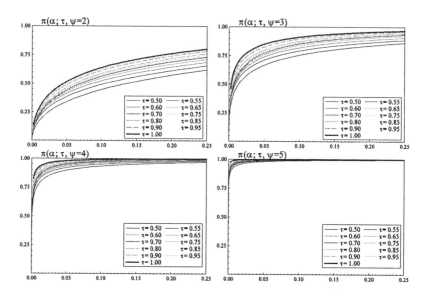

Figure 3.3   Power-size trade-off under the $\min\{|t_1|,|t_2|\} > c_{\alpha,\tau T}^{\min}$ *selection*

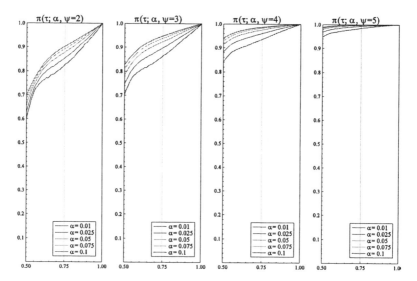

Figure 3.4   Relative power for given τ *under the* $\min\{|t_1|,|t_2|\} > c_{\alpha,\tau T}^{\min}$
        selection rule (T = 1,000)

The power loss is quite substantial (up to 40% for $\tau = 0.5$), but it is worth noting that analysing overlapping sub-samples can retrieve part of the power loss.

The power of the test relative to the full-sample case,

$$\frac{\pi(\alpha;\tau,\psi)}{\pi(\alpha;1,\psi)} \text{ with } \psi > 0,$$

is illustrated in Figure 3.4 for sub-sample sizes of $\tau = 0.5$ to 1.0. The power is found to be a monotonically increasing function in τ, so we can conclude that the sub-sample-based selection rule of Hoover and Perez (1999) is dominated by the simple full-sample t-test.

PcGets Approach

Reliability statistic
In *PcGets*, a variable is selected if it is significant in the full-sample, i.e., $|t_0| > c_{\gamma,T}$.[4] After selection, the relevance of variables in the final model is explored by post-selection reliability checks to ascertain whether 'significance' is substantive or adventitious.

The reliability of a regressor, which is normalized to be bounded between zero (no reliability) and one (full reliability), is a function of the full sample $|t_0|$-value and the significance of that regressor in the two sub-samples:

$$r(|t_0|,|t_1|,|t_2|) \in [0,1],$$

where the partial derivatives $r_i \geq 0$ for $i = 1,2,3$, $r(|t_0|,\cdot,\cdot) = 0$ if $|t_0| < c_{\gamma,T}$ and $r(\cdot) = 1$ if $|t_i| > c_{\delta,\tau T}^{sub}$ for all i. In the following, we consider parameterizations of the reliability function which are based on a constant penalty ρ for insignificance in sub-samples:

$$r(|t_0|,|t_1|,|t_2|) = I(|t_0| > c_{\gamma,T})\left[1 - \rho I(|t_1| < c_{\delta,\tau T}^{sub}) - \rho I(|t_2| < c_{\delta,\tau T}^{sub})\right], (3.17)$$

where $I(\cdot)$ is an indicator function with $I(C) = 1$ if C is true and 0 otherwise. We allow here for different significance levels for the full sample (γ) and the sub-samples (δ). *PcGets* sets $\rho = 0.3$ and $c_{\delta,\tau T}^{sub} = c_{1.5\gamma,\tau T}$, where – for typical macroeconomic sample sizes – the significance level γ is 0.05 for the liberal and 0.01 for the conservative strategy.

Note that we can write (3.17) as:

$$r\left(|t_0|,|t_1|,|t_2|\right)$$

$$= I\left(|t_0| > c_{\gamma,T}\right)\left[1 - \rho I\left(\min\left\{|t_1|,|t_2|\right\} < c_{\delta,\tau T}^{sub}\right) - \rho I\left(\max\left\{|t_1|,|t_2|\right\} < c_{\delta,\tau T}^{sub}\right)\right]$$

which can easily be compared to the Hoover–Perez rule:

$$r^{HP}\left(|t_1|,|t_2|\right) = I\left(\min\left\{|t_1|,|t_2|\right\} > c_{\alpha,\tau T}^{min}\right).$$

For $r^{HP}(|t_1|,|t_2|)$, we defined size as:

$$\alpha = \Pr\left(\min\left\{|t_1|,|t_2|\right\} > c_{\alpha,\tau T}^{min} \,|\, \psi = 0\right) = E\left[r^{HP}\left(|t_0|,|t_1|,|t_2|\right)|\psi = 0\right].$$

In an analogous fashion, we can define size and power for the *PcGets* approach as follows:

Size ($\psi=0$):

$$\alpha(\gamma,\delta) = E\left[r\left(|t_0|,|t_1|,|t_2|\right)|\psi = 0\right]$$

$$= \Pr\left(|t_0| > c_{\gamma,T} \,|\, \psi = 0\right)\left[1 - \rho\sum_{i=1}^{2}\Pr\left(|t_i| < c_{\delta,\tau T}^{sub} \,\big|\, |t_0| > c_{\gamma,T}, \psi = 0\right)\right];$$

Power ($\psi>0$):

$$\pi(\gamma,\delta,\tau,\psi) = E\left[r\left(|t_0|,|t_1|,|t_2|\right)|\psi\right]$$

$$= \Pr\left(|t_0| > c_{\gamma,T} \,|\, \psi\right)\left[1 - \rho\sum_{i=1}^{2}\Pr\left(|t_i| < c_{\delta,\tau T}^{sub} \,\big|\, |t_0| > c_{\gamma,T}, \psi\right)\right],$$

which can be rewritten, for the size say, as:

$$\alpha(\gamma,\delta) = E\left[r\left(|t_0|,|t_1|,|t_2|\right)|\psi = 0\right]$$

$$= \Pr\left(|t_0| > c_{\gamma,T} \,|\, \psi = 0\right)\left[1 - \rho\Pr\left(\min\left\{|t_1|,|t_2|\right\} < c_{\delta,\tau T}^{sub} \,\big|\, |t_0| > c_{\gamma,T}, \psi = 0\right)\right.$$

$$\left. - \rho\Pr\left(\max\left\{|t_1|,|t_2|\right\} < c_{\delta,\tau T}^{sub} \,\big|\, |t_0| > c_{\gamma,T}, \psi = 0\right)\right]$$

$$\simeq \Pr\left(\left|t_0\right| > c_{\gamma,T} \,\middle|\, \psi = 0\right)$$
$$\left[(1-\rho) + \rho\Pr\left(\min\left\{\left|t_1\right|,\left|t_2\right|\right\} > c_{\delta,\tau T}^{sub} \,\middle|\, \left|t_0\right| > c_{\gamma,T}, \psi = 0\right)\right]$$
$$= (1-\rho)\Pr\left(\left|t_0\right| < c_{\gamma,T} \,\middle|\, \psi = 0\right)$$
$$+ \rho\Pr\left(\min\left\{\left|t_1\right|,\left|t_2\right|\right\} > c_{\delta,\tau T}^{sub}, \left|t_0\right| > c_{\gamma,T} \,\middle|\, \psi = 0\right)$$

since $\Pr(\max\{\left|t_1\right|,\left|t_2\right|\} < c_{\delta,\tau T}^{sub} \,\|\, t_0 \,| > c_{\gamma,T}, \psi) \simeq 0$ for $\delta \simeq \gamma$.

Before investigating the power-size trade-off implied by the *PcGets* reliability statistic (3.17), we proceed by analysing the properties of the density of the sub-sample $\left|t_i\right|$-value given its significance in the full sample, i.e., $\left|t_0\right| > c_{\gamma,T}$.

Deriving the conditional distribution of $|t_i|$ given $|t_0| > c_{\gamma,T}$ by simulation

Design. Using the same framework as above, we now investigate the sub-sample properties of a single t-test when the analysis is conditioned on its significance in the full sample. The Monte Carlo study again consists of $M = 5,000,000$ replications of the experiment with $t(\tau T, \tau^{1/2}\psi)$ distributed

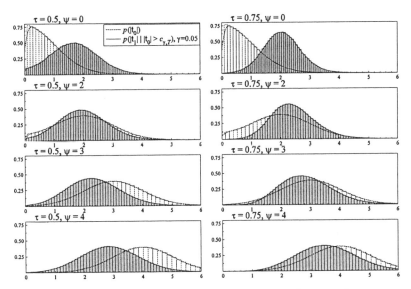

Figure 3.5 *The density of $|t_i|$ and $\min_i\{|\,t_i\,|\}$ conditional on significance in the full sample*

random variables with a full-sample non-centrality $\psi \in \{0, 2, 3, 4, 5\}$ and sample size $T = 100$. The size of the sub-samples is $[\tau T]$, where $\tau \in [0.5, 1]$, such that $\tau = 0.5$ denotes the case of non-overlapping sub-samples, $\tau \in (0.5, 1)$ implies overlapping sub-samples and $\tau = 1$ is the borderline case with the sub-samples and the full sample coinciding.

Figure 3.5 plots the conditional density of $|t_i|$ in non-overlapping ($\tau = 0.5$) and overlapping ($\tau = 0.75$) sub-samples conditional on significance in the full sample. When compared to the density of the simple (full sample) t-test, two effects become evident:

(i) For non-DGP variables, conditioning on significance in the full sample makes the pdf of its sub-sample $|t|$-value more similar to the unconditional density of a DGP variable with non-centrality close to the critical value of the full-sample test, $\psi \approx c_{\gamma, T}$. Thus, probability mass is dramatically shifted to the right.

(ii) For DGP variables with a sufficiently high population $|t|$-value, $\psi > c_{\gamma, T}$, the probability of being selected is close to one. So knowing the fact that the variable is significant in the full sample does not have any significant information value attached. Thus, the effect just described, which is so powerful for non-DGP variables, does not play a role here. Instead the 'curse of sub-samples' is due to shifting the probability mass to the left.

The two effects greatly complicate the selection problem: if a regressor is significant in the full sample, $|t_0| > c_{\gamma, T}$, the distribution of the sub-sample $|t|$-values of a variable that matters ($\psi > 0$) is hardly distinguishable from that of a nuisance variable ($\psi = 0$). A comparison of the two depicted cases ($\tau = 0.5$ versus $\tau = 0.75$) suggests the use of information from overlapping sub-samples for the reliability statistic.

The resulting size of the conditional sub-sample $|t_i|$ test at critical values corresponding to the reported nominal significance levels of a simple t-test is reported in Table 3.4 for $\gamma = 0.05$ and in Table 3.5 for a full-sample significance level of $\gamma = 0.01$. In the split-sample analysis of *PcGets*, the size of the sub-sample is $0.75T$ and the nominal significance level is 1.5γ, where γ is the significance level in the full sample. Thus, a nuisance parameter which is significant in the full sample has a 64.97% probability of passing the sub-sample test using the *PcGets* liberal strategy (54.1% for the conservative strategy).

Table 3.4 Size δ of $|t_1| > c_{\eta,\tau T}$ given $|t_0| > c_{0.05,T}$

τ	$\alpha = 1\%$	2.5%	5%	7.5%	10%
0.50	0.1108	0.2174	0.3404	0.4299	0.5006
0.65	0.1536	0.2985	0.4559	0.5618	0.6396
0.70	0.1641	0.3236	0.4947	0.6068	0.6858
0.75	0.1720	0.3465	0.5322	0.6497	0.7309
0.80	0.1804	0.3730	0.5751	0.6981	0.7787
0.85	0.1881	0.4011	0.6254	0.7532	0.8307
1.00	0.1989	0.4993	1.0000	1.0000	1.0000

Table 3.5 Size δ of $|t_1| > c_{\eta,\tau T}$ given $|t_0| > c_{0.01,T}$

τ	$\alpha = 1\%$	2.5%	5%	7.5%	10%
0.50	0.2401	0.3051	0.3545	0.3962	0.5423
0.65	0.3613	0.4449	0.5075	0.5577	0.7130
0.70	0.4002	0.4912	0.5582	0.6102	0.7645
0.75	0.4439	0.5412	0.6129	0.6664	0.8160
0.80	0.4881	0.5933	0.6676	0.7225	0.8623
0.85	0.5438	0.6569	0.7320	0.7834	0.9047
1.00	1.0000	1.0000	1.0000	1.0000	1.0000

To illustrate the procedure, we also report here the results for the hypothetical case of $\tau = 1$. This results in a two-stage test, where on the first stage a simple t-test is performed at a significance level of 0.05. Conditional on the outcome of that test, a further t test is applied to significant variables at a nominal size of δ. Clearly all t_0-values with $|t_0| > c_{\gamma,T}$ are going to pass this test if $\delta \geq \gamma$.

Table 3.6 reports the critical value $c_{\delta,\tau T}^{sub}$ of the sub-sample t-test conditional on significance in the full sample $|t| > c_{\gamma,T}$, when the size of the sub-sample test is calibrated to equalize the size in the full sample, i.e., $\delta = \gamma$. It illustrates the shift of the pdf to the right, when compared to the pdf of an unconditional t-test.

Table 3.6 Critical values $c^{sub}_{\gamma,\tau T}$ of the sub-sample t-test conditional on $|t_0| >$
        $c_{\gamma,T}$

τ	$\alpha = 1\%$	2.5%	5%	7.5%	10%	20%	30%	40%	50%
0.50	4.148	3.526	3.049	2.743	2.520	1.926	1.522	1.194	0.912
0.65	4.148	3.588	3.130	2.840	2.619	2.034	1.635	1.311	1.021
0.70	4.167	3.590	3.136	2.846	2.630	2.051	1.657	1.337	1.051
0.75	4.141	3.583	3.132	2.848	2.634	2.065	1.677	1.360	1.078
0.80	4.120	3.569	3.128	2.847	2.636	2.075	1.690	1.379	1.102
0.85	4.113	3.570	3.127	2.846	2.638	2.082	1.703	1.396	1.124
1.00	4.089	3.532	3.099	2.828	2.624	2.081	1.712	1.416	1.157

Table 3.7 corresponds to the previous table. It reports the nominal significance level of a simple t-test when the critical values $c^{sub}_{\gamma,\tau T}$ given by Table 3.6 are used. For reference, we also report the results for the sequential test implied by $\tau = 1$.

Table 3.7 Nominal $t(\tau T)$-tail probability $\eta(\gamma,\tau)$ for the critical values $c^{sub}_{\gamma,\tau T}$

τ	$\alpha = 1\%$	2.5%	5%	7.5%	10%	20%	30%	40%	50%
0.50	0.0001	0.0009	0.0037	0.0084	0.0150	0.0598	0.1344	0.2381	0.3660
0.65	0.0001	0.0006	0.0026	0.0060	0.0110	0.0460	0.1069	0.1945	0.3110
0.70	0.0001	0.0006	0.0025	0.0058	0.0105	0.0440	0.1019	0.1855	0.2970
0.75	0.0001	0.0006	0.0025	0.0057	0.0102	0.0423	0.0977	0.1778	0.2846
0.80	0.0001	0.0006	0.0025	0.0056	0.0101	0.0412	0.0949	0.1717	0.2736
0.85	0.0001	0.0006	0.0024	0.0055	0.0099	0.0403	0.0922	0.1664	0.2642
1.00	0.0001	0.0006	0.0025	0.0057	0.0101	0.0400	0.0900	0.1599	0.2501

Analogously to Tables 3.6 and 3.7, Tables 3.8 and 3.9 report critical values $c^{sub}_{\delta,\tau T}$ and nominal simple t-test significance levels of the conditional sub-sample t-test, but now under the assumption that the full-sample evidence has been evaluated at a given significance level of $\gamma = 0.05$. For $\tau = 0.75$, an actual size of 0.05 requires a critical value of 3.132, which corresponds to a nominal size of 0.25% in a simple t-test. For $\tau = 1$, the critical values can be taken from a $t(T,\psi)$-distribution evaluated at the two-sided tail-probability $\eta = \delta\gamma$.

Table 3.8 Critical values $c_{\gamma,\tau T}^{sub}$ of the sub-sample t-test conditional on $|t_0| >$ $c_{0.05,T}$

τ	$\alpha = 1\%$	2.5%	5%	7.5%	10%	20%	30%	40%	50%
0.50	3.662	3.324	3.049	2.866	2.728	2.362	2.101	1.880	1.677
0.65	3.689	3.382	3.130	2.970	2.850	2.522	2.291	2.098	1.919
0.70	3.688	3.383	3.136	2.981	2.865	2.533	2.336	2.155	1.986
0.75	3.668	3.364	3.132	2.983	2.873	2.574	2.369	2.198	2.042
0.80	3.649	3.361	3.128	2.986	2.877	2.593	2.402	2.243	2.097
0.85	3.652	3.363	3.127	2.985	2.880	2.610	2.430	2.283	2.151
1.00	3.598	3.319	3.099	2.967	2.868	2.624	2.474	2.364	2.275

Table 3.9 Nominal $t(\tau T)$-tail probability $\eta(\gamma,\tau)$ for the critical values $c_{\delta,\tau T}^{sub}$

τ	$\alpha = 1\%$	2.5%	5%	7.5%	10%	20%	30%	40%	50%
0.50	0.0006	0.0017	0.0037	0.0061	0.0088	0.0221	0.0407	0.0659	0.0998
0.65	0.0005	0.0012	0.0026	0.0042	0.0058	0.0141	0.0252	0.0398	0.0594
0.70	0.0004	0.0012	0.0025	0.0040	0.0055	0.0129	0.0224	0.0346	0.0510
0.75	0.0005	0.0012	0.0025	0.0039	0.0053	0.0120	0.0204	0.0310	0.0447
0.80	0.0005	0.0012	0.0025	0.0037	0.0052	0.0113	0.0186	0.0277	0.0391
0.85	0.0004	0.0012	0.0024	0.0037	0.0050	0.0107	0.0172	0.0249	0.0343
1.00	0.0005	0.0013	0.0025	0.0038	0.0050	0.0101	0.0151	0.0200	0.0250

Power size trade-off
We now derive the power of the reliability statistic for given size α and with
the sub-sample size being a fraction τ of the full sample:

$$\pi\left(\gamma,\tau,\psi\right) = \Pr\left(|t_0| > c_{\gamma,T} \mid \psi\right)\left[1 - 0.3\sum_{i=1}^{2}\Pr\left(|t_i| < c_{1.5\gamma,\tau T} \mid |t_0| > c_{\gamma,T},\psi\right)\right],$$

where

$$\alpha\left(\gamma,\tau\right) = \Pr\left(|t_0| > c_{\gamma,T} \mid \psi = 0\right)\left[1 - 0.3\sum_{i=1}^{2}\Pr\left(|t_i| < c_{1.5\gamma,\tau T} \mid |t_0| > c_{\gamma,T},\psi = 0\right)\right].$$

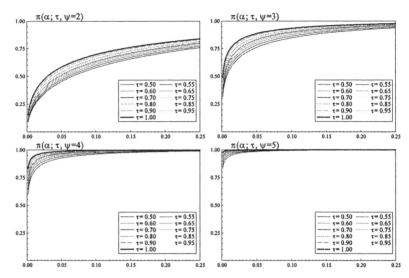

Figure 3.6   Power-size trade-off for the PcGets reliability function
            (T = 1,000).

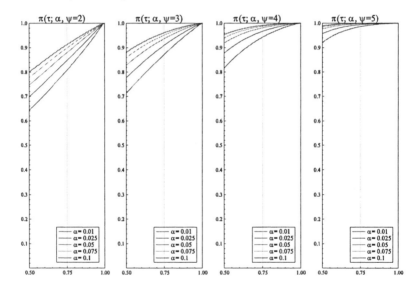

Figure 3.7   Relative power for given τ for the PcGets reliability function
            (T = 1,000)

For the derivation of the power-size trade-off $\pi(\alpha;\psi,\tau)$ shown in Figure 3.6, we use the same approach as before. The $(\alpha,\pi(\psi,\tau))$ functional is produced by parametric variation of the nominal significance level γ.

Figure 3.6 reports the resulting power-size trade-off for $T = 1,000$. The efficient frontier is again given by the full-sample analysis ($\tau = 1$). While using non-overlapping sub-samples ($\tau = 0.5$) delivers the worst power at any size α, analysing overlapping sub-samples can retrieve part of the power loss. This is illustrated in Figure 3.7, which plots the power of the *PcGets* reliability statistic $\pi(\alpha;\tau,\psi)$ relative to the power of the full-sample analysis $\pi(\alpha;1,\psi)$ for sub-sample sizes of $\tau = 0.5$ to 1.0. The power is found to be a monotonically increasing function in τ. For the sub-sample size used by *PcGets* (i.e., $\tau = 0.75$), the power loss is less than 20% for $\psi > 2$.

While the loss in power is as severe as in the case of the Hoover and Perez (1999) sub-sample-based selection rule, it is less damaging, since the reliability statistics are only provided as an additional information source: The *PcGets* model selection process proceeds on the basis of the full-sample evidence; then, the reliability of the selected variables is reported, and the user's own model choice might take this into consideration. For the size and power calculations presented here, we assumed that the reliability statistics are translated into retention probabilities in a linear fashion. It is also worth noting that we derived the simulation results under the assumption of structural stability. In practice, models are subject to structural breaks, so gains from analysing sub-sample information can be expected in that setting.

4. CONCLUSION

Model selection is an important and rapidly progressing part of a progressive research strategy. The sub-sample reliability procedure appears in Monte Carlo studies to reduce size at a small cost in power, but does not in fact result in a trade-off that is genuinely beneficial, although it certainly seems relatively costless, and has successfully controlled the null rejection frequency for selection problems that were previously deemed almost intractable (see, e.g., Lovell, 1983).

NOTES

1. *PcGets* by Hendry and Krolzig (2001) is an Ox Package (see Doornik, 2001) based on the theory of reduction (Hendry, 1995, chapter 9) implementing automatic general-to-specific (*Gets*) modelling for linear models.
2. We neglect the small percentage of the time where retained variables enter insignificantly because their elimination would induce a significant diagnostic test value.

3.   Hoover and Perez (1999) analysed the related problem as to whether the use of sub-sample evidence can mitigate the potential impact of data snooping on the distribution of test statistics. Comparing sub-sample and entire sample R^2 tests, Lynch and Vital-Ahuja (1998) found that the full-sample test has a less distorted size and more power than the multi-sample test.
4.   We abstract here from the possibility that a variable might be selected to ensure congruence, although it is not significant in the full sample.

REFERENCES

Brüggemann, R., H.-M. Krolzig and H. Lütkepohl (2002), 'Comparison of Model Selection Procedures for VAR Processes', Discussion Paper, Humboldt University, Berlin.

Doornik, J.A. (2001), *Object-oriented Matrix Programming using Ox*, 4th edn., London: Timberlake Consultants Press.

Hendry, D.F. (1995), *Dynamic Econometrics*, Oxford: Oxford University Press.

Hendry, D.F. and H.-M. Krolzig (1999), 'Improving on "Data Mining Reconsidered" by K.D. Hoover and S.J. Perez', *Econometrics Journal*, **2**, 202–219.

Hendry, D.F. and H.-M. Krolzig (2001), *Automatic Econometric Model Selection with PcGets*, London: Timberlake Consultants Press.

Hendry, D.F. and H.-M. Krolzig (2002), 'New Developments in Automatic General-to-Specific Modelling', in B.P. Stigum (ed.), *Econometrics and the Philosophy of Economics*, Princeton: Princeton University Press, 379–420.

Hendry, D.F. and H.-M. Krolzig (2003), 'The Properties of Automatic *Gets* modelling', Discussion Paper, Department of Economics, University of Oxford.

Hoover K.D. and S.J. Perez (1999), 'Data Mining Reconsidered: Encompassing and the General-to-Specific Approach to Specification Search', *Econometrics Journal*, **2**, 167–191.

Hoover K.D. and S.J. Perez (2000), 'Truth and Robustness in Cross-country Growth Regressions', Unpublished Paper, Economics Department, University of California, Davis.

Krolzig, H.-M. (2001), 'General-to-Specific Reductions in Vector Autoregression Processes', in R. Friedmann, L. Knüppel and H. Lütkepohl (eds.), *Econometric Studies – A Festschrift in Honour of Joachim Frohn*, Münster: LIT Verlag, 129–157.

Krolzig, H.-M. (2003), 'General-to-Specific Model Selection Procedures for Structural Vector Autoregressions', Discussion Paper, Department of Economics, University of Oxford.

Krolzig, H.-M. and D.F. Hendry (2001), 'Computer Automation of General-to-Specific Model Selection Procedures', *Journal of Economic Dynamics and Control*, **25**, 831–866.

Lovell, M.C. (1983), 'Data Mining', *Review of Economics and Statistics*, **25**, 1–12.

Lynch, A.W. and T. Vital-Ahuja (1998), 'Can Subsample Evidence Alleviate the Data-snooping Problem? A Comparison to the Maximal R^2 Cutoff Test', Discussion Paper, Stern Business School, New York University.

4. A Gibbs' Sampler for the Parameters of a Truncated Multivariate Normal Distribution

William Griffiths

1. INTRODUCTION

The truncated multivariate normal distribution is a reasonable distribution for modelling many natural occurring random outcomes. An example, and the one pursued in this chapter, is the distribution of rainfalls in adjacent geographical areas. The usefulness of modelling rainfall in this way, and the way in which it contributes to wheat yield uncertainty, is illustrated in Griffiths et al. (2001). Another area where truncated normal distributions have been used is in the modelling of firm efficiencies through stochastic production frontiers. For a general review see Greene (1997), and for one with a Bayesian flavour see Koop and Steel (2001). Posterior inferences about the location vector and scale matrix for a truncated multivariate normal distribution are complicated by the presence of a multivariate normal integral that depends on these unknown parameters. We show how to solve this problem by using latent variables that are corresponding non-truncated multivariate normal random variables; a relatively simple Gibbs' sampler involving only draws from conditional non-truncated normal distributions is set up.

The plan of the chapter is as follows. Some notation and preliminaries are established in Section 2. Section 3 contains a description of the Gibbs' sampler for a truncated univariate normal distribution. This algorithm is generalized to a multivariate distribution in Section 4. An application to shire-level rainfall is given in Section 5.

2. NOTATION AND PRELIMINARIES

Let y be an $(N \times 1)$ normal random vector with mean vector μ and covariance matrix Σ. Its probability density function (pdf) is given by

$$f(y \mid \mu, \Sigma) = (2\pi)^{-N/2} |\Sigma|^{-1/2} \exp\left\{ -\frac{1}{2}(y-\mu)' \Sigma^{-1}(y-\mu) \right\} \qquad (4.1)$$

Suppose x is a truncated version of y; it has the same location and scale parameters μ and Σ, but is truncated to the region $R = \{(a_i < x_i < b_i),\ i = 1, 2, \ldots, N\}$. We include cases where some or all of the a_i could be $-\infty$ and some or all of the b_i could be $+\infty$. The pdf for x is given by

$$f(x \mid \mu, \Sigma) = \left[P(\mu, \Sigma) \right]^{-1} (2\pi)^{-N/2} |\Sigma|^{-1/2}$$
$$\exp\left\{ -\frac{1}{2}(x-\mu)' \Sigma^{-1}(x-\mu) \right\} I_R(x) \qquad (4.2)$$

where $I_R(x)$ is an indicator function equal to one when x is in the region R and zero otherwise, and $P(\mu, \Sigma)^{-1}$ is a modification to the normalizing constant, attributable to the truncation. Specifically,

$$P(\mu, \Sigma) = \int_{a_1}^{b_1} \int_{a_2}^{b_2} \cdots \int_{a_N}^{b_N} f(y \mid \mu, \Sigma)\, dy \qquad (4.3)$$

Let $\mathbf{x} = (x_1, x_2, \ldots, x_T)$ denote a random sample from the truncated multivariate normal pdf $f(\mathbf{x} \mid \mu, \Sigma)$. The pdf for this random sample $\mathbf{x}$ (likelihood function for μ and Σ) is

$$f(\mathbf{x} \mid \mu, \Sigma) = \left[P(\mu, \Sigma) \right]^{-T} (2\pi)^{-TN/2} |\Sigma|^{-T/2}$$
$$\exp\left\{ -\frac{1}{2} \sum_{t=1}^{T}(x_t - \mu)' \Sigma^{-1}(x_t - \mu) \right\} I_R(\mathbf{x}) \qquad (4.4)$$
$$= \left[P(\mu, \Sigma) \right]^{-T} (2\pi)^{-TN/2} |\Sigma|^{-T/2} \exp\left\{ -\frac{1}{2} tr(S_x \Sigma^{-1}) \right\} I_R(\mathbf{x})$$

where $S_x = \sum_{t=1}^{T}(x_t - \mu)(x_t - \mu)'$.

As a prior pdf for (μ, Σ), we will use the conventional non-informative diffuse prior (see, for example, Zellner, 1971, p. 225)

$$f(\mu, \Sigma) \propto |\Sigma|^{-(N+1)/2} \qquad (4.5)$$

Combining this prior with the likelihood function yields the posterior pdf for (μ, Σ)

$$f(\mu, \Sigma \mid \mathbf{x}) \propto f(\mathbf{x} \mid \mu, \Sigma) f(\mu, \Sigma)$$
$$\propto \left[P(\mu, \Sigma) \right]^{-T} |\Sigma|^{-(T+N+1)/2} \exp\left\{ -\frac{1}{2} tr\left(S_x \Sigma^{-1} \right) \right\} \qquad (4.6)$$

The presence of the term $P(\mu, \Sigma)$ in this function makes posterior analysis difficult. There is no direct way to integrate out Σ to obtain the marginal posterior pdf for μ, or to integrate out μ to obtain the marginal posterior pdf for Σ. Also, single elements in μ and or Σ are likely to be of interest; there is no direct analytical way of obtaining the marginal posterior pdfs of such single elements. As an alternative, we can sample from these posterior pdfs and use the samples to estimate the marginal posterior pdfs and their moments. The objective of this chapter is to describe and illustrate a method of doing so.

3. THE UNIVARIATE CASE

It is convenient to begin by considering the case where x is a truncated univariate normal random variable, truncated from below at a and above at b (a could be $-\infty$ or b could be $+\infty$). Let y be the corresponding non-truncated version of x, with $y \sim N(\mu, \sigma^2)$. In this case equation (4.3) becomes

$$P(\mu, \sigma) = \Pr(a < y < b) = \Phi\left(\frac{b - \mu}{\sigma} \right) - \Phi\left(\frac{a - \mu}{\sigma} \right) \qquad (4.7)$$

where $\Phi(\cdot)$ is the standard normal cumulative distribution function (cdf). The posterior pdf for (μ, σ^2), equation (4.6), becomes

$$f\left(\mu,\sigma^2 \mid \mathbf{x}\right) \propto \left[\Phi\left(\frac{b-\mu}{\sigma}\right)-\Phi\left(\frac{a-\mu}{\sigma}\right)\right]^{-T}\left(\sigma^2\right)^{-(T+2)/2}$$

$$\exp\left\{-\frac{1}{2\sigma^2}\sum_{t=1}^{T}\left(x_t-\mu\right)^2\right\}$$

(4.8)

It is not possible to analytically integrate out μ or σ^2 from this pdf to obtain the marginal posterior pdfs $f\left(\sigma^2 \mid \mathbf{x}\right)$ and $f\left(\mu \mid \mathbf{x}\right)$. Also, because the conditional posterior pdfs $f\left(\sigma^2 \mid \mu, \mathbf{x}\right)$ and $f\left(\mu \mid \sigma^2, \mathbf{x}\right)$ are not recognizable, it is not possible to set up a Gibbs' sampling algorithm that draws from these conditional pdfs.

Our solution to this problem is to introduce a vector of latent variables $\mathbf{y} = (y_1, y_2, ..., y_T)'$ that can be viewed as drawings from the non-truncated normal distribution $N(\mu, \sigma^2)$ and that have a direct (deterministic) correspondence with the truncated observations $\mathbf{x}$. To appreciate this correspondence, consider the inverse cdf method for drawing observations y_t from $N(\mu, \sigma^2)$ and observations x_t from $N(\mu, \sigma^2) \times I_{(a,b)}(x_t)$. Given a uniform random draw U from $(0,1)$, draws for y_t and x_t are given respectively by

$$y_t = \mu + \sigma\,\Phi^{-1}\left(U\right)$$

(4.9)

and

$$x_t = \mu + \sigma\,\Phi^{-1}\left[\Phi\left(\frac{a-\mu}{\sigma}\right)+U\left(\Phi\left(\frac{b-\mu}{\sigma}\right)-\Phi\left(\frac{a-\mu}{\sigma}\right)\right)\right]$$

(4.10)

The result in equation (4.9) is well known; the result in equation (4.10) can be found, for example, in Albert and Chib (1996). Equations (4.9) and (4.10) can be used for generating a value for the latent variable y_t. Given a value x_t from the truncated distribution, and given (μ, σ^2), we can use equation (4.10) to compute a value for U.

$$U = \frac{\Phi\left(\dfrac{x_t-\mu}{\sigma}\right)-\Phi\left(\dfrac{a-\mu}{\sigma}\right)}{\Phi\left(\dfrac{b-\mu}{\sigma}\right)-\Phi\left(\dfrac{a-\mu}{\sigma}\right)}$$

(4.11)

Then a corresponding value y_t from the non-truncated distribution can be computed from equation (4.9)

$$y_t = \mu + \sigma \Phi^{-1}(U) = \mu + \sigma \Phi^{-1}\left(\frac{\Phi\left(\dfrac{x_t - \mu}{\sigma}\right) - \Phi\left(\dfrac{a - \mu}{\sigma}\right)}{\Phi\left(\dfrac{b - \mu}{\sigma}\right) - \Phi\left(\dfrac{a - \mu}{\sigma}\right)}\right) \qquad (4.12)$$

We are now in a position to use the values y_t in a Gibbs' sampling algorithm. From Bayes' theorem, we can write the joint posterior pdf for μ, σ^2 and **y** as

$$\begin{aligned} f\left(\mu, \sigma^2, \mathbf{y} \mid \mathbf{x}\right) &\propto f\left(\mathbf{x} \mid \mathbf{y}, \mu, \sigma^2\right) f\left(\mathbf{y}, \mu, \sigma^2\right) \\ &= f\left(\mathbf{x} \mid \mathbf{y}, \mu, \sigma^2\right) f\left(\mathbf{y} \mid \mu, \sigma^2\right) f\left(\mu, \sigma^2\right) \end{aligned} \qquad (4.13)$$

Given the deterministic relationship between **x** and **y** defined in equation (4.12), $f(\mathbf{x}|\mathbf{y},\mu,\sigma^2) = 1$ when (4.12) holds, and is zero otherwise. The remaining terms on the right side of equation (4.13) involve **y** not **x**, and so it is possible to express $f(\mu,\sigma^2,\mathbf{y}|\mathbf{x})$ in terms of the more readily manipulated non-truncated distribution. Specifically,

$$\begin{aligned} f\left(\mu, \sigma^2, \mathbf{y} \mid \mathbf{x}\right) &\propto \left(\sigma^2\right)^{-(T+2)/2} \exp\left\{-\frac{1}{2\sigma^2} \sum_{t=1}^{T} \left(y_t - \mu\right)^2\right\} \\ &= \left(\sigma^2\right)^{-(T+2)/2} \exp\left\{-\frac{1}{2\sigma^2}\left[\sum_{t=1}^{T}\left(y_t - \bar{y}\right)^2 + T\left(\mu - \bar{y}\right)\right]\right\} \end{aligned} \qquad (4.14)$$

where $\bar{y}$ is the sample mean of the y_t and the relationship between **y** and **x** is given by equation (4.12). The conditional posterior pdfs from equation (4.14), required for the Gibbs' sampler, are

$$f\left(\mu \mid \sigma^2, \mathbf{y}, \mathbf{x}\right) \propto \exp\left\{-\frac{T}{2\sigma^2}\left(\mu - \bar{y}\right)^2\right\} \qquad (4.15)$$

$$f\left(\sigma^2 \mid \mu, \mathbf{y}, \mathbf{x}\right) \propto \left(\sigma^2\right)^{-(T+2)/2} \exp\left\{-\frac{1}{2\sigma^2} \sum_{t=1}^{T}\left(y_t - \mu\right)^2\right\} \qquad (4.16)$$

$$f\left(\mathbf{x} \mid \mathbf{y}, \mu, \sigma^2\right) = 1 \qquad \text{when equation (4.12) holds} \qquad (4.17)$$

These pdfs suggest the following steps for generating (μ, σ^2) from the posterior pdf.

1. Choose starting values for (μ, σ^2).
2. Compute y_t, $t = 1, 2, \ldots, T$ from equation (4.12).
3. Draw μ from the $N(\bar{y}, \sigma^2 / T)$ distribution in equation (4.15).
4. Draw σ^2 from the inverted gamma pdf in equation (4.16).
5. Continue repeating steps 2 to 4, with the conditioning variables being the most recent draws of μ and σ^2, and the most recently calculated values for y.

The above procedure is suitable for posterior inferences on the parameters of a univariate truncated normal distribution. To make posterior inferences about the parameters of a multivariate truncated normal distribution we do not employ the above Gibbs' sampler directly, but we build on the results from the univariate case to derive an algorithm for the multivariate case.

4. THE MULTIVARIATE CASE

We return to the posterior pdf for μ and Σ in the multivariate case, namely

$$f(\mu, \Sigma \mid \mathbf{x}) \propto \left[P(\mu, \Sigma) \right]^{-T} |\Sigma|^{-(T+N+1)/2} \exp\left\{ -\frac{1}{2} tr\left(S_x \Sigma^{-1} \right) \right\} \quad (4.18)$$

where $y_t \sim N(\mu, \Sigma)$ and $x_t \sim N(\mu, \Sigma) \times I_R(x_t)$ are now N-dimensional vectors. To use the inverse cdf method to establish a deterministic relationship between $y_t = (y_{1t}, y_{2t}, \ldots, y_{Nt})'$ and $x_t = (x_{1t}, x_{2t}, \ldots, x_{Nt})'$ we consider a sequence of conditional distributions for the elements in these vectors. Beginning with x_{1t} and y_{1t}, we can write

$$y_{1t} = \tau_1 + \omega_1 \Phi^{-1} \left(\frac{\Phi\left(\dfrac{x_{1t} - \tau_1}{\omega_1} \right) - \Phi\left(\dfrac{a_1 - \tau_1}{\omega_2} \right)}{\Phi\left(\dfrac{b_1 - \tau_1}{\omega_1} \right) - \Phi\left(\dfrac{a_1 - \tau_1}{\omega_1} \right)} \right) \quad (4.19)$$

where $\omega_1 = \sqrt{\sigma_{11}}$ is the square root of the first diagonal element in Σ and $\tau_1 = \mu_1$.

To compute a value for y_{2t} we consider the distribution of y_{2t} conditional on y_{1t}. This distribution has mean and standard deviation given by

$$E\left(y_{2t} \mid y_{1t}\right) = \mu_2 + \sigma_{12}\sigma_{11}^{-1}\left(y_{1t} - \mu_1\right) = \tau_{2t} \tag{4.20}$$

$$sd\left(y_{2t} \mid y_{1t}\right) = \left(\sigma_{22} - \sigma_{12}\sigma_{11}^{-1}\sigma_{21}\right)^{1/2} = \omega_2 \tag{4.21}$$

where σ_{ij} is the (i,j)-th element of Σ and μ_i is the i-th element of μ. The value for y_{2t} can be calculated from

$$y_{2t} = \tau_2 + \omega_2\Phi^{-1}\left|\frac{\Phi\left(\dfrac{x_{2t} - \tau_{2t}}{\omega_2}\right) - \Phi\left(\dfrac{a_2 - \tau_{2t}}{\omega_2}\right)}{\Phi\left(\dfrac{b_2 - \tau_{2t}}{\omega_2}\right) - \Phi\left(\dfrac{a_2 - \tau_{2t}}{\omega_2}\right)}\right| \tag{4.22}$$

We can continue this way, considering the distribution of $(y_{3t}|y_{1t},y_{2t})$, then $(y_{4t}|y_{1t},y_{2t},y_{3t})$ and so on. Expressions for the conditional means and standard deviations can be found, for example, in Judge et al. (1998, p. 50). Those for $(y_{3t}|y_{1t},y_{2t})$ are

$$E\left(y_{3t} \mid y_{1t}, y_{2t}\right) = \tau_{3t} = \mu_3 + \begin{pmatrix}\sigma_{31} & \sigma_{32}\end{pmatrix}\begin{pmatrix}\sigma_{11} & \sigma_{12} \\ \sigma_{21} & \sigma_{22}\end{pmatrix}^{-1}\begin{pmatrix}y_{1t} - \mu_1 \\ y_{2t} - \mu_2\end{pmatrix} \tag{4.23}$$

$$sd\left(y_{3t} \mid y_{1t}, y_{2t}\right) = \omega_3 = \left[\sigma_{33} - \begin{pmatrix}\sigma_{31} & \sigma_{32}\end{pmatrix}\begin{pmatrix}\sigma_{11} & \sigma_{12} \\ \sigma_{21} & \sigma_{22}\end{pmatrix}^{-1}\begin{pmatrix}\sigma_{13} \\ \sigma_{23}\end{pmatrix}\right]^{1/2} \tag{4.24}$$

The generalization to $i = 4,5,...,$etc. is straightforward.

Proceeding in this way for all sample observations establishes a relationship between $\mathbf{x} = (x_1,x_2,...,x_T)$ and $\mathbf{y} = (y_1,y_2,...,y_T)'$. Analogous to equation (4.13), we can write Bayes' theorem as

$$\begin{aligned} f\left(\mu,\Sigma,\mathbf{y} \mid \mathbf{x}\right) &\propto f\left(\mathbf{x} \mid \mathbf{y},\mu,\Sigma\right)f\left(\mathbf{y},\mu,\Sigma\right) \\ &= f\left(\mathbf{x} \mid \mathbf{y},\mu,\Sigma\right)f\left(\mathbf{y} \mid \mu,\Sigma\right)f\left(\mu,\Sigma\right) \end{aligned} \tag{4.25}$$

The pdf $f\left(\mathbf{x} \mid \mathbf{y},\mu,\Sigma\right)$ is equal to one with the exact relationship between $\mathbf{x}$ and $\mathbf{y}$ being defined by equations (4.19) and (4.22) and their extensions to the later elements in x_t and y_t. Then, the posterior pdf for μ and Σ, written in terms of the y_t, is

$$f\left(\mu,\Sigma,\mathbf{y}\mid\mathbf{x}\right)\propto\left|\Sigma\right|^{-(T+N+1)/2}\exp\left\{-\frac{1}{2}tr\left(S_y\Sigma^{-1}\right)\right\}\qquad(4.26)$$

where $S_y=\sum_{t=1}^{T}(y_t-\mu)(y_t-\mu)'$.

For a Gibbs' sampling algorithm we need the conditional posterior pdfs from (4.26). The conditional posterior pdf for Σ is the inverted Wishart pdf

$$f\left(\Sigma\mid\mu,\mathbf{y},\mathbf{x}\right)\propto\left|\Sigma\right|^{-(T+N+1)/2}\exp\left\{-\frac{1}{2}tr\left(S_y\Sigma^{-1}\right)\right\}\qquad(4.27)$$

To establish the conditional posterior pdf for μ, note that

$$S_y=\sum_{t=1}^{T}(y_t-\overline{y})(y_t-\overline{y})'+T(\mu-\overline{y})(\mu-\overline{y})'\qquad(4.28)$$

where $\overline{y}$ is the sample mean of the y_t. Also,

$$tr\left(T(\mu-\overline{y})(\mu-\overline{y})'\Sigma^{-1}\right)=(\mu-\overline{y})'\left(\frac{\Sigma}{T}\right)^{-1}(\mu-\overline{y})\qquad(4.29)$$

Using equations (4.28) and (4.29) in equation (4.26), we can establish that the conditional posterior pdf for μ is the multivariate normal distribution

$$f\left(\mu\mid\Sigma,\mathbf{y},\mathbf{x}\right)\propto\exp\left\{-\frac{1}{2}(\mu-\overline{y})'\left(\frac{\Sigma}{T}\right)^{-1}(\mu-\overline{y})\right\}\qquad(4.30)$$

We are now in a position to summarize the Gibbs' sampling procedure for drawing observations (μ,Σ) from their posterior pdf.

1. Choose starting values for (μ,Σ).
2. Compute y_{it}, $i=1,2,...,N$ and $t=1,2,...,T$ using the expressions in (4.19) and (4.22) and their generalizations, and using the values for τ_{it} and ω_i defined below equation (4.19) and in equations (4.20), (4.21), (4.23), (4.24) and their extensions.
3. Draw μ from the $N\left(\overline{y},\Sigma/T\right)$ distribution in equation (4.30).
4. Draw Σ from the inverted Wishart distribution in equation (4.27).
5. Continue repeating steps 2 to 4, with the conditioning variables being the most recent draws of μ and Σ, and the most recently calculated values of $\mathbf{y}$.

5. THE APPLICATION

The variable chosen for an example is rainfall over the four months from January to April in five shires in the northern part of the Western Australian wheat belt: Northampton, Chapman Valley, Mullewa, Greenough and Irwin. Rainfall data were obtained from the Western Australian office of the Bureau of Meteorology as part of another study concerned with predictive densities for shire-level wheat yield (Griffiths et al., 2001). However, that study used rainfall data over the months May to October, not the first four months of the year that we are considering here. The vector x_t is of dimension (5×1) containing the four-month rainfalls for each of the five shires in year t. There are 49 observations ranging from 1950 to 1998. The rainfall for a given shire was taken as the measured rainfall at a site considered representative of that shire. These sites were Northampton P.O. (for Northampton shire), Chapman Research Station at Nabawa (for Chapman Valley shire), Mullewa (for Mullew shire), Geraldton airport (for Greenough shire), and Dongara (for Irwin shire). Each rainfall distribution is assumed to be truncated from below at zero and not truncated from above. Thus, we have $a_i = 0$ and $b_i = \infty$ for $i = 1,2,...,5$. The Gibbs' sampler was used to generate a total of 12,000 observations with the first 2,000 discarded as a burn in. Plots of the generated observations showed no evidence of non-stationarity.

Histograms and summary statistics for the rainfall data are graphed in Figure 4.A.1. The unit of measurement is millimetres. The rainfall distributions tend to be concentrated between zero and 50 millimetres and then tail off to the right. In shires 2 and 3 there is some evidence of a second mode, around 90 and 140 millimetres, respectively. The bimodality could be attributed to the fineness of the histograms, however. It seems unlikely that bimodality would persist if a larger sample was taken and so we proceed with the truncated normal distribution assumption. The marginal posterior pdfs for the parameters μ_i for each shire, and summary statistics for these pdfs, appear in Figure 4.A.2, adjacent to the rainfall graphs for each shire. In all shires except the first, the posterior pdf for each μ_i is approximately symmetric and, as one would expect for the mode of a truncated distribution, centred around a value to the left of the sample mean. The posterior pdf for μ_1 is skewed to the left and has a mean of -44.76. Ignoring the effect of correlations with other shires, this outcome suggests a mode at zero and that rainfall is modelled via the right tail of a normal distribution.

As an example of the posterior pdfs for some of the elements in Σ, those for $\sqrt{\sigma_{33}}$ and $\sqrt{\sigma_{44}}$, and related summary statistics, appear in Figure 4.A.3. These pdfs are skewed to the right and centred around values higher than the sample standard deviations of the truncated distributions. Finally, to give an idea of the correlation between rainfalls of adjacent shires the posterior pdfs for $\rho_{12} = \sigma_{12} / \sqrt{\sigma_{33}\sigma_{22}}$ and $\rho_{34} = \sigma_{34} / \sqrt{\sigma_{33}\sigma_{44}}$ are presented in Figure 4.A.4. These pdfs are skewed to the left and with means of 0.89 and 0.72, they suggest high correlations between the rainfalls.

6. CONCLUDING REMARKS

We have demonstrated how a relatively simple Gibbs' sampler can be set up to find posterior pdfs for the parameters of a truncated multivariate normal distribution. In the rainfall example this information could be utilized further to obtain predictive pdfs for rainfall. These predictive pdfs can then be used to incorporate rainfall uncertainty into predictive pdfs for wheat yield or into other models with outcomes that depend on rainfall. The algorithm is potentially useful in other areas where truncated distributions are utilized, such as in the area of stochastic frontier production functions.

REFERENCES

Albert, J.H. and S. Chib (1996), 'Computation in Bayesian Econometrics: An Introduction to Markov Chain Monte Carlo', in R.C. Hill (ed.), *Advances in Econometrics*: 'Computation Methods and Applications', Vol. 11A, Greenwich: JAI Press, pp. 3–24.

Greene, W.H. (1997), 'Frontier Production Functions', in M.H. Pesaran and P. Schmidt (eds.), *Handbook of Applied Econometrics, Volume II: Microeconometrics*, Malden: Blackwell, pp. 81–166.

Griffiths, W.E., L.S. Newton and C.J. O'Donell (2001), 'Predictive Densities for Shire Level Wheat Yield In Western Australia', paper contributed to the Australian Agricultural and Resource Economics Society Conference, Adelaide.

Judge, G.G., R.C. Hill, W.E. Griffiths, H. Lütkepohl, T.-C. Lee (1988), *Introduction to the Theory and Practice of Econometrics*, 2nd edn, New York: John Wiley and Sons.

Koop, G. and M.F.J. Steel (2001), 'Bayesian Analysis of Stochastic Frontier Models', in B.H. Baltagi (ed.), *A Companion to Theoretical Econometrics*, Oxford: Blackwell, pp. 520-537.

Zellner, A. (1971), *An Introduction to Bayesian Inference in Econometrics*, New York: John Wiley and Sons.

APPENDIX

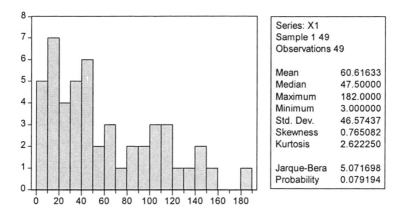

Figure 4.A.1a   Histogram and summary statistics for rainfall data in Shire 1

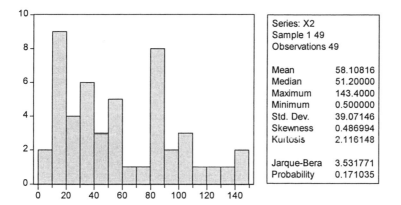

Figure 4.A.1b   Histogram and summary statistics for rainfall data in Shire 2

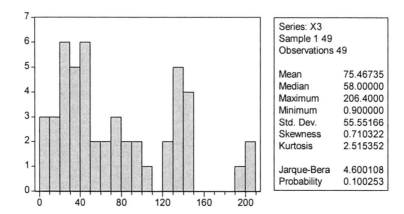

Figure 4.A.1c   Histogram and summary statistics for rainfall data in Shire 3

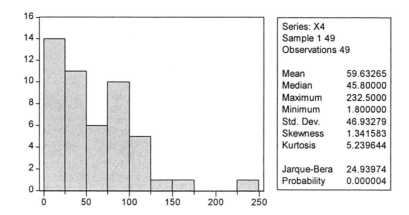

Figure 4.A.1d   Histogram and summary statistics for rainfall data in Shire 4

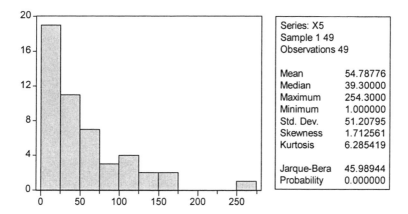

Figure 4.A.1e   Histogram and summary statistics for rainfall data in Shire 5

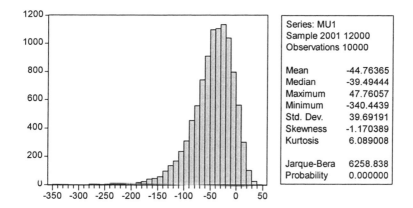

Figure 4.A.2a   Posterior pdfs and summary statistics for μ_1

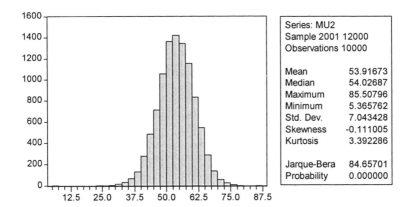

Figure 4.A.2b   Posterior pdfs and summary statistics for μ_2

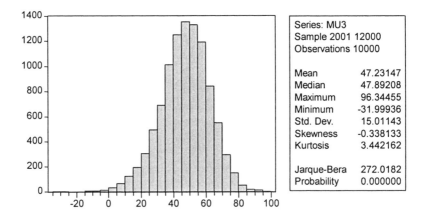

Figure 4.A.2c   Posterior pdfs and summary statistics for μ_3

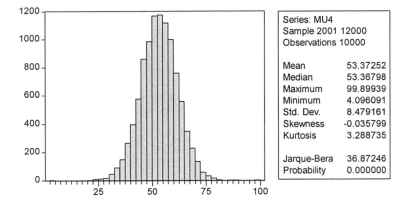

Figure 4.A.2d   Posterior pdfs and summary statistics for μ_4

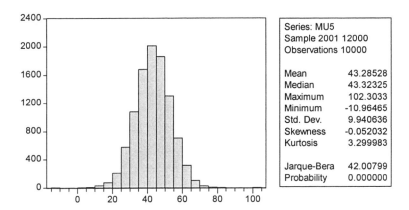

Figure 4.A.2e   Posterior pdfs and summary statistics for μ_5

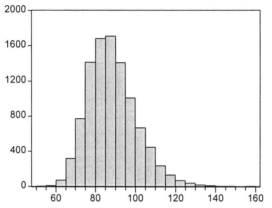

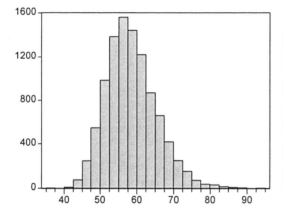

Figure 4.A.3   Posterior pdfs for $\sqrt{\sigma_{33}}$ and $\sqrt{\sigma_{44}}$

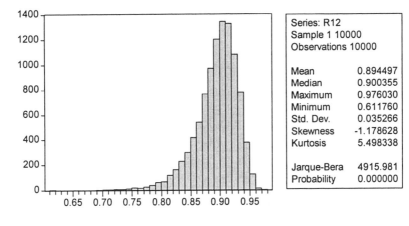

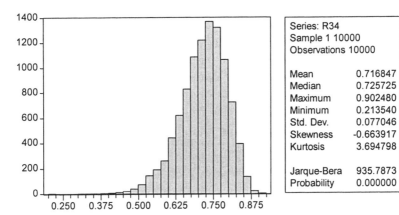

Figure 4.A.4   Posterior pdfs for ρ_{12} and ρ_{34}

5. A Necessary and Sufficient Condition for Weak Exogeneity in Vector Error Correction Models

Christophe Rault

1. INTRODUCTION

During the last decade considerable interest has been shown in the issue of weak exogeneity testing in a linear Vector Error Correction Model (VECM) with I(1) variables (see for instance Ericsson and et al., 1998; Hecq et al., 2002; Hendry and Mizon, 1993; Johansen, 1992, 1995; Urbain, 1992, 1995; Rault and Pradel, 2003). Weak exogeneity has also been extensively discussed in the two special issues of the *Journal of Policy Modeling* (1992), volume 14, issue 3 and *The Journal of Business and Economic Statistics* (1998), volume 6, issue 4, and is now widely recognized as a crucial concept for applied economic modelling. Indeed, when economists undertake practical modelling they are not equally interested in describing the behaviour of all the variables of the system. They are typically interested in building a model of either a single variable or a small subset of the variables. Many of the variables are there because economists think they are relevant to the determination of the variables they want to model but they are not interested in explaining them. For instance, when modelling wage and price determination, economists often include unemployment because they believe that unemployment affects wages, but they don't include the many variables which they think might explain unemployment. It would therefore be quite surprising if a cointegrated vector existed which would explain unemployment. Even though in the real world, we have no doubt that wages affect unemployment, in such models unemployment can often be treated as weakly exogenous.[1]

This simple example illustrates quite well the practical interest of partial or conditional ECMs, which have the same optimality properties as full VECM when weak exogeneity conditions are satisfied (cf. Johansen, 1995). It is however well-known that incorrect weak exogeneity assumptions invalidate any subsequent inference so that testing for exogeneity should be an integral and unavoidable step in any partial system modelling exercise.

The motivation of this chapter rests upon two key observations on recent theoretical works in VECM.

The first is that the usual weak exogeneity conditions which can be expressed in terms of coefficient nullities are only sufficient. They are certainly easily testable but sometimes imply 'overly strong' restrictions. The conditions of Johansen (1992) and Urbain (1992) for instance, which are widely used in applied works, forbid the existence of long-run relationships in equations describing the evolution of (weakly) exogenous variables. These equations are thus a vector autoregression (VAR) model in first differences. This implies that under these conditions the cointegration properties of the full VECM are determined solely by the conditional model. Besides, Johansen makes the assumption that macro-economists have a potential economic interest in all cointegrating relations existing between the variables being investigated. But it is actually far from being always the case and a typical difficulty sometimes arises when cointegration tests suggest in empirical applications the existence of r cointegrating vectors, whereas according to economic theory there should only exist m, with $m < r$.

The second is that the sufficient weak exogeneity conditions of Hendry and Mizon (1993) and Ericsson et al. (1998), which only consider a subset of the cointegrating relationships, impose a priori a partition of the r cointegrating vectors into r_1 and r_2. The r_1 vectors then belong to the equations of the endogenous variables and the r_2 vectors appear in the equations of the exogenous variables. Furthermore, only the long-run parameters of the conditional model are considered as possible economic parameters of interest for macro-economists. Yet in some applied studies, for a structural purpose, macro-economists can also be interested in short-run parameters and may wish, for example, to model dynamic adjustment towards long-run equilibrium.

To address the above issues we propose in this chapter an extension of the existing weak exogeneity conditions which is based on a canonical decomposition of the long-run matrix Π. This representation exploits the fact that the β cointegrating and α loading factor matrices are not unique in so far as $\Pi = \alpha\beta' = (\alpha\Psi^{-1})(\Psi\beta')$ for any $r \times r$ non-singular matrix Ψ. An interesting feature of this representation is that it enables us to give a necessary and sufficient condition for weak exogeneity. An appealing aspect of this condition for the practitioner is that it can be tested using asymptotically chi-squared distributed test statistics which can easily be computed with most statistical computer packages such as CATS in Rats or MALCOLM 2.4 (see Mosconi, 1998) for instance. Note that we do not address in this chapter the identification problem of cointegrating vectors nor the issue of testing over-identifying restrictions on long-run parameters, even if these questions are of course crucial in any dynamic structural econometric modelling, since our primary aim here is to give an intrinsic weak exogeneity condition.

The plan of the chapter is as follows. Section 2 sets out the general VECM framework. Section 3 introduces the canonical representation of the long-run matrix Π and proposes a necessary and sufficient condition for weak exogeneity. Section 4 deals with inference and testing which are conducted within the setting proposed by Johansen. Section 5 reports some Monte Carlo simulations and analyses the asymptotic and finite sample properties of the sequential procedure developed in Section 4. Finally, concluding remarks are presented in Section 6 and specific recommendations are provided for applied researchers. Proofs of important results are relegated to Appendix 1.

2. COINTEGRATED VARs

We begin by setting out the basic framework and thus consider an n-dimensional VECM(p) process $\{X_t\}$, generated by

$$\Delta X_t = \sum_{i=1}^{p-1} \Gamma_i \Delta X_{t-i} + \alpha \beta' X_{t-1} + \varepsilon_t, t = 1, ..., T \qquad (5.1)$$

where Γ_i, α, β are, respectively $n \times n$, $n \times r$, $n \times r$, $0 < r < n$ matrices such that $\Pi = \alpha\beta'$. The r linear combinations of X_t, the cointegrating vectors, $\beta'X_t$, are often interpreted as deviations from equilibrium and α is the matrix of adjustment or feedback coefficients, which measure how strongly the r stationary variables $\beta'X_{t-1}$ feed-back onto the system. ε_t is a normal, independent and identically distributed (i.i.d.) vector of errors, with a zero mean and a positive definite covariance matrix Σ; and p is a constant integer. To keep the notation as simple as possible we omit (without any loss of generality) deterministic components.

It is assumed in addition that (i)

$$\left| (I_n - \sum_{i=1}^{p-1} \Gamma_i z^i)(1-z) + \alpha\beta' z \right| = 0$$

implies either $|z| > 1$ or $z = 1$, and that (ii) the matrix $\alpha'_{\perp}(I_n - \sum_{i=1}^{p}\Gamma_i)\beta_{\perp}$ is invertible, where $\beta_{\perp}$ and $\alpha_{\perp}$ are both full rank $n \times n-r$ matrices satisfying $\alpha_{\perp}'\alpha_{\perp} = \beta_{\perp}'\beta_{\perp} = 0$, which rules out the possibility that one or more elements of X_t are I(2).[2]

These two conditions ensure that $\{X_t\}$ and $\{\beta'X_t\}$ are respectively I(1) and I(0) and that the conditions of the Granger theorem (1987) are satisfied.

Consider now the partition of the n-dimensional cointegrated vector time series $X_t = (Y_t', Z_t')'$ generated by equation (5.1), where Y_t and Z_t are distinct sub-vectors of dimension $g \times 1$ and $k \times 1$ respectively with $g + k = n$. In this writing Y_t and Z_t denote respectively the dependent and explanatory variables. Equation (5.1) can then easily be rewritten without loss of generality as a conditional model for Y_t given Z_t and a marginal model for Z_t, that is:

$$
\left\{
\begin{array}{c}
\text{conditional model} \\
\Delta Y_t = \sum_{i=1}^{p-1} \Gamma_{YY,i}^+ \Delta Y_{t-1} + \sum_{i=0}^{p-1} \Gamma_{YZ,i}^+ \Delta Z_{t-1} + \alpha_Y^+ \begin{bmatrix} \beta_Y' & \beta_Z' \end{bmatrix} \begin{bmatrix} Y_{t-1} \\ Z_{t-1} \end{bmatrix} + \eta_{Y,t} \\
\text{marginal model} \\
\Delta Z_t = \sum_{i=1}^{p-1} \Gamma_{ZY,i} \Delta Y_{t-1} + \sum_{i=0}^{p-1} \Gamma_{ZZ,i} \Delta Z_{t-1} + \alpha_Z \begin{bmatrix} \beta_Y' & \beta_Z' \end{bmatrix} \begin{bmatrix} Y_{t-1} \\ Z_{t-1} \end{bmatrix} + \varepsilon_{Z,t}
\end{array}
\right. \quad (5.2)
$$

with

$$
\left\{
\begin{array}{c}
\Gamma_{YY}^+(L) = \Gamma_{YY}(L) - \Sigma_{YZ}\Sigma_{ZZ}^{-1}\Gamma_{ZY}(L) = I_g - \sum_{i=1}^{p-1}\Gamma_{YY,i}^+ L^i \\
\Gamma_{YZ}^+(L) = \Gamma_{YZ}(L) - \Sigma_{YZ}\Sigma_{ZZ}^{-1}\Gamma_{ZZ}(L) = -\sum_{i=0}^{p-1}\Gamma_{YZ,i}^+ L^i \\
\alpha_Y^+ = \alpha_Y - \Sigma_{YZ}\Sigma_{ZZ}^{-1}\alpha_Z \\
\eta_{Yt} = \varepsilon_{Yt} - \Sigma_{YZ}\Sigma_{ZZ}^{-1}\varepsilon_{Zt} \\
\Sigma_{YY}^+ = \Sigma_{YY} - \Sigma_{YZ}\Sigma_{ZZ}^{-1}
\end{array}
\right.
$$

where L denotes the lag operator and

$$
\begin{pmatrix} \eta_{Yt} \\ \varepsilon_{Zt} \end{pmatrix} \sim N\left[\begin{pmatrix} 0 \\ 0 \end{pmatrix}, \begin{pmatrix} \Sigma_{YY}^+ & 0 \\ 0 & \Sigma_{ZZ} \end{pmatrix} \right]
$$

with the partitioning of the matrices Γ_i, α and β being conformable to that of X_t.

Equation (5.2) is known as the VECM block recursive form and its main interest is to provide the analytic expression of the conditional error correction model. Note that the disturbance orthogonalization doesn't affect the equations describing the evolution of the Z_t variables, that is the marginal model.

3. A NECESSARY AND SUFFICIENT CONDITION FOR WEAK EXOGENEITY IN VECM MODELS

As pointed out briefly in the Introduction, the existing conditions for weak exogeneity[3] in the literature, including the less restrictive ones proposed by Hendry and Mizon (1993) and Ericsson et al. (1998), are only sufficient conditions. In this section a necessary and sufficient condition for weak exogeneity is proposed, based on a canonical decomposition of the Π matrix.

As a precursor to deriving the necessary and sufficient condition for weak exogeneity, it is necessary to consider the following preliminary theorem:

Theorem 1. *Let $\Pi = \alpha\beta'$ be a $n \times n$ reduced rank matrix of rank r $(0 < r < n)$ and partition α into $\left(\alpha_Y', \alpha_Z'\right)'$.*

(i)   *If we define $m_1 = rank(\alpha_Y)$, with $m_1 > 0$ and $n - m_1 > 0$[4] then the α and β matrices can always be reparametrized as follows :*

$$\beta = [\beta_1 \quad \beta_2] = \begin{bmatrix} \beta_{Y1} & \beta_{Y2} \\ \beta_{Z1} & \beta_{Z2} \end{bmatrix}$$

$$\alpha = [\alpha_1 \quad \alpha_2] = \begin{bmatrix} \alpha_{Y1} & 0_{(g, r-m_1)} \\ \alpha_{Z1} & \alpha_{Z2} \end{bmatrix},$$

where $\beta_{Y1}, \alpha_{Y1}, \beta_{Z1}, \alpha_{Z1}, \beta_{y2}, \beta_{Z2}, \alpha_{Z2}$ are respectively $g \times m_1$, $g \times m_1$, $k \times m_1$, $k \times m_1$, $g \times r - m_1$, $g \times r - m_1$, $g \times r - m_1$ with $rank\left(\alpha_{Y1}\right) = m_1$ and $rank\left(\alpha_{Z2}\right) = r - m_1$.

(ii)   *m_1 is uniquely defined and is invariant to the chosen reparametrization. It is such as[5]*

$$\max\left(0, r - k\right) \le m_1 \le \min\left(g, r\right).$$

Under the reparametrization of the α and β matrices of Theorem 1, the conditional and marginal models (cf. equation 5.2) become:

$$\begin{cases} \qquad\qquad\qquad \text{conditional model} \\ \Delta Y_t = \sum_{i=1}^{p-1} \Gamma_{YY,i}^{+} \Delta Y_{t-1} + \sum_{i=0}^{p-1} \Gamma_{YZ,i}^{+} \Delta Z_{t-1} + \alpha_{Y1}^{+} \beta_1' X_{t-1} + \eta_{Y,t} \\ \qquad\qquad\qquad \text{marginal model} \\ \Delta Z_t = \sum_{i=1}^{p-1} \Gamma_{ZY,i} \Delta Y_{t-1} + \sum_{i=0}^{p-1} \Gamma_{ZZ,i} \Delta Z_{t-1} + \alpha_{Z1} \beta_1' X_{t-1} + \alpha_{Z2} \beta_2' X_{t-1} + \varepsilon_{Z,t} \end{cases} \qquad (5.3)$$

Theorem 1 gives an indication of the m_1 long-run relationships which necessarily belong to the conditional model and the $(r - m_1)$ long-run relationships which do not obligatorily appear in it. This canonical representation is obtained by a basis change in the adjustment space. To this partition corresponds a new β partitioned into $\begin{bmatrix} \beta_1 & \beta_2 \end{bmatrix}$. Actually, this representation exploits the indeterminacy existing on the α and β matrices: it is indeed now well-known that the parameters of these two matrices are not separately identified without r^2 additional restrictions (cf. Bauwens and Lubrano, 1994), since for any non-singular matrix Ψ of dimensions $(r \times r)$, we could define $\Pi = \left(\alpha \Psi^{-1} \right) \left(\Psi \beta' \right)$, and $\alpha^* = \alpha \Psi^{-1}$, $\beta^* = \beta \Psi'$ would be equivalent matrices of adjustment coefficients and cointegrating vectors. Theorem 1 implies no loss of generality, and only requires the determination of the m_1 rank of the upper block of the α matrix, denoted $\alpha_Y{}^6$ and reparametrized into $\begin{bmatrix} \alpha_{Y1} & 0_{(g,r-m_1)} \end{bmatrix}$.

We are in a position to state the following result:

Proposition 1. *Necessary and sufficient weak exogeneity condition. Suppose $m_1 > 0$, and that the parameters of interest Ψ are those of the conditional model, then Z_t is weakly exogenous for Ψ if and only if $\alpha_{Z1} = 0$ in the canonical representation given by Theorem 1.*

Contrary to Hendry and Mizon's weak exogeneity condition (1993) which assumes a priori a partition of β into $\begin{bmatrix} \beta_1 & \beta_2 \end{bmatrix}$, so that β_1 and β_2 appear respectively in the conditional and marginal models, we determine this partition explicitly, exploiting the fact that α and β are not unique. Note that our necessary and sufficient condition for weak exogeneity remains of course unchanged if only a subset of the parameters of the conditional model (for instance the long-run parameters) are of economic interest to the applied researcher. Furthermore, if the parameters of interest are given by the first g equations of the conventional VECM partitioned into Y_t and Z_t, it only requires in addition that $\Sigma_{YZ} = 0 .^6$

This latter case may turn out not to be very useful in practice since it is actually seldom the case that an empirical researcher has a structural interest in the unrestricted short-run dynamic parameters of the reduced form VECM, an exception perhaps being separation analyses (cf. Granger and Haldrup, 1997).

4. INFERENCE AND TESTING

The necessary and sufficient condition for weak exogeneity introduced in Proposition 1 requires the Π matrix to have been previously rewritten under the canonical decomposition given in Theorem 1. Then, in this framework, the condition is expressed in terms of coefficients of the α matrix being zero, which permits the use of conventional chi-squared statistics (see Johansen, 1995). As we have already noticed, this representation requires the determination of the m_1 rank of the α_Y sub-matrix. The following subsection develops a sequential procedure to determine this specific rank. Then, the next subsection describes how to test the weak exogeneity condition introduced in Proposition 1. Note that it is assumed that the cointegrating rank is known, that is, has been estimated along the lines of Johansen (1988), at a preliminary stage (cf. Section 2).

Determination of the M_1 Rank

The sequential procedure developed here is based on extensive use of a special class of tests of structural hypotheses proposed by Johansen and Juselius (1992), Johansen (1995) and Hunter (1992), which enables the linear restrictions on the parameters of the α matrix to be tested. The model is defined by the restrictions

$$\alpha = \left(H_1 \varphi, \Psi \right),$$

where H_1 is an $n \times k$ known matrix and φ and Ψ are respectively $k \times j$, $n \times r - j$ matrices of parameters to be estimated, with $0 \leq r - j \leq k$. In other words we impose $g = n - k$ restrictions on one set of j vectors in the adjustment space, the remaining $r - j$ vectors varying freely. This test turns out to be asymptotically chi-squared distributed and for detailed discussions the reader is referred to Johansen and Juselius (1992), or Konishi and Granger (1993). As our aim is to determine the m_1 rank of the α_Y matrix, the only restrictions considered here are zero ones. We know that rank$(\alpha) = r$, and then

$$\max\left(0, r - k\right) \leq rank\left(\alpha_Y\right) \leq \min\left(g, r\right).$$

More precisely, let us define $m_a = \min(g, r)$, $m_b = \min(0, r - k)$ and consider the following sequences of null hypotheses:

$$\left\{\begin{array}{l} H_{0,1} \left\{\begin{array}{l} \text{There exists a basis of the adjustment space such as} \\ \alpha = \left(H_1 \theta_{r-m_a+1}, \kappa_{r-m_a+1} \right) \\ \text{with } H_1 = \left(0'_{(g,k)} \quad I'_k \right)', \text{that is } m_b \le rank\left(\alpha_Y \right) \le m_a - 1. \end{array}\right. \\ \vdots \\ \text{for } j = 2,\dots, m_a - m_b, \text{ as long as } H_{0,j-1} \text{ is not rejected} \\ H_{0,j} \left\{\begin{array}{l} \text{There exists a basis of the adjustment space such as} \\ \alpha = \left(H_1 \theta_{r-m_a+j}, \kappa_{r-m_a+j} \right) \\ \text{with } H_1 = \left(0'_{(g,k)} \quad I'_k \right)', \text{that is } m_b \le rank\left(\alpha_Y \right) \le m_a - j. \end{array}\right. \end{array}\right.$$

To test these different hypotheses, we adopt the following sequential test procedure:

$$\left\{\begin{array}{l} \text{Step 1: test } H_{0,1} \text{ with the } \xi_1 \text{ statistic at the } \alpha_1 \text{ level} \\ \text{and reject } H_{0,1} \left(\Rightarrow rank\left(\alpha_Y \right) = m_a \right) \text{ if } \xi_j \ge \chi^2_{1-\alpha_j}\left(\upsilon_1 \right) \\ \vdots \\ \text{for } j = 2,\dots, m_a - m_b, \text{ as long as } H_{0,j-1} \text{ is not rejected} \\ \text{Step } j\text{: test } H_{0,j} \text{ with the } \xi_j \text{ statistic at the } \alpha_j \text{ level} \\ \text{and reject } H_{0,j} \left(\Rightarrow rank\left(\alpha_Y \right) = m_a - j + 1 \right) \text{ if } \xi_j \ge \chi^2_{1-\alpha_j}\left(\upsilon_j \right), \\ \text{else accept } H_{0,j} \left(\Rightarrow rank\left(\alpha_Y \right) = m_a - j \right) \text{ if } \xi_j < \chi^2_{1-\alpha_j}\left(\upsilon_j \right), \\ \text{where } \upsilon_j = \left(g - r + j \right) j \end{array}\right.$$

Each statistic is a likelihood ratio test :

$$\xi_j = -2\ln Q\left(H_j / H_1 \right) = T\left[\sum_{i=1}^{j} \ln\left(1 - \hat{p}_i \right) + \sum_{i=1}^{r-j} \ln\left(1 - \hat{\lambda}_i \right) - \sum_{i=1}^{r} \ln\left(1 - \tilde{\lambda}_i \right) \right] \quad (5.4)$$

which is asymptotically distributed under H_{0j} as a $\chi^2_{\upsilon_j}$ with $\upsilon_j = \left(g - r + j \right) j$ degrees of freedom. H_1 corresponds to the cointegrating hypothesis $\Pi = \alpha\beta'$, $\tilde{\lambda}_i$ denotes the eigenvalues of the unrestricted VECM and $\hat{p}_i$, $\tilde{\lambda}_i$ correspond to the eigenvalues associated respectively with the j restricted and the $r - j$ unrestricted vectors of the adjustment space.

It should be emphasized that as the ξ_j statistic is derived under asymptotic arguments and it seems to provide a bad approximation to the limit distribution in finite samples, since it tends to over-reject true nulls in small samples (see Psaradakis, 1994). Therefore, as one often encounters small size samples in empirical applications, we also consider the adjusted Likelihood Ratio (LR) test statistics, which is given by replacing T by $T - (s/n) + 0.5[n - r(n-k)/(n+1)]$ in equation (5.4), where s denotes the number of parameters to be estimated in equation (5.1). This small sample correction performs better in terms of size distortion when testing for linear restrictions on a multivariate gaussian model (see Anderson, 1984, chapter 8 for the stationary case, and the simulations of Psaradakis, 1994 for the non-stationary case).

Weak Exogeneity Testing

Having determined the m_1 rank of the α_Y sub-matrix, the Π matrix can be rewritten under the canonical representation given by Theorem 1 and the weak exogeneity hypothesis then implies the following parametric restrictions:

$$H_{0,we} : \alpha_{Z1} = 0.$$

As these restrictions only correspond to coefficient in the marginal model being zero several conventional tests can be carried out (LR test, Lagrange multiplier (LM) test, Wald test). Such tests can easily be implemented in empirical applications using most statistical computer packages.

5. THE MONTE CARLO DESIGN AND RESULTS

This section reports some Monte Carlo replications and analyses the size distortions and power of the sequential procedure of rank tests introduced in Section 4. Artificial data were generated from five data generation processes (DGPs) depicted in Table 5.A.1, each containing 11 variables ($g = 5$, $k = 6$), integrated of order 1, cointegrated of order 4, expressed in VECM forms. They only differ from the others by the rank m_1 of the α_Y matrix, which varies from 0 to 4, and have no short-run dynamics.

For each Monte Carlo simulation, we generated 10,000 series of length $T + 100 + p$, where p denotes the lag length in the estimated VECM. We discarded the first 100 observations to eliminate start-up effects. The vector of innovations ε_t was a gaussian 11-dimensional white noise, with zero mean and covariance matrix I_{11}. The initial values ($t = 0$) have been set to zero for all variables in the model, that is, $X_0 = 0_{11}$, and $X_1 = e_1 \sim N(0_{11}, I_{11})$. All simulations were carried out on a 266 Pentium II, using the matrix programming language GAUSS, the ε_t were generated by the function 'RNDN' and the nominal level of all tests was 5%. Some routines are partly adapted from Sam Ouliaris's COINT GAUSS program. For each DGP, five sample sizes were included; $T \in \{50, 100, 200, 500, 1000\}$, and the adjusted LR test statistics were used for $T \leq 100$. In each replication, the lag length p and the dimension of the cointegrating rank r are (in a first stage) treated as known, so that we can exclusively focus on the performance of our sequential test procedure. The tabulated results of the experiments are reported respectively in Tables 5.A.2 and 5.A.3 (cf. Appendix 2). These two tables contain the estimated empirical size and power of the $H_{0,j}$ null hypothesis tests, and the global sample empirical size of the sequential test procedure. More precisely, the numbers in the body of Tables 5.A.2 and 5.A.3 are respectively the percentage of rejections of the null hypotheses and the percentage of acceptance of the true rank m_1 of α_Y (that is, the proportion of 'success' of α_Y actual rank determination) at the 5% level.

We now discuss the performance of our sequential test procedure. Note that actually the results are very close to those reported in Rault (2000) for the sequential procedure of rank tests related to non-causality testing.[8] In Rault (2000), it is the rank of a sub-matrix extracted from the β matrix which is investigated and not an α sub-matrix rank, as is the case here.

These results can be summarized as follows: all $H_{0,j}$ null hypothesis tests ($j = 1,..,4$) still suffer from size distortion in small samples ($T = 50, 100$). As the sample size increases they approximate the correct size quite well. It must be underlined that the approximation accuracy to the asymptotic distribution depends on the number of restrictions tested: for the least restricted null hypothesis $H_{0,1}$, the empirical size is close to the nominal size of the tests for samples of size larger or equal to 500 (5.09% for $T = 500$), whereas for the most restricted null hypothesis $H_{0,4}$ the empirical size reduces to 5.19% only at a sample size of 1,000. Furthermore, the percentage of null hypothesis rejection when they are not true goes to 100% for all sample sizes considered in the experiment, indicating both finite distance and asymptotic power equal to one.

As far as the sequential test procedure is concerned, the multiplicity of tests can lead to a global size problem. Our simulations effectively show this phenomenon which is however more evident for small samples ($T = 50, 100$), since the sequential procedure estimated global size turns out to be highly dependent on the number of tests it is necessary to conclude (respectively 6.23%, 7.14%, 9.74%, 11.2% for $m_1 = 3,...,1$ and $T = 100$). On the contrary for large samples ($T = 200, 500$ or 1000), the estimated global size doesn't seem to vary a lot, indicating that the test procedure doesn't suffer from size distortion in large samples: for any possible m_1 true rank, the estimated global size is always very close to 5% (respectively 5.05%, 5.20%, 5.53%, 5.66% for $m_1 = 1,...,4$ and $T = 500$). This result is due to the fact that the $H_{0,j}$ null hypothesis tests ($j = 1,..,4$) are extremely powerful and never reject any null hypothesis $H_{0,j}$ when it is true. Note that a 'success' is obtained by both rejecting and not rejecting certain hypotheses in combination, and therefore the probability of success is controlled by adjusting the size of the tests to match the available power. It means, in other words, that if we need to perform up to j tests to determine the m_1 rank of the α_Y matrix, the global size of the sequential test procedure is simply given in large samples by $\alpha = 1 - (1 - \alpha_j)$. Note that this result is not true for finite samples.

Since in most practical applications it is inappropriate to assume that the cointegrating rank (r) is known a priori, we finally conducted additional simulations when r is unknown and determined using Johansen's trace test. The results of the simulation experiments reported in Table 5.A.4 show that restricting the cointegrating rank has little impact on the performance of the sequential test procedure, at least as long as it is not restricted to be less than the true rank. More precisely, if r is overestimated the sequential procedure estimated size is very close to the case where the cointegrating rank is correctly specified. This finding should not surprise us since, if one supposes for instance that $r = 5$ instead of $r = 4$, it is then possible to produce by linear combination a column of zeros in the β and α matrices, which only adds a supplementary step in the sequential procedure of rank tests, but doesn't alter its performance since the $H_{0,j}$ null hypothesis tests are very powerful. However the performance of the sequential test procedure is severely distorted by underestimating the cointegrating rank. A similar result concerning the effectiveness of restriction testing on long-run parameters in the Johansen's framework has also been obtained by Greenslade et al. (1999) when r is underestimated. This is a useful and significant result for the practitioner as it suggests that the sequential procedure may be conducted under the assumption that the Π matrix has full rank without affecting its performance.

6. CONCLUDING REMARKS

In this chapter we have provided a necessary and sufficient condition for weak exogeneity in a VECM model. This condition has been given in the setting of a canonical decomposition of the Π matrix and requires the determination of a specific sub-matrix rank, which can easily be done by the practitioner using a simple sequential test procedure based on asymptotically chi-squared statistics, whose properties have been analysed with Monte Carlo experiments.

Our Monte Carlo exercises have shown that the performance of the sequential test procedure is heavily dependent on the choice of the rank of the cointegrating matrix (Π). Indeed, provided this rank is correctly selected or overestimated, sequential testing to determine the 'true' α_Y rank has asymptotically a frequency of success comparable to linear restriction testing on cointegrating parameters by the usual Johansen's tests (1991). By contrast, the performance of the sequential procedure is distorted when underestimating the cointegrating rank and performs poorly with respect to size distortion, whatever the size of the sample.

Our conclusions therefore are to recommend investigating the α_Y matrix rank under the assumption that the the cointegrating matrix has full rank since Monte Carlo simulations have shown that in small samples of the sort typically used by the applied researcher (about 100 quarterly observations, say), there is a very good chance of successfully detecting the true α_Y matrix rank. More precisely, our advice to the practitioner is to (i) apply the standard Johansen tests for detecting the number of cointegrating vectors in the full system, (ii) investigate the rank of the α_Y matrix using our sequential test procedure in the way advocated above, and (iii) decide on the endogeneity and weak exogeneity status of the variables, keeping in mind that weak exogeneity is not invariant to the marginalization of the model. Indeed, it is not an absolute property of a variable, rather it is a property of a particular model.

NOTES

1. In this chapter, we shall confine ourselves to the concepts of weak exogeneity proposed by Richard (1980) and Engle et al. (1983).
2. A review of the econometric analysis of I (2) variables is provided in Haldrup (1998)
3. Let us remember that Engle et al. (1983) define a vector of Z_t variables to be weakly exogenous for the parameters of interest, if (i) the parameters of interest only depend on those of the conditional model, (ii) the parameters of the conditional and marginal models are variation-free, that is there exists a sequential partition of the two parameter spaces (cf. Florens and Mouchart, 1980).
4. We assume that β_1 and β_2 each contain at least one cointegrating vector to exclude the case where $\beta_1 = \beta_2$, which entails that β_2 is a null set.
5. This condition is derived from $\text{rank}(\alpha) = r$.
6. The way this rank can be determined in applied studies is discussed in Section 4.
7. The proof is straightforward since as $\alpha_{Y1}^+ = \alpha_{Y1} - \Sigma_{YZ}\Sigma_{ZZ}^{-1}\alpha_{Z1}$, $\alpha_{Z1} = 0 \Rightarrow \alpha_{Y1}^+ = \alpha_{Y1}$.
8. In Rault (2000), it is the rank of a sub-matrix extracted from the β matrix which is investigated and not an α sub-matrix rank, as is the case here.

REFERENCES

Anderson, T.W. (1984) *An Introduction to Multivariate Statistical Analysis*, New York: Wiley.

Barndorff-Nielsen, O.E. (1978), *Information and Exponential Families in Statistical Theory*, Chichester: John Wiley.

Bauwens L. and M. Lubrano (1994), 'Identification Restrictions and Posterior Densities in Cointegrated Gaussian VAR Systems', Discussion paper, Université Catholique de Louvain.

Engle, R.F., D.F. Hendry and J.F. Richard (1983), 'Exogeneity', *Econometrica*, **51**, 277–304.

Ericsson, N.R. (1995), 'Conditional and Structural Error Correction Models', *Journal of Econometrics*, **69**, 159–171.

Ericsson, N.R., D.F. Hendry, G.E. Mizon (1998), 'Exogeneity, Cointegration, and Economic Policy Analysis: An Overview', *Journal of Business and Economic Statistics*, **6**, 370–387.

Florens, J.P and M. Mouchart (1980), 'Initial and Sequential Reduction of Bayesian Experiments', *CORE Discussion Paper no. 8015*, Université Catholique de Louvain.

Granger C.W.J and N. Haldrup (1997), 'Separation in Cointegrated Systems and P-T Decompositions', *Oxford Bulletin of Economics and Statistics*, **59**, 449–463.

Greenslade J.F, S.G. Hall and S.G.B. Henry (1999), 'On the Identification of Cointegrated Systems in Small Samples: Practical Procedures with an Application to UK Wages and Prices', Working paper, London Business School.

Haldrup, N. (1998), 'A Review of the Econometric Analysis of I(2) Variables', *Journal of Economic Surveys,* **12**, 595–650.

Hecq A., F.C. Palm and J.P. Urbain (2002), 'Separation, Weak Exogeneity and P-T Decomposition in Cointegrated VAR Systems with Common Features', *Econometric Reviews*, **21**, 273-307.

Hendry, D.F and G.E. Mizon (1993), 'Evaluating Dynamic Models by Encompassing the VAR', in P.C.B Phillips, (ed.), *Models, Methods, and Applications of Econometrics*, Oxford: Basil Blackwell, 272–300.

Hunter, J. (1992), 'Tests of Cointegrating Exogeneity for PPP and Uncovered Interest Rate Parity in the United Kingdom', *Journal of Policy Modeling*, **4**, 453–463.

Johansen, S. (1988), 'Statistical Analysis of Cointegration Vectors', *Journal of Economic Dynamics and Control*, **12**, 231–254.

Johansen, S. (1991), 'Estimation and Hypothesis Testing of Cointegration Vectors in Gaussian Vectors Autoregressive Models', *Econometrica*, **6**, 1551–1580.

Johansen, S. (1992), 'Cointegration in Partial Systems and the Efficiency of Single-Equation Analysis', *Journal of Econometrics*, **52**, 389–402.

Johansen, S. (1995), *Likelihood-based Inference in Cointegrated Vector Auto-regressive Models*, Oxford: Oxford University Press.

Johansen, S. and K. Juselius (1992), 'Testing Structural Hypotheses in a Multivariate Cointegration Analysis of the PPP and UIP for UK', *Journal of Econometrics*, **53**, 211–244.

Konishi, T. and C.W.J. Granger (1993), 'Separation in Cointegrated System', Manuscript, University of California, San Diego.

Mosconi, R. (1998), *MALCOLM: The Theory and Practice of Cointegration Analysis in RATS*, Venice: Ca Foscarina. Available online at http//www.greta.it/malcolm.

Psaradakis, Z. (1994), 'A Comparison of Tests of Linear Hypotheses in Cointegrated Vector Autoregressive Models', *Economic Letters*, **45**, 137–144.

Rault, C. (2000), 'Noncausality in VAR-ECM Models with Purely Exogenous Long Run Paths', *Economics Letters*, 67–72.

Rault, C. and J. Pradel (2003), 'Exogeneity in VAR-ECM Models with Purely Exogenous Long Run Paths', *Oxford Bulletin of Economics and Statistics*, **65**, 629–653.

Richard, J.F. (1980), 'Models with Several Regimes and Changes in Exogeneity', *Review of Economic Studies*, **7**, 1–20.

Urbain, J.P. (1992), 'On Weak Exogeneity in Error Correction Models', *Oxford Bulletin of Economics and Statistics*, **54**, 187–207.

Urbain, J.P. (1995), 'Partial Versus Full System Modelling of Cointegrated Systems: An Empirical Illustration', Journal of Econometrics, **69**, 177–210.

APPENDIX 1 MATHEMATICAL DETAILS

Proof of Theorem 1

(i) First note that if we make a basis change in the dual space of the cointegrating space (that is in the adjustment space) such as $\alpha^* = \alpha P$, where P is a non-singular (r,r) matrix, then the β^* matrix is completely determined by:

$$\alpha\beta' = \alpha^*\beta^{*'} \Leftrightarrow \alpha\left(P\beta^{*'} - \beta' \right) = 0$$

$$\Leftrightarrow \left(P\beta^{*'} - \beta' \right) = 0, \text{ because } \alpha \text{ is of full column rank } k$$

$$\Leftrightarrow \beta^* = \beta\left(P' \right)^{-1}$$

Next consider an α basis of the adjustment space (EA) of dimension r:

$$EA = \left\{ \upsilon \in R^n : \upsilon = a_1\alpha_1 + \ldots + a_r\alpha_r, a_i \in R \right\}.$$

and let U_k be a vectorial subspace of R^n spanned by the set of vectors of the form $(O'_{(g,k)} \quad I'_k)'$. The intersection of U_k with the adjustment space is also a vectorial subspace. This implies that an EA basis can be determined in completing an α_2 basis of $EC \cap U_k$ with α_1 vectors. We define m_1 as the rank of α_1 and $r - m_1$ as the rank of α_2. Moreover, since α_1 is also a supplementary space basis, it follows that $\alpha_{\gamma 1}$ is of full rank column m_1: indeed, if a linear combination of the $\alpha_{\gamma 1}$ columns that produces a column of zeros existed, this would mean that a vector of U_k spanned by the α_1 vectors would exist, which has been excluded by construction.

It is then easily shown that the transformation matrix from the α basis to $\alpha^* = \alpha P$ basis can be written as

$$P = \begin{bmatrix} I_{m_1} & -B \\ 0 & I_{r-m} \end{bmatrix}$$

and then one deduces $\beta^* = \beta\left(P' \right)^{-1}$.

Finally, the expressions of the reparametrized matrices α and β are given by Theorem 1.

(ii) Let us now consider a reparametrization of the form $\alpha^* = \alpha P$, where P is a non-singular matrix of dimension (r,r). In this case,

$$\alpha^* = \begin{bmatrix} \alpha_Y \\ \alpha_Z \end{bmatrix} P = \begin{bmatrix} \alpha_Y P \\ \alpha_Z P \end{bmatrix} = \begin{bmatrix} \alpha_Y^* \\ \alpha_Z^* \end{bmatrix}$$

implies $rank\left(\alpha_Y^*\right) = rank\left(\beta_Y P\right) = rank\left(\alpha_Y\right)$, if the P matrix is invertible.■

APPENDIX 2   SIMULATION RESULTS

Table 5.A.1   Data generation processes (DGP) (n = 11, g = 5, k =6)

DGP(1): $m_1 = 4$				DGP(2): $m_1 = 3$				DGP(3): $m_1 = 2$			
Beta				Beta				Beta			
0.10	1.70	0.60	−0.10	0.10	1.70	0.60	−0.10	0.10	1.70	0.60	−0.10
−0.10	−2.00	−0.40	−0.40	−0.10	−2.00	−0.40	−0.40	−0.10	−2.00	−0.40	−0.40
−0.30	0.50	−0.20	0.50	−0.30	0.50	−0.20	0.50	−0.30	0.50	−0.20	0.50
−1.00	0.10	0.20	0.20	−1.00	0.10	0.20	0.20	−1.00	0.10	0.20	0.20
0.10	−1.00	−0.80	0.30	0.10	−1.00	−0.80	0.30	0.10	−1.00	−0.80	0.30
0.20	−0.10	−0.20	0.10	0.20	−0.10	−0.20	0.10	0.20	−0.10	−0.20	0.10
0.10	0.20	0.10	0.20	0.10	0.20	0.10	0.20	0.10	0.20	0.10	0.20
0.10	−0.20	−0.30	−0.20	0.10	−0.20	−0.30	−0.20	0.10	−0.20	−0.30	−0.20
0.20	−0.10	0.20	−0.10	0.20	−0.10	0.20	−1.10	0.20	−0.10	0.20	−0.10
0.60	0.50	0.30	0.00	0.60	0.50	0.30	0.00	0.60	0.50	0.30	0.00
0.10	−0.30	−0.30	0.00	0.10	−0.30	−0.30	0.00	0.10	−0.30	−0.30	0.00
Alpha				Alpha				Alpha			
−0.50	−0.30	−0.40	0.30	−0.50	−0.30	−0.40	0.00	−0.50	−0.30	−0.60	0.00
0.30	0.20	0.60	0.50	0.30	0.20	0.60	0.00	0.30	0.20	0.40	0.00
−0.20	−0.20	−0.20	0.00	−0.20	−0.20	−0.20	0.00	−0.20	−0.20	−0.40	0.00
0.70	0.10	0.50	0.10	0.70	0.10	0.50	0.00	0.70	0.10	0.20	0.00
−0.90	−0.50	−1.10	0.00	−0.90	−0.50	−1.10	0.00	−0.90	−0.50	−1.00	0.00
−1.00	0.00	−0.20	0.10	−1.00	0.00	−0.20	0.10	−1.00	0.00	−0.20	0.10
−0.20	0.40	0.00	0.10	−0.20	0.40	0.00	0.10	−0.20	0.40	0.00	0.10
−0.50	−0.50	0.60	0.00	−0.50	−0.50	0.60	0.00	−0.50	−0.50	0.60	0.00
0.10	0.50	0.10	−0.20	0.10	0.50	0.10	−0.20	0.10	0.50	0.10	−0.20
0.10	0.30	−0.30	0.20	0.10	0.30	−0.30	0.20	0.10	0.30	−0.30	0.20
−0.90	0.40	0.30	−0.50	−0.90	0.40	0.30	−0.50	−0.90	0.40	0.30	0.50
DGP(4): $m_1 = 1$				DGP(5): $m_1 = 0$							
Beta				Beta							
0.10	1.70	0.60	−0.10	0.10	1.70	0.60	−0.10				
−0.10	−2.00	−0.40	−0.40	−0.10	−2.00	−0.40	−0.40				
−0.30	0.50	−0.20	0.50	−0.30	0.50	−0.20	0.50				
−1.00	0.10	0.20	0.20	−1.00	0.10	0.20	0.20				
0.10	−1.00	−0.80	0.30	0.10	−1.00	−0.80	0.30				
0.20	−0.10	−0.20	0.10	0.20	−0.10	−0.20	0.10				
0.10	0.20	0.10	0.20	0.10	0.20	0.10	0.20				
0.10	−0.20	−0.30	−0.20	0.10	−0.20	−0.30	−0.20				
0.20	−0.10	0.20	−0.10	0.20	−0.10	0.20	−0.10				
0.60	0.50	0.30	0.00	0.60	0.50	0.30	0.00				
0.10	−0.30	−0.30	0.00	0.10	−0.30	−0.30	0.00				
Alpha				Alpha							
−0.90	−0.30	−0.60	0.00	0.00	0.00	0.00	0.00				
0.60	0.20	0.40	0.00	0.00	0.00	0.00	0.00				
−0.60	−0.20	−0.40	0.00	0.00	0.00	0.00	0.00				
0.30	0.10	0.20	0.00	0.00	0.00	0.00	0.00				
−1.50	−0.50	−1.00	0.00	0.00	0.00	0.00	0.00				
−1.00	0.00	−0.20	0.10	−1.00	0.00	−0.20	0.10				
−0.20	0.40	0.00	0.10	−0.20	0.40	0.00	0.10				
−0.50	−0.50	0.60	0.00	−0.50	−0.50	0.60	0.00				
0.10	0.50	0.10	−0.20	0.10	0.50	0.10	−0.20				
0.10	0.30	−0.30	0.20	0.10	0.30	−0.30	0.20				
−0.90	0.40	0.30	−0.50	−0.20	0.50	0.30	0.30				

Notes: DGP(1), (2) and (5) can easily be seen to be respectively of rank $m_1 = 4, 3, 0$. However the fact that DGP(3) and (4) are of rank $m_1 = 2$ and $m_1=1$ is less straightforward: it requires noticing that the α_Y columns of these two DGPs are not linearly independent since they are respectively linked by $C_3 = 2 C_2$, for DGP(3) and by $C_3 = 2 C_2, C_1 = C_2 + C_3$ for DGP(4).

Table 5.A.2 *Empirical size and power of the $H_{0,j}$ null hypothesis tests ($j = 1,..,4$) (rejection per 100), with 10,000 replications at the 5% nominal level of significance[1]*

	Hypothesis tested	$H_{0,1}$: {rank(α_Y) ≤ 3} versus {rank(α_Y) = 4}	$H_{0,1}$: {rank(α_Y) ≤ 3} versus {rank(α_Y) = 4}	$H_{0,1}$: {rank(α_Y) ≤ 3} versus {rank(α_Y) = 4}	$H_{0,1}$: {rank(α_Y) ≤ 3} versus {rank(α_Y) = 4}
	Sample Size	α_1 $W_1 = \Psi_1 > A_1{}^2$	α_2 $W_2 = \Psi_2 > A_2$	α_3 $W_3 = \Psi_3 > A_3$	α_4 $W_4 = \Psi_4 > A_4$
DGP(1):					
$m_1 = 4$	50	100	100	100	100
	100	100	100	100	100
	200	100	100	100	100
	500	100	100	100	100
	1000	100	100	100	100
DGP(2):					
$m_1 = 3$	50	7.87	100	100	100
	100	6.35	100	100	100
	200	5.23	100	100	100
	500	5.09	100	100	100
	1000	5.03	100	100	100
DGP(3):					
$m_1 = 2$	50	0.00	12.4	100	100
	100	0.00	7.22	100	100
	200	0.00	6.12	100	100
	500	0.00	5.27	100	100
	1000	0.00	5.11	100	100
DGP(4):					
$m_1 = 1$	50	0.10	0.21	17.5	100
	100	0.00	0.00	9.57	100
	200	0.00	0.00	7.02	100
	500	0.00	0.00	5.58	100
	1000	0.00	0.00	5.11	100
DGP(5):					
$m_1 = 0$	50	0.20	0.42	1.30	20.4
	100	0.00	0.00	1.05	9.86
	200	0.00	0.00	0.40	7.12
	500	0.00	0.00	0.00	5.72
	1000	0.00	0.00	0.00	5.19

Notes:
1. The adjusted version of the test statistic was used for $T = 50, 100$.
2. A_i, $i = 1,..,4$ denotes the critical value from the χ^2 distribution at the 5% level of significance.

Econometric Theory

Table 5.A.3 *Empirical size of the sequential test procedure (rejection per 100), with 10,000 replications at the 5% nominal level of significance in the case where the cointegrating rank (that is $r = 4$) is known*

	DGP(2): $m_1 = 3$, $P(W_1)$				
Sample size T	50	100	200	500	1000
m_1 estimated $= m_1$	7.44	6.23	5.19	5.05	5.01
	DGP(3): $m_1 = 2$, $P(\overline{W}_1\ W_2)$ [1]				
Sample size T	50	100	200	500	1000
m_1 estimated $= m_1$	12.8	7.14	5.99	5.2	5.05
	DGP(4): $m_1 = 1$, $P(\overline{W}_1\ \overline{W}_2\ W_3)$				
Sample size T	50	100	200	500	1000
m_1 estimated $= m_1$	18.6	9.74	6.91	5.53	5.13
	DGP(5): $m_1 = 0$, $P(\overline{W}_1\ \overline{W}_2\ \overline{W}_3\ W_4)$				
Sample size T	50	100	200	500	1000
m_1 estimated $= m_1$	20.9	11.2	7.09	5.66	5.18

Notes:
1. $P(\overline{W}_1\ W_2)$ represents the probability of being simultaneously in the acceptance region $\overline{W}_1$ of test 1 and in the critical region W_2 of test 2.

Table 5.A.4 *Empirical size of the sequential test procedure (rejection per 100), with 10,000 replications at the 5% nominal level of significance in the case where the cointegrating rank (that is r = 4) is not correctly selected.*

		DGP(2): $m_1 = 3, P(W_1)$				
	Sample Size T	50	100	200	500	1000
$r = 2$	m_1 estimated $= m_1$	24.7	21.8	19.6	16.3	13.8
$r = 3$	m_1 estimated $= m_1$	15.7	13.94	12.4	11.4	10.1
$r = 5$	m_1 estimated $= m_1$	7.95	6.63	5.50	5.26	5.12
$r = 6$	m_1 estimated $= m_1$	8.26	6. 77	5.64	5.42	5.26
		DGP(3): $m_1 = 2, P(\overline{W}_1\ W_2)$				
$r = 2$	m_1 estimated $= m_1$	32.2	24.3	20.8	18.8	15.5
$r = 3$	m_1 estimated $= m_1$	22.1	15.9	13.9	12.4	11.7
$r = 5$	m_1 estimated $= m_1$	13.5	7.75	6.40	5.51	5.24
$r = 6$	m_1 estimated $= m_1$	14.0	8.12	6.65	5.71	5.36
		DGP(4): $m_1 = 1, P(\overline{W}_1\ \overline{W}_2\ W_3)$				
$r = 2$	m_1 estimated $= m_1$	39.2	27.6	22.4	20.0	16.3
$r = 3$	m_1 estimated $= m_1$	28.9	18.5	14.8	13.9	12.1
$r = 5$	m_1 estimated $= m_1$	19.2	10.1	7.31	5.78	5.28
$r = 6$	m_1 estimated $= m_1$	19.7	10.5	7.66	5.99	5.42
		DGP(5): $m_1 = 0, P(\overline{W}_1\ \overline{W}_2\ \overline{W}_3\ W_4)$				
$r = 2$	m_1 estimated $= m_1$	43.2	30.4	25.3	22.1	18.1
$r = 3$	m_1 estimated $= m_1$	31.1	20.4	16.1	14.1	12.4
$r = 5$	m_1 estimated $= m_1$	22.1	12.0	7.78	6.11	5.32
$r = 6$	m_1 estimated $= m_1$	22.9	12.7	8.37	6.52	5.60

6. Bayesian Graphical Inference for Economic Time Series that may have Stochastic or Deterministic Trends

John Marriott, John Naylor and Andy Tremayne

1. INTRODUCTION

A considerable literature has grown around the problem of testing for the existence of unit roots. Fuller (1976) and Dickey and Fuller (1979) based their tests on regressions of the form

$$y_t = \alpha + \rho y_{t-1} + u_t,$$

where u_t is assumed to be white noise. Said and Dickey (1984) demonstrated that if the $\{u_t\}$ followed some unknown autoregressive moving average model (ARMA) process an adequate approximation could be obtained by using the regression

$$y_t = \alpha + \rho y_{t-1} + \sum_{i=1}^{p} \phi_i \Delta y_{t-i} + u_t,$$

where p is $O(T^{1/3})$ for a series of length T. Tests that employ this correction for serial correlation are referred to as augmented Dickey–Fuller tests. Other authors (see for example Schwert, 1987; Kwiatkowski and Schmidt, 1990; and Said, 1991) have considered extensions of these tests to the case in which the regression includes a time trend where, under the null hypothesis of a unit root, the trend parameter, β, is set to zero. Pantula and Hall (1991) developed an approach based on an instrumental variable estimator and Ahn (1993) has developed Lagrange multiplier tests; both of these approaches allow for β to be non-zero under the null hypothesis. In all of the work referred to above the alternative hypothesis is that the series is stationary (or trend stationary).

Bayesian analyses of unit root models have also been developed (see for example Phillips, 1991; Poirier, 1991; Schotman and Van Dijk, 1991; Koop, 1992; Zivot, 1994; Uhlig, 1994; and Lubrano, 1995; and the references therein). A clear and useful exposition of the Bayesian analysis of stochastic trends, that summarises many of these references, is provided by Maddala and Kim (1998, chapter 8). More recently, Koop and Van Dijk (2000) have considered a Bayesian analysis using a state space model, but we do not consider this case here.

Several authors have suggested that the framework within which the analysis takes place may be unsatisfactory. Schotman and Van Dijk (1991), for example, indicate that an appropriate response to evidence of explosive roots may be to consider other, possibly non-linear, models. Sims (1991, p. 430) points out that the hypotheses considered are actually a proxy for 'classes of nearby models' and expresses a preference for work that uses richer models. Kwiatkowski et al. (1992), in discussing their inconclusive conclusions for several of the Nelson and Plosser (1982) data series, again suggest the consideration of alternative models. Andrews (1993) and Stock (1991) have also raised these concerns and adopt an estimative (rather than testing) approach that leads to interval, as well as point, estimators to provide additional information.

The approach developed here is Bayesian, using proper priors and is also estimative in nature. The method proposed should not be thought of as providing a formal inference with respect to the presence of a unit root and/or a deterministic trend; rather it should be viewed from the perspective of a data exploratory device. We use a structural form discussed by Lubrano (1995) among others and develop a graphical approach based on the marginal joint posterior density of the unit root and trend parameters. We explicitly do not exclude the possibility of explosive non-stationary behaviour. By considering the graph of this joint posterior we obtain useful indications of whether difference or trend stationary models are appropriate. In addition, the graph gives a clear indication of whether the investigator should consider a different line of enquiry, a task that is beyond the scope of this chapter.

The model we employ and its associated likelihood are discussed in Section 2. Section 3 presents the Bayesian analysis and a discussion of the graphical approach, together with presentations based on simulated data from known data generating mechanisms. In Section 4 we illustrate the approach in the context of the familiar data set first discussed by Nelson and Plosser (1982) and used by many investigators in this field.

2. THE MODEL

Model Specification

We start by following Davidson and MacKinnon (1993) in considering the formulation first advocated by Bhargava (1986)

$$y_t = \mu + \delta t + u_t$$
$$u_t = \rho u_{t-1} + \varepsilon_t; \quad \varepsilon_t \sim iid\, N\left(0, \sigma^2\right) \tag{6.1}$$

which is a structural form of the type investigated by Schotman and Van Dijk (1991). The reduced form of (6.1) is

$$y_t = \left[(1-\rho)\mu + \rho\delta\right] + (1-\rho)\delta t + \rho y_{t-1} + \varepsilon_t; \tag{6.2}$$

see also Franses (2001) for related discussion. This can be written using a different parametrisation, in what Zivot (1994) refers to as the 'linear' version of the reduced form,

$$y_t = \alpha + \beta t + \rho y_{t-1} + \varepsilon_t. \tag{6.3}$$

Regressions based on (6.3) form the basis of both the classical approach to discriminating between a difference stationary and a trend stationary process and the Bayesian approach to the analysis of the unit root problem proposed by Phillips (1991); see also the work of Zivot and Phillips (1994), who are expressly concerned with trend determination in a Bayesian setting.

We note here that the implication of using (6.3) rather than (6.1) is that when $\rho = 1$ β must be constrained to be zero; no such restriction applies to the parameters of (6.1). Ignoring this restriction in (6.3) can impose serious problems and it is primarily for this reason that Lubrano (1995) argues that (6.1) should be used in a Bayesian framework. Another problem can arise in the context of (6.2), for the intercept, or mean, parameter μ is not identified as $\rho \rightarrow 1$. As has been indicated by Schotman and Van Dijk (1991) this can be overcome in a Bayesian analysis by specifying a proper prior for μ.

In order to allow for autocorrelation at higher lags Lubrano (1995) and Geweke (1994) consider the following generalisation of (6.1)

$$y_t = \mu + \delta t + u_t$$
$$A(L)u_t = \varepsilon_t, \tag{6.4}$$

where

$$A(L) = 1 - \sum_{i=1}^{p} a_i L^i.$$

L is the lag operator and ε_t is as defined in (6.1). It is straightforward to show that (6.4) can be rewritten as

$$y_t = \mu + \delta t + u_t; \quad u_t = \rho u_{t-1} + \sum_{i=1}^{p-1} \phi_i \Delta u_{t-i} + \varepsilon_t, \tag{6.5}$$

where

$$\rho = \sum_{i=1}^{p} a_i \text{ and } \phi_j = -\sum_{i=1}^{p-j} a_{i+j}.$$

This is the model we use here and we note in passing that it is similar to the model considered by Ahn (1993) in developing a Lagrange multiplier test; see also Schmidt and Phillips (1992). The reduced form of (6.5) is

$$y_t = \left[(1-\rho)\mu + \rho\delta\right] + \rho y_{t-1} + (1-\rho)\delta t + \sum_{i=1}^{p-1} \phi_i \left(\Delta y_{t-i} - \delta\right) + \varepsilon_t \tag{6.6}$$

which clearly involves non-linearity in both ρ and δ. This model has also been used in a Bayesian context by Hoek (1997, section 4.2).

Specification of the Likelihood

To obtain the likelihood for sample data $\mathbf{y} = (y_1, y_2, \ldots, y_T)$ we employ the well-known factorisation

$$p(\mathbf{y} \mid \theta) = p(\mathbf{y}_p \mid \theta) \times p(\mathbf{y}_{\bar{p}} \mid \theta, \mathbf{y}_p) \tag{6.7}$$

where $\mathbf{y}_p = (y_1, y_2, \ldots, y_p)$, $\mathbf{y}_{\bar{p}} = (y_{p+1}, \ldots, y_T)$ and we denote the, as yet unspecified, vector of parameters by θ. It is clear from (6.5) and (6.6) that the first term on the right-hand side of (6.7) will depend on the *unobserved* values $\mathbf{u} = (u_0, u_{-1}, \ldots, u_{1-p})$, which must be specified in some way. Naylor and Marriott (1996) have shown that the exact likelihood can be obtained by treating these unobserved values as additional parameters and then marginalising the resulting likelihood by integration. We follow Marriott et al. (1996) in writing the likelihood as

$$p(\mathbf{y} \mid \theta) = p(y_1 \mid \theta) p(y_2 \mid \theta, y_1) \ldots p(y_j \mid \theta, \mathbf{y}_{j-1}) \ldots p(y_T \mid \theta, \mathbf{y}_{T-1}) \tag{6.8}$$

with $\mathbf{y}_t$ comprising the first t points in the sample, and write

$$p(y_t \mid \theta, \mathbf{y}_{t-1}) = \frac{1}{\sqrt{2\pi}\sigma} \exp\left\{-\frac{S(\theta, \mathbf{y}_t)}{2\sigma^2}\right\}, \tag{6.9}$$

where

$$S(\theta, \mathbf{y}_t) = \left(y_t - \rho y_{t-1} - \left[(1-\rho)\mu + \rho\delta \right] - (1-\rho)\delta t - \sum_{i=1}^{p-1} \phi_i \left(\Delta y_{t-i} - \delta \right) \right)^2$$

is completely specified in terms of the model parameters, $\theta = (\mu, \delta, \rho,$ $\phi_1, ..., \phi_{p-1}, \mathbf{u}_-)$ and observed sample data. Clearly, using (6.9), both terms in (6.7) are readily found.

Within the above formulation of the problem we are obviously not constrained to assume a normal density for ε_t. For example, one alternative might be to model ε_t / σ as Student's t with v degrees of freedom. In this case we would replace (6.9) with

$$p(y_t \mid \theta, \mathbf{y}_{t-1}) = \frac{\Gamma\left[(v+1)/2 \right]}{\sqrt{v}\Gamma\left[1/2 \right]\Gamma\left[v/2 \right]} \left[1 + \frac{S(\theta, \mathbf{y}_t)}{v\sigma^2} \right]^{-(v+1)/2}$$

and could then either specify a value for v or include it as a parameter to be estimated. Such an approach may have fruitful application in empirical finance where fat-tailed distributions are commonplace.

Given the joint prior for θ, the joint posterior for ρ and δ can be obtained under the unconditional likelihood by integrating out the unobserved values. A different approach to inference is to use Monte Carlo Markov Chain (MCMC) techniques to generate large samples from the posterior density. In the context of (6.5), Hoek (1997) has adopted this alternative methodology though his treatment of the initial values does not lead to the exact likelihood in our sense. Hoek takes the first pre-sample value, u_0, as $N(0,\sigma^2/(1-\rho^2))$ and sets all other pre-sample values to zero (Hoek 1997, p. 33). This has the effect of treating the single pre-sample value u_0 as a parameter, with the specified normal distribution as a prior. Here we follow a numerical integration strategy and plot contours of the exact joint posterior of interest. In order to obtain contours that even approach the precision available to us, extremely large MCMC samples may be needed. Additionally, in this case the exact joint posterior density is available and we have chosen to employ it rather than attempt to take, and use, a sample from it.

3. A BAYESIAN APPROACH

The Priors and Resultant Posteriors

Our Bayesian analysis of model (6.5) now follows Naylor and Marriott (1996), with the augmented parameter vector θ and prior of the form

$$p(\theta) = p(\delta)\,p(\rho)\,p(\mu \mid \sigma)\,p(\phi_1) \cdots p(\phi_{p-1})\,p(\mathbf{u}_- \mid \sigma)\,p(\sigma). \quad (6.10)$$

We use proper densities that are not over-informative but do represent sensible choices. Of course, in any practical situation, problem-specific expertise may lead to different priors, or non-informative priors may be preferred. However it is straightforward to adapt the methodology to be described below so as to handle such alternative specifications. Our concern here is not to dwell on the elicitation of priors with a necessarily intuitive interpretation (though that will often be desirable in real applications). Rather we make illustrative choices that follow previous practice in some way, or seem defensible. This is so that our method can be exposited and we leave applied workers free to amend our selections whenever they wish.

For μ and σ we follow Monahan (1983) and use the normal and inverse gamma forms,

$$p(\mu \mid \sigma) = \frac{1}{\sqrt{2\pi}\,\tau\sigma}\exp\left\{-\frac{1}{2}\left(\frac{\mu - m_\mu}{\tau\sigma}\right)^2\right\}, \quad (6.11)$$

$$p(\sigma) = \frac{2}{\Gamma(\xi)\,\eta^\xi\,\sigma^{2\xi+1}}\exp\left(-\frac{1}{\eta\sigma^2}\right). \quad (6.12)$$

Monahan suggests values for the parameters ξ, η, and τ corresponding to various levels of information. For example, the weakest of the priors given is described as 'diffuse' and is defined by $\xi = 1/256$, $\eta = 256$, and $\tau = 16$ in our parametrisation (which differs in detail from that of Monahan). Though any choice of m_μ is possible, in all the examples presented here it is taken as zero. The prior for δ is taken as zero mean normal with unit variance. We specify an N(0,1) prior for ϕ_j, $j > 0$, which offers a proper, but not very informative prior centred on zero. The prior mean therefore corresponds to u_t in (6.5) being an AR(1) process, but the prior has substantial weight on alternatives with large correlations (negative or positive) at lags greater than one as well.

Viewing the history $\mathbf{u}_-$ purely as parameters, and regarding the process as having started at time $t = 1$ with this set of 'initial values', gives us a freedom of choice as to what aspects of the eventual model we might reflect in the

prior. The choice we make here for $\mathbf{u}_-$ is a multivariate Student t on $v = 2$
degrees of freedom, t_2, with location and scale $\boldsymbol{\mu}_0$ and $\sigma_0^2 \mathbf{R}$ respectively:

$$p\left(\mathbf{u}_- \mid \sigma\right) \propto \frac{1}{\sigma_0^p}\left(2 + \frac{1}{\sigma_0^2}\left(\mathbf{u}_- - \boldsymbol{\mu}_0\right)' \mathbf{R}^{-1}\left(\mathbf{u}_- - \boldsymbol{\mu}_0\right)\right)^{-\frac{p+2}{2}} \qquad (6.13)$$

$$\text{with } \mathbf{R} = \begin{bmatrix} 1 & k & k^2 & \cdots & k^{p-1} \\ k & 1 & k & \cdots & k^{p-2} \\ \vdots & \vdots & \vdots & & \vdots \\ k^{p-1} & k^{p-2} & k^{p-3} & \cdots & 1 \end{bmatrix}.$$

We have chosen this to model several aspects of $\mathbf{u}_-$. The non-finite
second moments on the unit root boundary have been accommodated, in that
the contribution of $\mathbf{u}_-$ to the likelihood is thereby well defined for all values
of ρ; this would not otherwise be the case when $\rho = 1$. Actual prior beliefs
about the process can be modelled by choice of $\boldsymbol{\mu}_0$; we view $\boldsymbol{\mu}_0 = 0$ as a
natural choice given the structural form (6.5). Some control over the plausible
range of values of $\boldsymbol{\mu}_0$ can be exercised via σ_0. If an expert witness cannot
offer a good constant value for σ_0 a natural choice would seem to be $\sigma_0 = \sigma$ to
at least ensure sensible scaling in relation to the variation in the data. Finally
our choice of $\mathbf{R}$ reflects the a priori mean AR(1) process referred to above in
that we choose $k = \mathrm{E}[\rho]$, the prior mean for ρ.

Zivot (1994) points out that inappropriate treatment of the initial value, x_0
in his notation, in models where it is unusually large can lead to incorrect
posterior inference. He further observes that 'One way to eliminate the
dependence of the posteriors on x_0 is to treat x_0 as stochastic', which we do
here. (Indeed, we have observed, for simulated data, that our graphical
inference is robust whether the initial observations are generated as Gaussian,
or even as t_2, with or without dependence structure.)

A considerable debate in the literature surrounds the prior specification
adopted for the 'unit root parameter' ρ. In a paper concerned with classical
confidence intervals, Stock (1991) argues that one advantage of such an
approach is that it sidesteps the debate over priors; see also Andrews (1993).
The classical approach is equivalent to allocating equal probability to
negative and positive values of ρ. In our view, if a researcher is seriously
considering models like (6.5) in the context of data which may have
stochastic trends, she/he is likely to regard negative values of ρ with extreme
scepticism.

In the Bayesian literature Phillips (1991) adapted a Jeffreys' prior as his
'critics prior' and argued that this was more appropriate than a flat prior for
considering unit roots. The ignorance priors suggested by Phillips put
considerable weight on values of ρ in excess of 1.0; this point is well

illustrated in Phillips (1991, figure 1). Zivot and Phillips (1994, section 2.3) discuss how this potentially undesirable feature can be attenuated. Schotman and Van Dijk (1991), Uhlig (1994) and Zivot (1994) all consider Jeffreys priors for different treatments of the initial value, y_0, in (6.1), (6.2) or (6.3). Schotman (1994) compares these priors with the maximal data information priors of Zellner (1977). Other authors consider proper priors and Poirier (1991) uses a normal distribution centred on the stationary boundary and with a point mass at $\rho = 1$. Berger and Yang (1994) adapt a reference prior (Bernardo, 1979) for the AR(1) model and Lubrano (1995) uses a degenerate beta density.

Clearly, various sensible proper priors may be available and in this chapter, for expository purposes, we use normal priors with a small prior belief in an explosive model as a subjective econometrician's prior. Non-stationary values are possible under our priors but we do not wish to put point probability mass on any point value of ρ, including $\rho = 1$. One of our priors is therefore chosen to place most of the probability in the range 0.70 to 1.05 with $P(\rho > 1) \approx 0.05$; we use $\rho \sim N(0.863, 0.083^2)$. One might envisage an econometrician using this prior when the time series plot of the data is suggestive of autoregressive behaviour exhibiting substantial persistence. In the results reported hereafter this prior serves as the default choice. However, in view of the considerable evidence of the effect of prior choice on posterior inferences in this problem, and mindful of the important issues raised by Stock (1991, section 5) and others, we also undertake sensitivity analyses, though retaining normality for the prior for ρ. For instance, when the default prior for ρ seems inappropriate for the data at hand, the more diffuse specification of $\rho \sim N(0.5, 0.25^2)$ is used.

Inference about θ is now obtained via the posterior density

$$p(\theta \mid \mathbf{y}) = p(\mathbf{y} \mid \theta) p(\theta) / p(\mathbf{y})$$

where

$$p(\mathbf{y}) = \int p(\mathbf{y} \mid \theta) p(\theta) \, d\theta$$

is a normalising constant.

The inference available from the posterior density $p(\theta \mid \mathbf{y})$ may not be in readily assimilated form. For example θ may be of high dimension, so that simple plots of the posterior density are not possible. In this case, plots of selected marginal posterior densities

$$p(\theta_j \mid \mathbf{y}) = \int p(\theta \mid \mathbf{y}) \, d\theta_j$$

where θ_j is some one or two dimensional sub-space, and $\theta_{\bar{j}}$ is its complement in θ, may be helpful.

Another convenient summary is provided by posterior moments, for example

$$E\left(\theta_j \mid \mathbf{y}\right) = \int \theta_j p\left(\theta \mid \mathbf{y}\right) d\theta \text{ and } E\left(\theta_i \theta_j \mid \mathbf{y}\right) = \int \theta_i \theta_j p\left(\theta \mid \mathbf{y}\right) d\theta.$$

The posterior means are often used as Bayes point estimates, while second order moments reveal something of the posterior correlation structure. Such posterior correlations may well arise as a consequence only of the data, having not been specified a priori. This will generally be the case for correlations between ρ and the ϕ's, which are assumed to be zero in our prior but will generally be non-zero in the posterior.

Of course, computation of both the posterior density and convenient summaries requires evaluation of integrals, generally over several dimensions. The integrals needed for this cannot be found analytically and so some computational method is needed. For $p \leq 3$ there are at most nine parameters and iterative Gauss Hermite quadrature (see for example Smith et al., 1985; and Shaw, 1988), can be used efficiently. For $p > 3$ the conditional likelihood described by (6.8) with pre-sample values set to zero, rather than treated as parameters, could be employed. This approach is used in the next section, for example, to deal with significant moving average components in data. Such features have often been observed with macroeconomic data; see, inter alia, Schwert (1987) and Leybourne (1994). For all the examples given here the 'Bayes Four' library (see Naylor, 1991) has been used. This facilitates computation of $p(\mathbf{y})$, first and second order posterior moments, univariate and bivariate marginal posterior densities, and predictive expectations. To improve performance of this method a functional transformation of σ to $\log(\sigma)$ was used.

The method basically uses a Gauss Hermite rule which is re-scaled by factors calculated from first and second order posterior moments. Values for these are determined by iterative application of the method. The system requires some initial 'starting values' to be provided and, particularly in time series applications, it can be difficult to obtain values that are 'good enough'. A linear search algorithm based on Gauss Hermite rules has been used in the analyses reported here.

Graphical Analysis of the Joint Posterior

In this chapter, attention focuses on exploratory assessment of δ (time trend parameter) and ρ (autoregressive or stochastic trend parameter) (although in principle researchers could concern themselves with any two elements of θ), for which estimative inference is based on the joint marginal posterior density

$$p(\delta, \rho \,|\, \mathbf{y}) = \int_{-\infty}^{\infty} \cdots \int_{-\infty}^{\infty} p(\theta \,|\, \mathbf{y}) \, d\theta_{\bar{\imath}}, \qquad (6.14)$$

where $\theta_{\bar{\imath}}$ denotes the entire parameter vector θ except for the 'trend' parameters δ and ρ. Contour plots of this density provide a powerful graphical tool for distinguishing between difference stationary series and trend stationary series where autoregressive persistence is not high. In addition they can provide an indication of whether any form of the model (6.5) is an adequate specification for the series under consideration.

Following on from the discussion in Ahn (1993) some observations are made about the behaviour of the process for different values of ρ and δ. When $\rho = 1$ Δu_t follows an AR($p - 1$) process and y_t has a stochastic trend, with Δy_t following $\phi(L)(\Delta y_t - \delta) = \varepsilon_t$. When $\rho < 1$ u_t is stationary AR(p) and y_t does not have a stochastic trend. When $\delta \neq 0$ y_t has a linear time trend whether $\rho = 1$ or not.

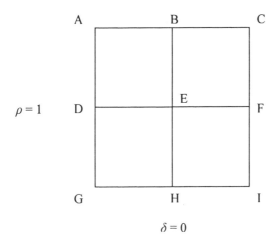

Figure 6.1 The $\rho - \delta$ parameter space

Figure 6.1 shows the $\rho - \delta$ parameter space on which we plot contours of the marginal bivariate density and the above discussion can be translated into observations that can be made on the basis of where on the graph the joint posterior density falls.

1. If the outermost contours lie along and on either side of the line DEF this would be suggestive of the presence of a unit root.
2. If the contours are concentrated along the line EH y_t follows a stationary process.
3. If the contours fall within the rectangle DFIG but not on the lines DEF or EH then y_t has a linear time trend and stationary disturbances.
4. If the contours straddle the line DEF, away from the line BEH, and have a substantial probability content above DEF this would be suggestive of a non-stationary explosive model for the time series in question. For any except very short series this conclusion is implausible. We would rather adopt the alternative interpretation that the model being used to derive the joint density is inappropriate and, hence, that a wider class of models should be entertained.

In all cases the joint posterior density should be examined in conjunction with at least a time series plot of the original data; space precludes this here, but we recommend our method is never used in isolation. Clearly if there are strong indications of non-linearity in the original series the fitting of (6.5) would not be appropriate. The purpose of our graphical device is to determine the admissibility or not of model (6.5) for the data at hand. Should 1, 2 or 3 arise then model (6.5) in some form may be appropriate, otherwise the search for an adequate model for the data must be renewed. Such an extended search is warranted if: there are indications of non-linearity in the data; there is evidence in the graph of the joint posterior that 4 above applies; or there is other irregular behaviour of the graph that is unanticipated if (6.5) is appropriate.

In order to illustrate the use of Figure 6.1 it is useful to 'calibrate' the performance of the joint posterior density of ρ and δ for different simulated stationary and non-stationary processes. We generated 100 observations from each of a range of models, some of which are generated from (6.5) and others which are not and obtained the joint posterior density arising from assuming model (6.5) in each case.

Inference Using Simulated Data from (6.5)

In this part of the investigation, the six models used were

$$(a) \quad y_t = y_{t-1} + \varepsilon_t \qquad (d) \quad y_t = 0.02 + 0.01t + \varepsilon_t$$

$$(b) \quad \begin{cases} y_t = 0.01t + u_t \\ u_t = u_{t-1} + \varepsilon_t \end{cases} \qquad (e) \quad \begin{cases} y_t = 0.01t + u_t \\ u_t = 0.7u_{t-1} + \varepsilon_t \end{cases}$$

$$(c) \quad y_t = 0.7y_{t-1} + \varepsilon_t \qquad (f) \quad \begin{cases} y_t = u_t \\ u_t = u_{t-1} + \Delta u_{t-1} + \varepsilon_t. \end{cases}$$

For all the above cases and those to be used in the next subsection $\varepsilon_t \sim N\left(0, 0.06^2\right)$. A choice of $\sigma = 0.06$ for the innovation standard deviation was made on the basis of fitting the same model to all of the Nelson and Plosser (1982) data sets and recording a point estimate of σ in each case. The median value of these point estimates was 0.0595. In these calibration examples we used values of $p = 2$ and $p = 3$ for the Dickey–Fuller style augmentation in (6.5) with the exact likelihood and generally found here that the inferences from our graphical device were qualitatively unaffected by the choice of p. In view of research evidence (see inter alia Hoek, 1997; Leybourne, 1994; Schwert, 1987, 1989), the use of these values of p is likely to be inadequate whenever there are substantial moving average components in the data. This is a matter we take up further below. All plots were obtained using 'Splus', see Becker et al. (1988) for an introduction.

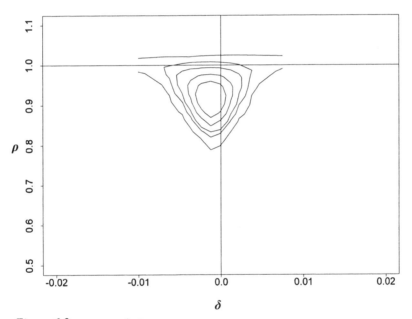

Figure 6.2 $y_t = y_{t-1} + \varepsilon_t$

The joint posterior densities of ρ and δ for (a) to (f) above, are plotted, respectively, in Figures 6.2 to 6.7. The five contours in these and other figures are drawn at 50%, 25%, 10%, 5% and 1% of the modal height of the estimated joint posterior distribution. These choices correspond to highest posterior density regions in a straightforward way. The graphs displayed are indicative of the results we obtained from a substantial number of realisations for each case.

The joint posterior densities depicted in Figures 6.2 to 6.6 behave as foreshadowed in discussion of Figure 6.1. Consider first Figures 6.2 and 6.3 for which the spreading of the outer contours along the line DEF of Figure 6.1 indicates the likelihood of a unit root. Notice that the mode of the joint posterior is indicative of a downward bias in the estimate of ρ. We note that Phillips (1991) uses a Jeffreys' prior in an attempt to offset this. In Figure 6.2, since the contours are centred around $\delta = 0$, the line BEH of Figure 6.1, we infer that there is no deterministic trend. In Figure 6.3, in addition to the spreading of the outer contours along DEF, they are centred around $\delta = 0.01$ and the mass of the joint posterior distribution is well to the right of the line $\delta = 0$ thereby indicating the presence of both a deterministic trend and a unit root. Of course, in the context of the reduced form (6.6) this takes the form of a non-zero drift parameter in a unit root model. It might also be pointed out that the behaviour of the contours in Figures 6.2 and 6.3 is robust both to a substantial sharpening of the marginal (normal) prior density for ρ by increasing the mean towards the unit root (retaining the small prior probability of explosive behaviour) as well as to the use of a more diffuse prior. These effects were investigated as sensitivity analyses in the light of the discussion in the subsection 'The Priors and Resultant Posteriors' relating to this point.

The joint posterior densities shown in Figures 6.4, 6.5 and 6.6 reflect cases where no unit root is present. The contours are more compact relative to those in the earlier two figures. This can be seen, for example, by noting that the distance between the 10% contours on either side of the mode of the joint posterior in the δ direction in Figure 6.4 is about 0.004 (compared with about twice that for Figure 6.2). A parallel notion of 'compactness' will also be used for the ρ direction below. In Figure 6.4 the contours are centred around $\delta = 0$, as was the case with Figure 6.2, but this time all plotted contours of the joint posterior density lie below the line DEF, thus leading to the graphical inference that there is neither deterministic nor stochastic trend. However the contours indicate a large probability mass between $\rho = 0.65$ and $\rho = 0.85$ indicating the possibility of a stable autoregressive structure in the disturbances of (6.5). Of course applied workers are often interested in analysing autoregressive series that prove to have roots close to, but not on, the unit circle, that is intermediate cases between those reflected in Figures 6.2 and 6.4. We have experimented with such data generating mechanisms, but the basic inference derived from Figure 6.4 remains robust until ρ takes values very close to 1.0.

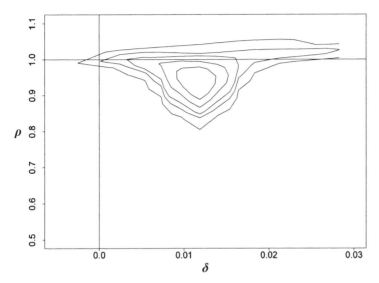

Figure 6.3 $y_t = 0.01t + u_t;\ u_t = u_{t-1} + \varepsilon_t$

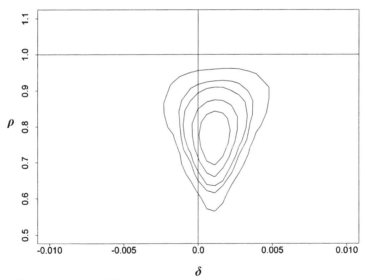

Figure 6.4 $y_t = 0.7y_{t-1} + \varepsilon_t$

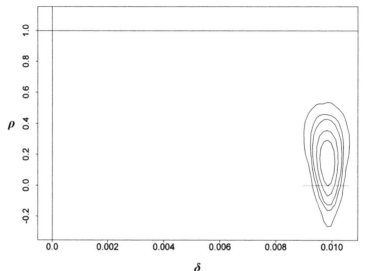

Figure 6.5 $y_t = 0.02 + 0.01t + \varepsilon_t$

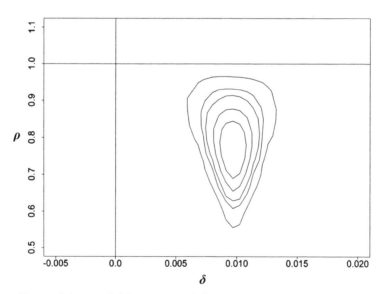

Figure 6.6 $y_t = 0.01t + u_t; \ u_t = 0.7u_{t-1} + \varepsilon_t$

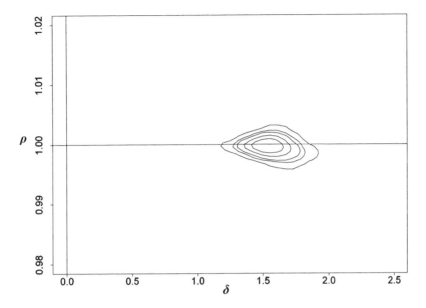

Figure 6.7 $y_t = u_t;$ $u_t = u_{t-1} + \Delta u_{t-1} + \varepsilon_t$

The plot in Figure 6.5, which was obtained using the more diffuse prior, clearly indicates that there is no unit root and that there is no strong evidence of autoregressive structure. The presence of a deterministic trend around $\delta = 0.01$ is self-evident. The contours of Figure 6.6 resemble those in 6.4 shifted to the right and, as might be expected, there is evidence of autoregressive structure (although no suggestion of a unit root) and a possible deterministic trend. The inferences described above all relate to processes arising from (6.5) and are qualitatively robust across all the realisations we examined.

The plot in Figure 6.7 derives from model (f) which is evidently a process with not one but two unit roots, that is y_t is integrated of order 2, I(2). In this case not only is $\rho = 1$ but there is also unit root behaviour in the first differences in (6.5). The figure indicates very strongly the presence of a unit root and a plot of the original data will generally be indicative of highly non-stationary behaviour anyway. If a modeller wishes to distinguish between I(1) and I(2) processes using our graphical inference, the qualitative difference between Figures 6.2 and 6.7 may be helpful. At any event, if a data realisation is I(2) and produces a figure similar to the latter, then the graph pertaining to the first differences of the data can be expected to more closely resemble the former.

Inference Using Data Not Simulated from (6.5)

In practical situations, one of a researcher's main aims will be to determine whether or not (6.5) is indeed appropriate. Of course, should (6.5) be inadequate, a vast range of other specifications could be entertained. This subsection considers artificially generated data from a range of models that might be considered particularly pertinent.

The first data generating mechanism is

$$(g) \quad y_t = 0.001 + y_{t-1} + 0.002t + \varepsilon_t$$

which can be thought of as the reduced form arising from the structural model (6.5) with the linear trend augmented by a quadratic term. The contours of the empirical joint posterior portrayed in Figure 6.8 all lie above the line DEF and we would clearly reject (6.5) as a plausible generating mechanism for the data.

The next two specifications involve explicitly non-linear data generating

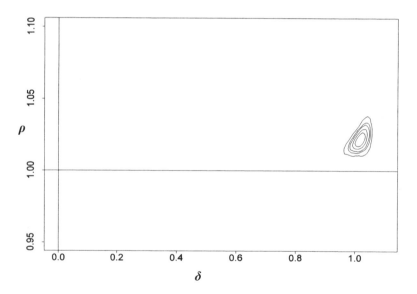

Figure 6.8 $y_t = 0.001 + y_{t-1} + 0.002t + \varepsilon_t$

mechanisms. The first of these is the bilinear process

$$(h) \quad y_t = (\alpha + \beta \varepsilon_t) y_{t-1} + \varepsilon_t$$

The arguments of Quinn (1982) indicate that parametric combinations of α and β admit different aspects of stationarity and ergodicity to these models. For instance strictly stationary data generating mechanisms can arise even when $|\alpha| > 1.0$. The situation is neatly summarised by figure 1 of Quinn (1982, p. 251).

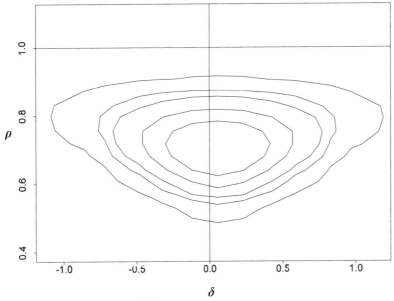

Figure 6.9 $y_t = (0.8 + 22\varepsilon_t)y_{t-1} + \varepsilon_t$

As emphasised earlier, we advocate the use of our estimative procedure only after preliminary consideration of the data (naturally including a time series plot). Generally speaking, whenever the variance contribution of the bilinear component to the dependence structure of y_t is non-negligible, this will be evident in the time series plot and the erratic behaviour of this plot will exclude (6.5) from further consideration. However it is still of some interest to explore the results of applying the procedure in such circumstances. Two representative examples are given here. The first of these derives from a realisation where $\alpha = 0.8$ and $\beta = 22$. The implied process is strictly stationary. The relevant graph is presented as Figure 6.9 and it is seen that, while the estimated value of ρ approximates α well, the estimated value of δ is completely unreliable with our compactness measure being in excess of 1.0! This figure provides strong evidence of the inappropriateness of (6.5). The plot in Figure 6.10 employs $\alpha = 1.21$ and $\beta = 22$ and this process is not strictly stationary. In this case the estimated value of ρ does not even provide useful information about α and we would point out in passing that the posterior mean of σ is around 11.15, compared to the (true) value of 0.06. A range of other plots is available on the web site (http://dcm.ntu.ac.uk/jmm/plots.html), but a succinct summary is that the plots seem to provide useful information about α via ρ only when α is less than 1.0 or the heteroscedastic effect introduced by the bilinear component is small.

Of some interest is the non-stationary random coefficient process of

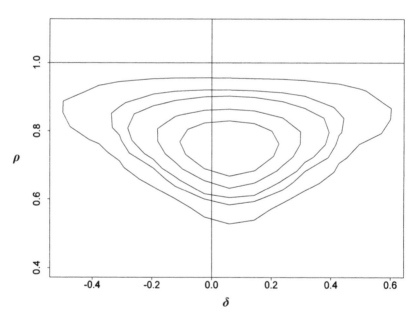

Figure 6.10 $y_t = (1.21 + 22\varepsilon_t)y_{t-1} + \varepsilon_t$

$$(i) \quad y_t = \alpha_t y_{t-1} + \varepsilon_t, \text{ with } \alpha_t \sim N\left(1, 0.1^2\right).$$

Leybourne et al. (1996) present a comprehensive discussion of these models in the context of testing for alternatives to unit root models. While some realisations give rise to even more volatile posterior joint densities, the result we portray in Figure 6.11 is typical of many. In this case there is substantially more probability content above the line DEF than is evident in either Figure 6.2 or Figure 6.3. Such unpredictable joint posterior plots suggest strongly that a wider class of models than any obtainable from (6.5) should be entertained. This feature is exhibited here for sample size 100; by virtue of the conditional linearity of the process (Grunwald et al., 2000), it may be the case that such volatile behaviour would not be evident in (possibly much) larger samples. We have not investigated this point here but maintain that (6.5) should not be entertained in small and moderate sample sizes. We believe that a researcher would be warned off doing so by using our procedure.

As a sensitivity analysis we used Student's t with five degrees of freedom, rather than Gaussian noise terms to generate data from each of models (a) to (h) in this and the previous subsection. Heavy-tailed distributions are often observed in practice with financial time series, where samples of size 500 and

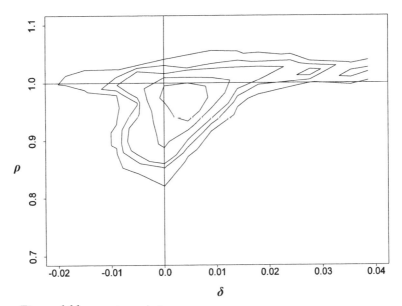

Figure 6.11 $y_t = \alpha y_{t-1} + \varepsilon_t$

more are frequently encountered. The resultant graphical inference is broadly similar to that reported above. We carried out experiments for T between 100 and 500 and found that, in the few cases where inferences were unreliable for the smallest samples ($T = 100$), they generally behaved predictably for the largest samples ($T = 500$). The exception to this is the case of unit root processes, where large samples are required for robustness to non-normal errors. In the case of process (i), inference with fat-tailed innovations still provides volatile plots at $T = 500$.

There are two further topics that are explored in this section. The first of these relates to one addressed in some detail in Hoek (1997, chapter 5), raised first by Schwert (1987, 1989) and subsequently by other authors. These authors discuss the presence of moving average components in macroeconomic data sets akin to those employed in the context of our graphical device in the next section. Hoek's ultimate conclusion is that 'some of the Nelson–Plosser series ... contain strong MA components'. But 'it appears that unit root inference for the extended Nelson–Plosser data is not much affected by considering ARMA instead of AR models' (Hoek, 1997, p.95). Using these data, Leybourne (1994) reports quite large MA components for three of the Nelson–Plosser series, one of which does not appear to have a unit root. Of course, any MA component, other than one with a unit root, can be expressed as an AR of sufficiently high order. Indeed, this is the spirit of the Dickey–Fuller augmentation methodology involving the ϕ_i parameters here. So, in principle, our proposal can handle such components by choosing p sufficiently large.

At the outset we experimented with our graphical device retaining p no larger than 3 in the presence of small MA components in the data generating process

$$(j) \quad y_t = y_{t-1} + \varepsilon_t - \gamma \varepsilon_{t-1}.$$

If this model is approximated by (6.5) for some chosen p, then the ϕ coefficients are given by $\phi_i = \gamma^p - \gamma^i$ and the value of ρ is $1 - \gamma^p$. It is therefore the case that we should still expect a joint posterior indicative of a value of ρ close to unity whenever either: p is sufficiently large; or γ is small. When the coefficient γ is less than 0.3 in absolute value we found our qualitative conclusions to be robust. The graphs are not presented here to save space. As γ increases above 0.3 the use of the exact likelihood becomes problematic since existing software constrains us to setting $p \leq 3$. To investigate this case further we therefore adopted the expedient, mentioned towards the end of the subsection, 'The Prior and Resultant Posteriors', of no longer treating $\mathbf{u}_-$ as a parameter to be estimated. Instead we substitute the

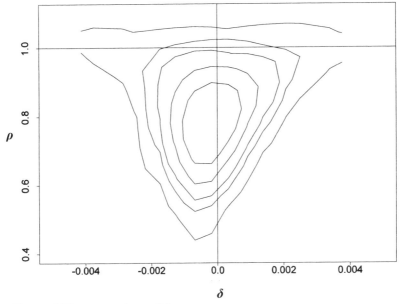

Figure 6.12 $y_t = y_{t-1} + \varepsilon_t - 0.5\varepsilon_{t-1}$

elements thereby freed up in θ with higher order autoregressive components implied by larger values of p. A maximum value of $p = 6$ is now available. Of course even this expedient may be inadequate (see, for example, the previous paragraph and Schwert, 1989, p. 148 for relevant discussion). Some programming effort could attenuate this further, but we do not pursue this here. We provide representative plots to show what may be expected. Since there may now be less reason to hold a prior belief that ρ is even close to 1 and likely uncertainty about its value, these plots are based on the more diffuse prior that incorporates a lower mean for ρ.

Figure 6.12 arises from a realisation with $\gamma = 0.5$ and is not unlike the simple random walk of Figure 6.2, except that the posterior mean of ρ is considerably lower and our measure of compactness in the direction of ρ is between two and three times as large. Increasing γ to 0.7 leads to Figure 6.13 The shape is qualitatively similar to what has gone before in Figures 6.2 and 6.12 but the posterior mean of ρ has been reduced.

Further graphs for these and even higher values of γ are available on the web site, but the qualitative inferences are completely predictable. If such large moving average components are suspected in real data, we recommend the use of software that can cope with very high values of p or, alternatively, that deals explicitly with moving average parameters in specifying the likelihood; the development of such software is beyond the scope of this chapter.

When a moving average operator with a root on the unit circle is considered, the familiar identification problem with ARMA models occurs when there is also a unit root in the AR operator. The root cancellation is exact in this case and approximate when either operator has a root close to unity. The cancellation leads to a data generating mechanism that no longer has unit roots in evidence and the parameter ρ now represents the remaining first order autocorrelation. Our graphical device indicates this reliably when (6.5) is otherwise appropriate.

The final issue to be raised here relates to the possible existence of structural breaks in the data. In order to investigate the effect of the different types of outlier sometimes found in macroeconomic series, we examined Models A and B of Perron (1989) together with their alternatives. These are

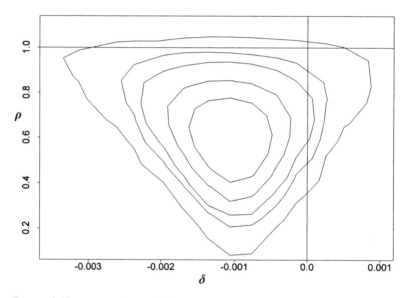

Figure 6.13 $y_t = y_{t-1} + \varepsilon_t - 0.7\varepsilon_{t-1}$

(k) Model A null $y_t = \mu + dD(TB)_t + y_{t-1} + \varepsilon_t$

(l) Model A alternative $y_t = \mu_1 + \beta t + (\mu_2 - \mu_1)DU_t + \varepsilon_t$

(m) Model B null $y_t = \mu_1 + y_{t-1} + (\mu_2 - \mu_1)DU_t + \varepsilon_t$

(n) Model A alternative $y_t = \mu + \beta_1 t + (\beta_2 - \beta_1)DT_t^* + \varepsilon_t$

where: $D(TB)_t = 1$, $t = 51$, 0 otherwise; $DU_t = 1$, $t \geq 51$; and $DT_t^* = t - 50$ if $t > 50$, 0 otherwise. Since $T = 100$, this implies that any structural break takes place in the middle of the realisation.

Perron referred to Model A as the 'crash model' and for the alternative to this model he considered the case $\mu_2 < \mu_1$. He referred to model B as the 'changing growth model' because, under the alternative, a change in slope is allowed.

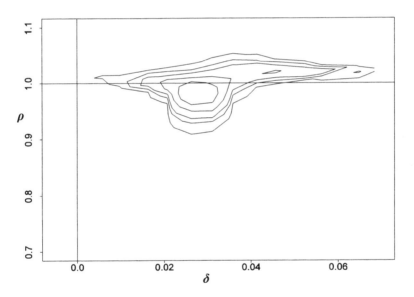

Figure 6.14 $y_t = 0.03 + y_{t-1} - 0.01DU_t + \varepsilon_t$

Processes generated by (k) will contain a single spike, or pulse, outlier at $t = 51$. In the absence of this outlier we would expect to see a picture similar to Figure 6.2. In the presence of the outlier the plots for the case $\mu = 0$ and $d < 0$ showed considerable volatility and one resembled Figure 6.3 with a different sign for δ. Our inference in this case would not suggest a simple unit root even though the only difference between (a) and (k) is the single pulse outlier. When $\mu > 0$ and $d < 0$ for this model, that is, in the presence of positive drift, the outlier takes the form of a crash, which seems to be the more likely event in macroeconomic series. The plot here still resembles Figure 6.2 even though it contains the outlier. In the case of a positive spike, $d > 0$, our plot clearly indicates that it is not a model of type (6.5). Perron's alternative to Model A is (l) which, in the absence of the crash, would resemble (e) with $\rho = 0$. For this reason we use the more diffuse prior with $\rho \sim N(0.5, 0.25^2)$. Our plots indicate a positive linear trend with AR(1) disturbances. However the evidence for a simple trend is noticeably weaker than is observed when a simple linear trend does in fact generate the data. Plots forming the basis of this and the following discussion can again be found on the web site referred to above.

The null changing growth model, Model B, is provided by (m). If the shift represented by $(\mu_2 - \mu_1)DU_t$ had no effect we would expect the plot to resemble that from a random walk with drift, as in Figure 6.3. In the presence of a structural shift the graphs become qualitatively dissimilar and unlike any others identified from models in the class of (6.5) and (6.6). Figure 6.14 provides the plot of the joint posterior density for a realisation from (m) when $\mu_1 = 0.03$ and $\mu_2 = 0.02$. The alternative for Model B is (n); if the regime shift had no effect in this case we would expect a linear trend, possibly with a non-zero intercept, as in Figure 6.5. However the graphs obtained are unlike those of Figures 6.2 or 6.6. In all except one of the structural change cases, namely when there is a negative crash and positive drift in (k), our graphical inference is able to determine quite readily that models in the class specified by (6.5) are inadequate.

We suggest that the figures presented in this and the previous subsection may be gainfully employed as templates when performing this analysis with real data.

4. THE NELSON–PLOSSER DATA

The data we use to illustrate this approach are taken from the seminal article of Nelson and Plosser (1982) and are listed in Table 6.1. These data have, of course, been subject to widespread analysis by many authors. We consider them here as a suitable test bed for our procedure and not with any realistic intention of generating new insights into their behaviour. The rightmost column headed (6.5)? in Table 6.1 reports: those series which may have been generated by (6.5) following our Bayesian graphical analysis (YES); and those for which the evidence suggests otherwise (NO).

Ordinarily, economic time series such as these, which are annual data averages for the year, would generally, with the exception of BND, be studied by first taking logarithms of the data in order to model rates of growth or to estimate elasticities. We have adopted this convention in the analyses reported here.

For each series the value of p, which determines the number of lagged differences included in the regression, is either 2 or 3 with the exact likelihood, or up to 6 if the conditional likelihood is employed. In the spirit of the arguments of Agiakloglou and Newbold (1992) that sampling properties of unit root tests are affected by increasing the order of the augmented Dickey–Fuller regressions, we anticipate our graphical inference may be less precise (perhaps conveniently described by our 'compactness' measure) for increasing values of p. However, in view of the effects of positive moving average components (Schwert, 1987, 1989) in real data, we feel that a range of values of p must be considered in practical exercises. It is, however, of some comfort to note that Leybourne (1994, p.727) and Hoek (1997, p.92) found that none of these 14 series evidenced a positive value of γ (in the notation of this chapter), which may be more problematic than a negative value. The value of p used in the graphs presented here is chosen to be one for which inference from the joint posterior plot is stable in the sense that incrementing p has no appreciable effect on the estimated posterior moments, particularly on the means.

Table 6.1   The Nelson and Plosser Data

Name	Series	Period	T	(6.5)?
RGNP	Real GNP	1909–1970	62	YES
GNP	Nominal GNP	1909–1970	62	YES
PCRGNP	Real per capita GNP	1909–1970	62	YES
IP	Industrial production	1860–1970	111	YES
EMP	Employment	1890–1970	81	YES
UN	Unemployment rate	1890–1970	81	YES
PRGNP	GNP deflator	1889–1970	82	YES
CPI	Consumer prices	1860–1970	111	NO
WG	Wages	1900–1970	71	YES
RWG	Real wages	1900–1970	71	YES
M	Money stock	1889–1970	82	YES
VEL	Velocity	1869–1970	102	NO
BND	Bond yield	1900–1970	71	NO
SP500	Common stock prices	1871–1970	100	YES

A selection of the plots of the joint posterior density for δ and ρ for the data series given in Table 6.1 is presented in Figures 6.15 to 6.20 The structure of the plots is similar to that used in the calibration exercises documented above. Following the discussions of Section 3 we can now offer initial comments on the possible structure of each series following our exploratory analysis.

Only the Bayesian graphical inference for UN, presented in Figure 6.15, appears to clearly support a stationary AR(1) model; compare Figure 6.4. This corresponds to what many authors find, including Nelson and Plosser (1982). The value of p here is 2. Increasing p to 6 has little effect on the estimated posterior mean of ρ and increases our compactness measure by about 8% in this dimension.

Figure 6.16 illustrates our graphical device in the context of series M and is suggestive of stationary behaviour around a linear trend, so that (6.5) may be appropriate; compare Figure 6.6. (The industrial production series produces directly comparable inference; this and other plots not presented to save space are available from the web site.) It is sometimes suggested that M may be an I(2) series and there are some similarities between Figures 6.16 and 6.7, though the probability content of the former in the ρ direction is much less concentrated around the line DEF of Figure 6.1 than the latter. Repeating the analysis using the first differences of M results in a graph strikingly similar to Figure 6.4 that is based on data generated from a stationary AR(1) model and so we do not believe the evidence of I(2) behaviour for M is convincing.

The posterior density plot for GNP with $p = 3$ is presented in Figure 6.17. It most closely resembles the template Figure 6.3 and we infer that there may be evidence of a unit root, unlike the three series discussed above. The plots for RGNP, PCRGNP, EMP, WG, RWG, PRGNP and SP500 are qualitatively quite similar; that for SP500 is presented in Figure 6.18 as an exempler. Many of these series, for example RGNP, have been widely discussed and we are mindful of the difficulty of discriminating data with a unit root from that which is near non-stationary. We do not regard our procedure as an inference for confirming a unit root, rather we look on it as providing confirmatory information about the reasonableness of (6.5), together with (in these cases) evidence of a need to investigate unit root behaviour more closely. The evidence for a unit root varies a little from one of these series to another, but in every case it appears that (6.5) represents a plausible maintained model.

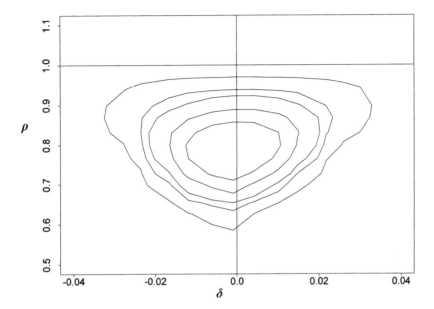

Figure 6.15   UN, p = 2

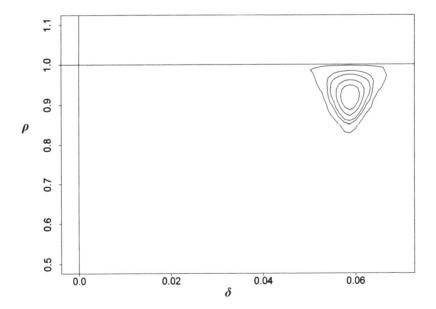

Figure 6.16   M, p = 2

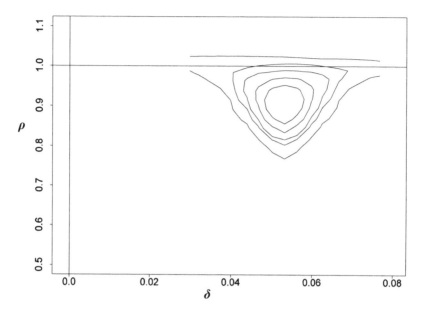

Figure 6.17   GNP, p = 3

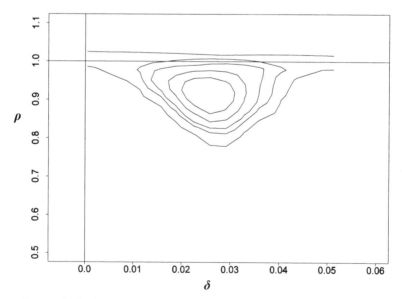

Figure 6.18   SP500, p = 2

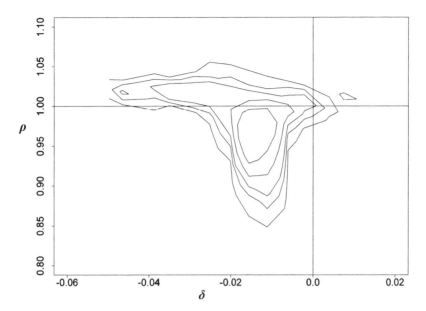

Figure 6.19   VEL, p = 2

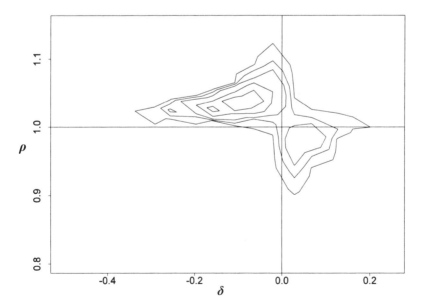

Figure 6.20   BND, p = 2

The remaining three series show strong departures from what would be expected under (6.5). Figure 6.19 ($p = 2$) clearly indicates that the VEL series is not likely to be well represented by (6.5). Indeed the plot shown here bears a marked resemblance to that of Figure 6.11. The plot for CPI is very similar. Finally Figure 6.20 for the BND series is an even less regular bivariate posterior probability distribution, being distinctly bimodal. While we do not propose a parametric specification appropriate for such a series, any economic modeller would be clearly led to conclude that a richer class of models than (6.5) should be entertained with this series.

5. CONCLUSION

The proposed Bayesian graphical analysis, by allowing a probabilistic examination of the joint behaviour of two parameters of specific interest, provides a flexible and powerful tool in the analysis of economic time series. In particular we have seen that data generated from (6.5) with a unit root can be discriminated from certain models without this structure on the basis of these plots. We have also seen that data from non-linear processes that are widely discussed in the literature give rise to samples that can be identified by this approach as not belonging to the class of models described by (6.5). The experiments and portrayals of Section 3 provide templates for a range of models that are and are not based on (6.5) and that may be of importance in practice. Application of the methodology to the famous 14 Nelson and Plosser (1982) US annual data sets indicates that (6.5) may be an inadequate maintained model in at least three cases. Given the availability of suitable software we feel that the proposed procedure provides a powerful new exploratory inference technique for applied economic researchers.

REFERENCES

Agiakloglou, C. and P. Newbold (1992), 'Empirical Evidence on Dickey–Fuller-Type Tests', *Journal of Time Series Analysis*, **13**, 471–483.

Ahn, S.K. (1993), 'Some Tests for Unit Roots in Autoregressive-Integrated-Moving Average Models with Deterministic Trends', *Biometrika*, **80**, 855–868.

Andrews, D.W.K. (1993), 'Exactly Median-Unbiased Estimation of First Order Autoregressive/Unit Root Models', *Econometrica*, **61**, 139–165.

Becker, R.A., J.M. Chambers and A.R. Wilks (1988), *The New S Language*, Pacific Grove, CA: Wadsworth.

Berger, J.O. and R. Yang (1994), 'Noninformative Priors and Bayesian Testing for the AR(1) Model', *Econometric Theory*, **10**, 461–482.

Bernardo, J.M. (1979), 'Reference Posterior Distributions for Bayes Inference', *Journal of the Royal Statistical Society*, **B 41**, 113–147.

Bhargava, A. (1986), 'On the Theory of Testing for Unit Roots in Observed Time Series', *Review of Economic Studies*, **LIII**, 369–384.

Davidson, R. and J.G. MacKinnon (1993), *Estimation and Inference in Econometrics*, Oxford: Oxford University Press.

Dickey, D.A. and W.A. Fuller (1979), 'Distribution of the Estimators for Autoregressive Time Series with a Unit Root', *Journal of the American Statistical Association*, **74**, 427–431.

Franses, P.H. (2001), 'How to Deal with Intercept and Trend in Practical Cointegration Analysis?', *Applied Economics*, **33**, 577–579.

Fuller, W.A. (1976), *Introduction to Statistical Time Series*, New York: Wiley.

Geweke, J. (1994), 'Priors for Macroeconomic Time Series and their Application', *Econometric Theory*, **10**, 609–632.

Grunwald, G.K., R.J. Hyndman, L. Tedesco and R.L. Tweedie (2000), 'Non-Gaussian Conditional Linear AR(1) Models', *Australian and New Zealand Journal of Statistics*, **42**, 479–495.

Hoek, H. (1997), 'Variable Trends: A Bayesian Perspective', *Ph.D. Thesis*, no.147 of the Tinbergen Institute Research Series, Amsterdam: Thesis Publishers.

Koop, G. (1992), '"Objective" Bayesian Unit Root Tests', *Journal of Applied Econometrics*, **7**, 65–82.

Koop, G. and H.K. Van Dijk (2000), 'Testing for Integration Using Evolving Trend and Seasonal Models: A Bayesian Approach', *Journal of Econometrics*, **97**, 261–291.

Kwiatkowski, D., P.C.B. Phillips, P. Schmidt. and Y. Shin (1992), 'Testing the Null Hypothesis of Stationarity Against the Alternative of a Unit Root', *Journal of Econometrics*, **54**, 159–178.

Kwiatkowski, D. and P. Schmidt (1990), 'Dickey–Fuller Tests with Trend', *Communications in Statistics Theory and Methods*, **19**, 3645–3656.

Leybourne, S.J. (1994), 'Testing for Unit Roots: A Simple Alternative to Dickey–Fuller', *Applied Economics*, **26**, 721–729.

Leybourne, S.J., B.P.M. McCabe and A.R. Tremayne (1996), 'Can Economic Time Series be Differenced to Stationarity?' *Journal of Business and Economic Statistics*, **14**, 435–446.

Lubrano, M. (1995), 'Testing for Unit Roots in a Bayesian Framework', *Journal of Econometrics*, **69**, 81–109.

Maddala, G.S. and I.-M. Kim (1998), *Unit Roots, Cointegration and Structural Change*, Cambridge: Cambridge University Press.

Marriott, J.M., N. Ravishanker, A.E. Gelfand and J.S. Pai (1996), 'Bayesian Analysis for ARMA Processes: Complete Sampling Based Inference Under Exact Likelihoods', in D. Barry, K. Chaloner and J. Geweke (eds.), *Bayesian Statistics and Econometrics: Essays in Honour of Arnold Zellner*, New York: Wiley, pp. 243–256.

Monahan, J.F. (1983), 'Fully Bayesian Analysis of ARMA Time Series Models', *Journal of Econometrics*, **21**, 307–331.

Naylor, J.C. (1991), *Bayes Four User Guide, Technical Report*, Nottingham Trent University.

Naylor, J.C. and J.M. Marriott (1996), 'A Bayesian Analysis of Non-stationary Autoregressive Series', in J.M. Bernardo, J.O. Berger, A.P. Dawid and A.F.M. Smith (eds.), *Bayesian Statistics 5*, Oxford: Oxford University Press, pp. 705–712.

Nelson, C.R. and C.I. Plosser (1982), 'Trends and Random Walks in Macroeconomic Time Series', *Journal of Monetary Economics*, **10**, 139–162.

Pantula, S.G. and A. Hall (1991), 'Testing for Unit Roots in Autoregressive Moving Average Models: An Instrumental Variable Approach', *Journal of Econometrics*, **48**, 325–353.

Perron, P. (1989), 'The Great Crash, the Oil Price Shock and the Unit Root Hypothesis', *Econometrica*, **57**, 1361–1401.

Phillips, P.C.B. (1991), 'To Criticize the Critics: An Objective Bayesian Analysis of Stochastic Trends', *Journal of Applied Econometrics*, **6**, 333–364.

Poirier, D.J. (1991), 'A Comment on "To Criticize the Critics: An Objective Bayesian Analysis of Stochastic Trends"', *Journal of Applied Econometrics*, **6**, 381–386.

Quinn, B.G. (1982), 'A Note on the Existence of Strictly Stationary Solutions to Bilinear Equations', *Journal of Time Series Analysis*, **3**, 249–252.

Said, E.S. (1991), 'Unit-Root Tests for Time-Series Data with a Linear Trend', *Journal of Econometrics*, **47**, 285–303.

Said, E.S. and D.A. Dickey (1984), 'Testing for Unit Roots in Autoregressive Moving-Average Models of Unknown Order', *Biometrika*, **71**, 599–607.

Schmidt, P. and P.C.B. Phillips (1992), 'LM Tests for a Unit Root in the Presence of Deterministic Trends', *Oxford Bulletin of Economics and Statistics*, **54**, 257–287.

Schotman, P.C. (1994), 'Priors for the AR(1) Model: Parameterization Issues and Time Series Considerations', *Econometric Theory*, **10**, 579–595.

Schotman, P.C. and H.K. Van Dijk (1991), 'On Bayesian Routes to Unit Roots', *Journal of Applied Econometrics*, **6**, 387–401.

Schwert, G.W. (1987), 'Effects of Model Specification on Tests for Unit Roots in Macroeconomic Data', *Journal of Monetary Economics*, **20**, 73–103.

Schwert, G.W. (1989), 'Tests for Unit Roots: A Monte Carlo Investigation', *Journal of Business and Economic Statistics*, **7**, 147–159.

Shaw, J.E.H. (1988), 'Aspects of Numerical Integration and Summarisation', in J.M. Bernardo, M.H. DeGroot, D.V. Lindley and A.F.M. Smith (eds.), *Bayesian Statistics 3*, Oxford: Oxford University Press, pp. 411–428 (with discussion).

Sims, C.A. (1991), 'Comment on "To Criticize the Critics"', by Peter C. B. Phillips', *Journal of Applied Econometrics*, **6**, 423–434.

Smith, A.F.M., A.M. Skene, J.E.H. Shaw, J.C. Naylor and M. Dransfield (1985), 'The Implementation of the Bayesian Paradigm', *Communications in Statistics*, **14**, 1079–1102.

Stock, J.H. (1991), 'Confidence Intervals for the Largest Autoregressive Root in US Macroeconomic Time Series', *Journal of Monetary Economics*, **28**, 435–459.

Uhlig, H. (1994), 'On Jeffreys Prior When Using the Exact Likelihood Function', *Econometric Theory*, **10**, 633–644.

Zellner, A. (1977), 'Maximal Data Information Prior Distributions', in A. Aykac and C. Brumat (eds.), *New Developments in the Applications of Bayesian Methods*, Amsterdam: North-Holland, pp. 211–232.

Zivot, E. (1994), 'A Bayesian Analysis of the Unit Root Hypothesis within an Unobserved Components Model', *Econometric Theory*, **10**, 552–578.

Zivot, E. and P.C.B. Phillips (1994), 'A Bayesian Analysis of Trend Determination in Economic Time Series', *Econometric Reviews*, **13**, 291–336.

PART III

Applications

7. The Impact of Monetary Policy in the UK on the Relationship between the Term Structure of Interest Rates and Future Inflation

Gunnar Bårdsen, Ralf Becker and Stan Hurn

1. INTRODUCTION

Much recent research has focused on the informational content of the term structure of interest rates. Specifically, the predictive power of yield spreads with respect to future inflation and real economic activity have been examined by numerous authors including Mishkin (1990a, 1990b, 1991), Estrella and Mishkin (1997) and more recently Siklos (2000) and Hamilton and Kim (2000). In general, it has been found that the term structure does contain useful information concerning these final goals of monetary policy, but that the relationship can change over time. In the context of European monetary policy, for example, Estrella and Mishkin (1997) make a strong argument for the use of interest rate spreads as simple but accurate indicators of real economic activity and inflation. From the perspective of monetary policy it is important to assess whether the informational content of interest rates with respect to future inflation is relatively robust, even invariant, to the conduct of monetary policy. This chapter investigates this aspect of the relationship between short-term, money-market spreads and future inflation in the UK for the period 1976 to 1999. Of particular interest is the change from a regime of exchange rate targeting to one of inflation targeting in 1992. One of the aims of the chapter is to assess whether or not this change is reflected in the informational content of London interbank interest rates.

The interest rate data used in this chapter are from the London interbank market, a highly competitive market in sterling term deposits that is also closely integrated with the markets for other liquid assets such as Treasury bills and commercial paper. Shorter-term LIBOR maturities,[1] such as 1- and 3-month interest rates, are influenced by the Bank of England as part of its monetary policy operations, but longer rates are determined in a highly competitive environment. It may be therefore that the informational content of the LIBOR interest rates will be sensitive to changes in the conduct of monetary policy. The UK experience should, therefore, constitute a fertile testing ground for the impact of monetary shocks on the predictive power of the yield curve for changes in inflation.

Of course the practical implementation of this investigation of the effects of monetary policy on the relationship between interest rates and inflation requires that any structural breaks in the relationship be identified accurately. Rather than dividing the sample into sub-periods, on grounds of economic priors, a combination of recursive estimation and formal testing is used to identify the number of significant changes over the sample period. As will become apparent, this method yields some interesting results in terms of the UK data. Once the relevant sub-periods have been identified, a second issue to be addressed concerns the statistical reliability of the information provided by the term structure during these periods of relative stability, given that these kinds of studies typically employ rather limited dynamic models. To try and ensure that the conclusions drawn from the estimation are robust, the moving-block bootstrap procedure (Carlstein, 1986; Künsch, 1989; Liu and Singh, 1992) is used to check the results obtained from asymptotic test procedures.

The structure of the chapter is as follows. Section 2 outlines the basic method for estimating the relationship between future inflation and the term structure of interest rates. Section 3 presents three sets of empirical results for this model, namely, the full-sample estimates, the results of the recursive estimation which is used to identify the appropriate number of sub-periods over which to estimate the model and then the sub-sample estimates. A discussion of the moving-block bootstrap procedure and the results from its implementation are contained in Section 4. Section 5 is a brief conclusion.

2. EMPIRICAL METHODOLOGY

The Inflation Change Equation

The standard approach to analysing the information in the term structure regarding future inflation is based on the Fisher equation

$$i_t^m = E\left[r_t^m\right] + E\left[\pi_t^m\right] \tag{7.1}$$

which expresses the nominal interest rate, i_t^m, in terms of the expected real interest rate, $E[r_t^m]$, and expected inflation, $E[\pi_t^m]$, over the relevant period. On the assumption of rational expectations, forecast and actual inflation will differ by some error term, say ε_t^m, which is uncorrelated with any information at time t. The difference between inflation over the next m periods and inflation over the next n periods can then be written in the form of the so-called 'inflation-change equation' proposed by Mishkin (1990a, 1990b):

$$\pi_t^m - \pi_t^n = \alpha_{m,n} + \beta_{m,n}\left[i_t^m - i_t^n\right] + e_t^{m,n} \tag{7.2}$$

where

$$\alpha_{m,n} = -\left(E\left[r_t^m\right] - E\left[r_t^n\right]\right)$$
$$e_t^{m,n} = \varepsilon_t^m - \varepsilon_t^n$$

and α and β are parameters to be estimated.

This equation purports to explain the inflation differential over a given time horizon in terms of an equivalent yield differential between two financial instruments on the assumption that the yield differential on real interest rates, over the time period concerned, is constant. As a model of changes in inflation, this regression will be misspecified. The argument is, however, that even though the model is misspecified, the effect of the spread on future inflation changes will be estimated consistently so long as the slope of the term structure of real interest rates, $\alpha_{m,n}$, is constant and omitted variables are uncorrelated with the interest rate spread. The literature concludes that the slope of the term structure contains information about changes in future inflation if the hypothesis $\beta = 0$ is rejected. It is clear from these remarks that correct inference in relation to the coefficient β is critical. In this regard there are two potential problems whose nature and suggested resolution are now discussed.

Structural Stability

The first of these potential problems relates to structural instability in the inflation change regression brought about by monetary policy shocks. Of particular importance will be the behaviour of the estimate of β at the time of entry and exit from the exchange rate mechanism of the European Community. In principle, when going from exchange rate targeting to inflation targeting, one would expect the predictive power of the term structure to disappear – since if monetary policy was successful, the change in inflation ex post should be zero. So if the hypothesis $\beta = 0$ can be rejected using the sample before inflation targeting and $\beta = 0$ cannot be rejected over the sub-sample after inflation targeting, this should imply that inflation targeting has been successful. In addition to the potentially important regime change in the early 1990s, however, there were a number of other unanticipated monetary events in the UK during the data sample period that may have influenced the informational content of the term structure. These would include, for example, the rapid interest rate increases following the election of the first Thatcher government in 1979–80, the sterling crisis of 1985 and the Deutschemark-shadowing experiment of 1987/88.

It is clear that the question of whether or not the relationship in equation (7.2) is constant over the entire sample period is an empirical one of critical importance. The evidence on the structural stability of the relationship between the term structure of interest rates and future inflation in other countries has only recently started to emerge. For example, Estrella et al. (2000) and Schich (1999) have recently investigated the temporal evolution of the informational content of the yield curve in Germany and the US. The results seem to suggest a single break point for the US (in late 1979) but a relatively stable relationship for Germany. It may be therefore that the relationship is not influenced by minor unanticipated events but only by significant regime changes.

This question of structural stability is not adequately addressed by constructing a series of sub-samples for estimating the value of β. In the first instance, the sub-samples would impose prior beliefs of the significance of particular events rather than allowing the data to determine the appropriate break points. In addition if all possible monetary shocks were to be catered for, many of the required sub-samples would be too small to allow reliable inference, especially when appeal is made to asymptotic results to justify hypothesis testing. This, in turn, would detract from investigating the major issue of the effect of the adoption of inflation targeting. To investigate the temporal evolution of the term structure, a better approach is to allow the data to indicate the significant breaks. Several tools will be employed to that end. Recursive estimation is frequently applied to gauge the constancy of parameter estimates. This approach is problematic, as the recursive coefficients will be biased after a structural break since they also reflect the history of the previous regime. One possible remedy is to employ a backward recursive scheme to reflect the information content under the most recent regime and thus complement the information gleaned in the forward-recursive estimates. In addition, recent tests for structural change with unknown break points following Andrews (1993) and Andrews and Ploberger (1994), and more traditional tests for structural change are used to formalize the information gleaned from the recursive estimation.

Inference

A second potential problem concerns statistical inference on the parameter. Even within regimes where stable relationships could exist, the standard error associated with the estimate of β is likely to be biased. Residuals from the inflation-change equation will probably be autocorrelated – because of equation misspecification and overlapping observations – and perhaps heteroscedastic. The standard solution has been to correct the standard errors, using the method of Newey and West (1987). Although the Newey–West standard errors correct for unknown forms of autocorrelation and heteroscedasticity, there is some evidence to suggest that the empirical size of the t-tests based on heteroscedasticity-corrected standard errors is too large (Horowitz, 2001). It may be, therefore, that a t or normal distribution does not approximate the actual empirical distribution of βs particularly well.

The approach taken here is to use the Newey–West correction for the basic results but to augment these by deriving confidence intervals for β by block bootstrapping – a bootstrapping procedure which is able to take account of dependence in the residuals. The dual approach to inference in this problem is not new. Mishkin (1990a) derives the critical values for his hypothesis tests by Monte Carlo simulation. The disadvantage of his Monte Carlo approach is that parametric models for the error process from the inflation-change equation need to be specified and estimated in order to implement the approach. This leaves scope for misspecifying the error process and introducing bias. Without a parametric model of error process, however, it is not possible to implement a residual-based bootstrap method. This conundrum may be overcome by implementing a bootstrap procedure that is capable of dealing with the correlation structure generally found in time series data. The moving-block bootstrap with overlapping blocks (Künsch, 1989; Liu and Singh, 1992) is used in this application.

3. DATA AND RESULTS

The data are continuously compounded interest rates and inflation rates. The interest rates used are monthly LIBOR data for 1-, 3-, 6- and 12-month deposits for the period 1976:1–1999:9. Although we will report results for spreads of all combinations of maturities, we will in the following be focusing on the data involving 12-month rates. The upper panel of Figure 3.1 illustrates that the variance of the inflation spreads decreases later in the sample, particularly after joining the exchange rate mechanism of the European Community on 8 October 1990. Although membership was suspended on 6 September 1992 a new framework for inflation targeting was announced in October of that year and the first *Inflation Report* by the Bank of England was published in February 1993. It appears therefore that volatility of inflation rates in the inflation-targeting regime has been more muted than in earlier monetary regimes. A second observation that may be made about the behaviour of inflation spreads concerns the regular pattern of spikes in the data. This indicates the likely presence of autocorrelation in the data. Given the very simple dynamic structure of the inflation-change equation, therefore, it is likely that correcting for both heteroscedasticity and autocorrelation will be an important factor in assessing the statistical significance of the information about future inflation contained in interest-rate spreads.

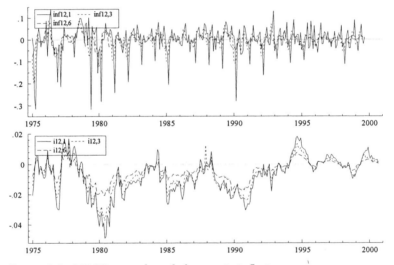

Figure 7.1   LIBOR spreads and changes in inflation

The corresponding interest rate spreads are plotted in the lower panel of Figure 7.1. As expected the most volatile of the three variables is the 12- and 1-month LIBOR spread. This is to be expected given the likely sensitivity of 1-month LIBOR interest rates to the short-term liquidity conditions in the interbank market and the influence of the Bank of England's monetary operations at the short end of the maturity spectrum. Although armed with institutional knowledge, one might claim that a change occurs in the behaviour of interest rate spreads after 1992, this information is not readily apparent from the raw data plots. There is thus a strong case for investigating the robustness of claims about the 'information' of interest rate spreads for predicting inflation both on statistical grounds.

Table 7.1 The effects of the slope of the yield curve on future inflation

	β (se$_\beta$)	p-value	R-squared
(3,1)	0.047 *(0.574)*	0.935	0.000
(6,1)	0.605 *(0.480)*	0.208	0.005
(12,1)	0.738 *(0.340)*	0.031	0.022
(6,3)	0.624 *(0.560)*	0.266	0.008
(12,3)	0.727 *(0.377)*	0.055	0.038
(12,6)	0.884 *(0.400)*	0.028	0.068

OLS Estimates 1976:1–2001:10 (Newey–West Standard Errors)

Notes: Left hand column represents the pairs of LIBOR maturities for which the estimation was undertaken.

Table 7.1 reports the full-sample estimates of the slope coefficient β of the inflation-change equation (7.2). There is virtually no information in the spreads at the lower end of the yield curve. However, when considering spreads including 12-month rates, the explanatory power increases, and the coefficient of interest becomes significant. The results seem to confirm those of Mishkin (1990a) and Siklos (2000) in the sense that only longer rates contain any information. This conclusion would, however, be premature, as the occurrence of numerous unexpected monetary shocks during the sample period has already been highlighted. Detailed investigation of the effects of these shocks is required before any firm conclusion can be made about the informational content of interest-rate spreads.

Figure 7.2 presents the forward (upper panels) and backward (lower panels) recursive estimates of the coefficient with 24 starting observations and error bands given by the Newey–West corrected standard errors. The results presented in Figure 7.2 are particularly instructive. The forward recursions of β do not indicate any particular changes in the coefficient estimates after the estimation procedure has settled down. Although there appears to be a downward trend in the mid-1990s, the estimates are surprisingly stable, with precision increasing over the sample. There is therefore no convincing evidence of structural breaks in the information content so far. This is, however, an example of the history of a previous regime dominating the coefficient estimates in the latter stages of the sample.

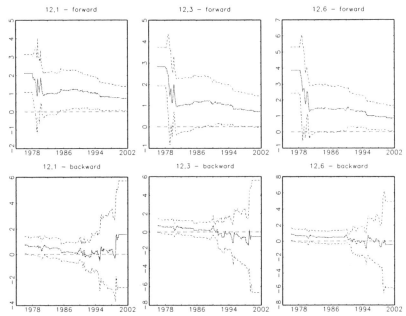

Figure 7.2   *Recursive coefficients +/- 2 Newey–West standard errors*
                 forward recursion in uppermost panel and backward
                 recursion below

When the recursion algorithm is run backwards, so that the sample starts
with the most recent information, there are a few things to note in relation to
structural breaks in the relationship once start-up effects are allowed for.

1. There appears to be a structural break in the relationship around 1990, the
   date at which sterling entered the exchange rate mechanism (ERM) of the
   European Community. Before 1990 the β coefficient is always greater
   than zero, while after this date the point estimate oscillates around zero.
2. The plots involving the shorter maturities, namely 1- and 3-month LIBOR,
   suggest a possible break in early 1985 corresponding to the sterling crisis
   which reached its peak in February of that year. Interestingly enough this
   break is not a major feature of the 12,6 maturity pair indicating that, for the
   most part, the crisis affected shorter-term LIBOR rates.
3. There appears to be a sharp change in the β estimates in 1980 but this
   effect is short-lived and does not appear to result in a sustained change in
   the value of the coefficient.

To confirm circumstantial evidence provided by the recursive estimation, the test for structural change with an unknown break-point (Andrews and Ploberger, 1994) was employed. The results of this exercise confirmed that the major breaks in the relationship occurred in February 1985 (for the maturity pairs 12,1 and 12,3) and October 1990, and that these breaks were statistically significant.[2] The sub-samples chosen as a result of this exercise are therefore 1976:1–1985:1, 1985:3–1990:9 and 1990:11–2001:12.

Table 7.2   The information content of interest rate spreads on future inflation for various sub-samples of interest

				OLS Estimates with Newey–West Standard Errors					
	1976:1–1985:1			1985:3–1990:9			1990:11–2001:12		
	β	p-value	R^2	β	p-value	R^2	β	p-value	R^2
(3,1)	−0.161	0.846	0.000	1.109	0.469	0.005	0.029	0.981	0.000
	(0.82)			(1.52)			(1.24)		
(6,1)	0.766	0.242	0.009	1.749	0.343	0.019	−0.127	0.881	0.000
	(0.65)			(1.83)			(0.84)		
(12,1)	1.088	0.054	0.044	1.768	0.052	0.048	0.045	0.917	0.000
	(0.56)			(0.89)			(0.43)		
(6,3)	0.867	0.296	0.016	0.903	0.357	0.012	−0.364	0.736	0.001
	(0.83)			(0.97)			(1.08)		
(12,3)	1.114	0.081	0.078	1.219	0.102	0.053	0.199	0.688	0.002
	(0.63)			(0.74)			(0.50)		
(12,6)	1.437	0.061	0.114	1.412	0.066	0.146	0.348	0.431	0.011
	(0.76)			(0.76)			(0.44)		

Table 7.2 presents the results obtained by estimating the inflation-change regression over these sub-samples of the data. It is clear that for the shorter end of the maturity spectrum, namely for maturity pairs (3,1), (6,1) and (6,3), there is little information to be gleaned about the immediate course of future inflation from LIBOR spreads. In all three of the sub-periods considered, the estimate of β is statistically insignificant. There is a different story for the maturity pairs involving 12-month LIBOR. Here the estimates of β are statistically significant at the 10% level for both the earlier two sub-samples, indicating that during these periods the longer end of the interbank interest-rate spectrum did contain information on the future course of UK inflation. Furthermore, it appears that the 1985 sterling crisis and the subsequent period of shadowing the Deutschemark in the late 1980s does not affect this relationship significantly as the coefficient estimates are broadly similar. Not surprisingly, this conclusion is perhaps not as strong for the (12,1) maturity pair, given that the effect of the sterling crisis would have had implications for the behaviour of 1-month LIBOR in particular. As a result of

this observation it was decided to estimate the inflation-change equation over the period 1976:1–1990:9. These results are reported in Table 7.3. The point estimates of β for the three maturity pairs involving 12-month LIBOR are slightly lower than expected but all are statistically significant, now at the 5% level.

Table 7.3   The effects of the slope of the yield curve on future inflation

| OLS Estimates 1976:1–1990:9 with Newey–West Standard Errors | | |
β (se$_\beta$)	p-value	R^2
(3,1)	0.047 *(0.574)*	0.935	0.000
(6,1)	0.605 *(0.480)*	0.208	0.005
(12,1)	0.738 *(0.340)*	0.031	0.022
(6,3)	0.624 *(0.560)*	0.266	0.008
(12,3)	0.727 *(0.377)*	0.055	0.038
(12,6)	0.884 *(0.400)*	0.028	0.068

Perhaps the most significant feature of the results reported in Table 7.2 concerns the period after entry to the ERM in 1990. After this date there is no evidence of any relationship whatsoever between spreads of interest rates and changes in future inflation, a result consistent with a regime of credible inflation targeting. This is an interesting result given that a firm commitment to inflation targeting was only given on exit from the ERM in 1992. One possible interpretation is that entry into the ERM represented a fundamental commitment to fighting inflation which exit from the ERM did not significantly alter.

4. BOOTSTRAPPED CONFIDENCE LEVELS

The point has already been made that the residuals from the inflation-change equation are likely to be autocorrelated because of equation misspecification and overlapping observations. It is also likely that the residuals are heteroscedastic. As a consequence, the question of the reliability of the inference drawn from models of this kind remains, especially if they are to be used in forecasting exercises (see for example, Jorion and Mishkin, 1991).

To check the conclusions reached on considering the results reported in Tables 7.4 and 7.5, the moving-block bootstrap was used to derive confidence intervals for the parameter β. The basic idea of the moving-block bootstrap as applied here is easily outlined. The method is as follows.

1. Estimate the inflation-change equation and generate the OLS residuals, $\hat{\varepsilon}_t$.
2. Resample blocks of $\hat{\varepsilon}_t$ with replacement using the overlapping blocks method suggested by Künsch's (1989) and stack the blocks together to yield a time series, $\hat{\varepsilon}_t^*$. of approximately the same length as the original. This method preserves the dependency structure in the residuals.
3. Use the bootstrapped residuals $\hat{\varepsilon}_t^*$ to generate bootstrap samples of the dependent variable using the OLS estimate of β and the observed values for the interest rate spreads.
4. Re-estimate β and repeat steps (2)–(4) to build up the distribution of this parameter. Once the bootstrapped distribution of β is available, a 95% confidence interval may be computed. Given that there remains lively debate in the literature as to which method of confidence interval construction is optimal, confidence intervals based on both the bootstrap-t and percentile method are used here (see, for example, Li and Maddala, 1996, and the associated discussion).

The optimal choice of block size in this bootstrap scheme has received some attention in the literature. Rather than appeal to any asymptotically correct block size we note that the main autocorrelation problems in our data stem from overlapping observation problems and the maximum possible order of this overlapping interval is 12 (for the (12,1) LIBOR pair). For the most part, the overlapping interval is less than 6 periods. As a result we use two block sizes of 12 and 6. The distributions of the estimates of β recovered from the full-sample bootstrap are illustrated in Figure 7.3. In general, the bootstrapped distributions appear relatively well behaved, and no clear choice in favour of one or other of the block sizes is apparent. As a result both block sizes are maintained for the construction of the interval estimates reported in Tables 7.4 and 7.5.

For the earlier sub-sample, 1976:1–1990: 9 and the pairs of maturities involving 12-month LIBOR, the interest rate spreads did contain significant information about the future course of inflation. Despite this statistical significance, however, the size of the confidence interval remains large – even though the estimation takes place within one regime. This poses questions as to the practical use of the method in terms of forecasting and certainly urges caution in the use of these severely misspecified equations for purposes other than drawing very broad conclusions.

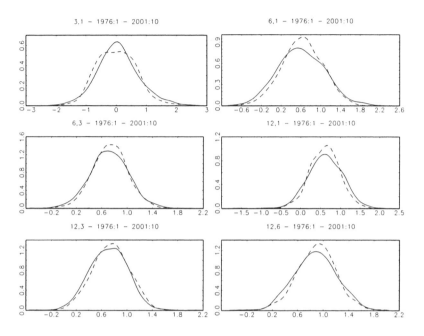

Figure 7.3   The bootstrap distributions of β based on the full sample.

Table 7.4   Bootstrap confidence intervals 1976:1–1990:11

	Point Estimate		Block Size = 12 95% CI			Block Size = 6 95% CI		
(3,1)	0.054	Bootstrap-t	1.321	↔	1.420	−1.345	↔	1.498
	(0.702)	Percentile	−1.663	↔	1.834	−1.845	↔	1.967
(6,1)	0.924	Bootstrap-t	−0.244	↔	2.164	−0.391	↔	2.238
	(0.635)	Percentile	−0.226	↔	2.108	−0.340	↔	2.258
(12,1)	1.207	Bootstrap-t	0.226	↔	2.256	0.112	↔	2.278
	(0.502)	Percentile	0.337	↔	2.034	0.360	↔	2.135
(6,3)	0.976	Bootstrap-t	−0.360	↔	2.205	−0.500	↔	2.382
	(0.702)	Percentile	−0.087	↔	2.064	−0.178	↔	2.205
(12,3)	1.148	Bootstrap-t	−0.044	↔	2.198	−0.093	↔	2.216
	(0.525)	Percentile	0.340	↔	2.039	0.332	↔	2.019
(12,6)	1.394	Bootstrap-t	0.226	↔	2.566	−1.010	↔	1.492
	(0.577)	Percentile	0.512	↔	2.331	-0.483	↔	1.292

Table 7.5 Bootstrap confidence intervals 1990:11–2001:10

	Point Estimate		Block Size = 12 95% CI		Block Size = 6 95% CI	
(3,1)	0.029	Bootstrap-*t*	−2.280 ↔ 2.381		−2.134 ↔ 2.346	
	(1.24)	Percentile	−2.190 ↔ 2.083		−2.183 ↔ 1.993	
(6,1)	-0.127	Bootstrap-*t*	−1.518 ↔ 1.372		−1.578 ↔ 1.460	
	(0.84)	Percentile	−1.361 ↔ 1.067		−1.484 ↔ 1.119	
(12,1)	0.045	Bootstrap-*t*	−0.652 ↔ 0.900		−0.715 ↔ 0.871	
	(0.43)	Percentile	−0.731 ↔ 0.752		−0.688 ↔ 0.783	
(6,3)	-0.364	Bootstrap-*t*	−2.072 ↔ 1.420		−2.487 ↔ 1.610	
	(1.08)	Percentile	−1.661 ↔ 0.902		−1.903 ↔ 1.152	
(12,3)	0.199	Bootstrap-*t*	−0.764 ↔ 1.235		−0.093 ↔ 2.216	
	(0.50)	Percentile	−0.632 ↔ 1.033		0.332 ↔ 2.019	
(12,6)	0.348	Bootstrap-*t*	−0.740 ↔ 1.347		−1.010 ↔ 1.492	
	(0.44)	Percentile	−0.466 ↔ 1.204		−0.483 ↔ 1.292	

Not surprisingly, the earlier results for the period of inflation targeting are confirmed and the hypothesis of $\beta = 0$ cannot be rejected. The fact that the timing of this change pre-dates the formal adoption of inflation targets in the UK is curious. One possible explanation concerns the role of the exchange rate in policymaking. When Nigel Lawson became Chancellor of the Exchequer after the election of 1983, the stage was set for a long conflict within the government over the EMS and this itself increased the prominence of the exchange rate in policymaking. Over the period the exchange rate became accepted as at least one of the guides for policy. Indeed market perceptions of the prospect of ERM membership grew as monetary policy was driven by the Deutschemark exchange rate. This led to the formal policy of 'shadowing' the Deutschemark between 1987 and March 1988. It appears from the results reported here that this change in monetary policy had the effect of decoupling the link between interest rates and future inflation even before ERM entry.

In any event, the results reported here may be taken as prima facie evidence that the UK inflation target is a credible one. This result is consistent with the conclusions of Siklos (2000), who found that in New Zealand, which has a firm inflation target, the term structure contains little information about future inflation in contrast to Australia which targets inflation but with a relatively weaker commitment. What this suggests is that the nominal UK term structure is now a yardstick for future real interest rates as opposed to inflation.

5. CONCLUSION

This chapter has examined the impact of changes in monetary policy on the informational content of the term structure with respect to future inflation in the UK. The results of combining of both forward and backward recursive estimation identified significant break points in the relationship between interest and inflation differentials, which may be related to significant changes in monetary policy. The use of the moving-block bootstrap, to guard against incorrect inference in an equation where the residuals are both autocorrelated and heteroscedastic, reinforced the conclusion of the unreliability of the informational content.

Summing up, the results from this modelling exercise are fairly clear-cut. The interest rates differentials involving the 12-month deposit rate contained information about future inflation prior to 1990. It also transpires, however, that the confidence interval for the crucial parameter governing this relationship is a broad one, a fact that would inhibit relying on this rather simple specification for rigorous forecasting purposes. The most interesting result to emerge is that there appears to be no information on future inflation in interest rate spreads after the entry into the ERM in 1990. The interest rate spreads in the later period signal changes in real interest rates rather than changes in future inflation. This result is consistent with empirical work from other countries, which shows that the information content of interest spreads is higher in countries with less formal inflation targets (the US and Australia) and non-existent in countries with a formal commitment to inflation targeting (New Zealand). Extracting information about the future path of inflation from the term structure is therefore to be considered a highly unreliable business.

NOTES

1.   LIBOR is an abbreviation of London Interbank Offer Rate. The interest rates in this data set are month-end middle rates.
2.   The actual months recording the highest values of the Andrews and Ploberger test varied slightly for different maturity pairs. As the maximum values of the tests were not uniformly located at a particular month we could see no reason not to use the months in which the economic event of interest occurred.

REFERENCES

Andrews, D.W.K. (1993), 'Tests for Parameter Instability and Structural Change with Unknown Change Point', *Econometrica*, **61**, 821–856.

Andrews, D.W.K. and W. Ploberger (1994), 'Optimal Tests when a Nuisance Parameter is Present Only under the Alternative', *Econometrica*, **62**, 1383–1414.

Carlstein, E. (1986), 'The Use of Subseries Values for Estimating the Variance of a General Statistic from a Nonstationary Sequence', *The Annals of Statistics*, **14**, 117–1179.

Estrella, A. and F.S. Mishkin (1997), 'The Predictive Power of the Term Structure of Interest Rates in Europe and the United States: Implications for the European Central Bank', *European Economic Review*, **41**, 1375–1201.

Estrella, A., A.P. Rodrigues and S. Schich (2000), 'How Stable is the Predictive Power of the Yield Curve? Evidence from Germany and the United States', mimeo, Federal Reserve Bank of New York.

Hamilton, J.D. and D.H. Kim (2000), 'A Re-examination of the Predictability of Economic Activity Using the Yield Spread', *NBER Working Paper*, No. W7954.

Horowitz, J. (2001), 'The Bootstrap', in J.J. Heckman and E. Leamer, *Handbook of Econometrics, Volume 5*, Amsterdam: Elsevier.

Jorion, P. and F.S. Mishkin (1991), 'A Multi-Country Comparison of Term Structure Forecasts at Long Horizons', *Journal of Financial Economics*, **29**, 59–80.

Künsch, H.R. (1989), 'The Jackknife and the Bootstrap for General Stationary Observations', *The Annals of Statistics*, **17**, 1217–1241.

Li, H. and G.S. Maddala (1996), 'Bootstrapping Time Series Models', *Econometric Reviews*, **15**, 115–158.

Liu, R.Y. and K. Singh (1992), 'Moving Blocks Jackknife and Bootstrap Capture Weak Dependence' in R. LePage and L. Billard (eds.), *Exploring the Limits of the Bootstrap*, John Wiley and Sons: New York.

Mishkin, F.S. (1990a), 'What Does the Term Structure Tell Us About Future Inflation?', *Journal of Monetary Economics*, **25**, 77–95.

Mishkin, F.S. (1990b), 'The Information in the Longer-Maturity Term Structure About Future Inflation', *Quarterly Journal of Economics*, **55**, 815–828.

Mishkin, F.S. (1991), 'A Multi-Country Study of the Information in the Term Structure About Future Inflation', *Journal of International Money and Finance*, **19**, 2–22.

Newey, W.K. and K.D. West (1987), 'A Simple Positive Semi-Definite, Heteroscedasticity and Autocorrelation Consistent Covariance Matrix', *Econometrica*, **55**, 703–708.

Politis, D.N., J.P. Romano and M. Wolf (1997), 'Subsampling for Heteroskedastic Time Series', *Journal of Econometrics*, **81**, 281–317.

Schich, S. (1999), 'What the Yield Curves say about Inflation: Does it Change Over Time?', *Working Paper*, OECD Economics Department.

Siklos, P.L. (2000), 'Inflation Targets and the Yield Curve: New Zealand and Australia versus the US', *International Journal of Finance and Economics*, **5**, 15–32.

8. Missing Data and Interpolation in Dynamic Term Structure Models

Vlad Pavlov

1. INTRODUCTION

One often-neglected problem when estimating term-structure models is the effect of measurement errors on the properties of the statistics of the particular theory of interest to an econometrician. Even default-free term-structure datasets often contain a large number of missing observations, which are due either to thin trading or the simple non-existence of bonds with certain maturities. Corporate-debt datasets are often much more thinly traded and sparse. The problem is particularly severe for longer-maturity bonds, in high-frequency (daily, weekly) datasets and for relatively small markets (such as Australia).

Most empirical studies rely on various cross-sectional interpolation techniques to reconstruct the missing observations. Simple cubic-spline interpolation, used by McCulloch and Kwon to construct a popular dataset of monthly US interest rates (McCulloch and Kwon, 1993), is still arguably one of the most accepted methods.

The ability of the interpolation procedure to extract information from the observed cross-sections has been studied by a number of authors. Bliss (1996), for example, reports that residuals of many such methods appear to contain omitted factors. The effect of interpolation on the properties of estimators in popular term-structure models, however, has not been investigated. The objective of this chapter, therefore, is to evaluate the effect of interpolation on some popular expectations theory statistics by means of a simple simulation experiment.

The structure of the experiment is straightforward. An interest-rate model is estimated using the US money-market interest rates of the McCulloch dataset (for maturities of one to twelve months). The estimated model is then simulated under specific restrictions to produce observations consistent with the expectations hypothesis. In each simulation, observations are dropped randomly from cross-sections to reproduce the missing data problem and then reconstructed using cubic-spline interpolation. Expectations-theory statistics are then computed using the reconstructed datasets and accumulated until enough data have been collected to examine their statistical properties under interpolation.

2. EXPECTATIONS THEORY

This section provides a brief exposition of the expectations theory (ET), its formalisations and popular testing strategies. The motivation for choosing ET is simple. The theory has been a popular subject for econometricians and the properties of popular statistics used to test the expectations hypothesis (EH) are well known.

Testing the expectations theory has generated a large empirical literature. Earlier papers (Fama and Bliss, 1987; Campbell and Shiller, 1987 and 1991) tended to produce emphatic rejections of the theory. Recently, however, the expectations theory has been brought back into the spotlight when some support for the theory was found at very short maturities (Longstaff, 2000), in international data (Hurn et al., 1995) and in data from market surveys (Froot, 1989). A recent comprehensive survey of the theory, with tests and applications, can be found in Bekaert and Hodrick (2000).

The expectations hypothesis has a long history in economics. It is based on the intuitively plausible idea that if long-term rates diverge too far from the expectations of future short rates the investors will trade until short and long rates are brought back in line with these expectations. Cox et al. (1981) noted however that this intuitive idea can be translated into a number of incompatible formulations. Much of the existing empirical literature circumvents the problem by postulating the ET in terms of yields rather than returns, in which case alternative ways to postulate the theory generate identical restrictions on the behaviour of interest rates.

Define the yield on an n-period bond as

$$r(t,n) = -\frac{1}{n} LnB(t,n)$$

and the holding period yield as

$$h(t,n) = \ln p(t+1, n-1) - \ln p(t,n).$$

Define the forward rate $f(t,n)$ as the yield on one-period investment at $t+n$ which can be contracted at time t. The ET can now be formulated in either of the two forms: local ET (LET) and unbiased ET (UET). LET states that expected holding-period yields on all bonds are equal, possibly up to time-invariant maturity-specific risk premia $\mu_1(n)$:

$$E_t\left(r(t,n)\right) = r(t) + \mu_1(n) \qquad (8.1)$$

Here $r(t)$ is the yield on the one-period (short) bond and E_t is the conditional expectation taken with respect to current information.

Re-arranging (8.1) we can write

$$E_t\left\{r(t+1,n-1) - r(t,n)\right\} = \frac{r(t,n) - r(t)}{n-1} + \mu_1(n). \qquad (8.2)$$

Thus, when long yields are high relative to the short yield, the market expects interest rates to rise. The expected capital loss on the long bond is the compensation required to induce investors to hold short bonds.

The UET hypothesis maintains that current forward rates reflect market expectations of future short rates:

$$f(t,n) = E_t\left[r(t+n)\right] + \mu(n). \qquad (8.3)$$

Here $\mu(n)$ is a maturity-specific risk premium.

The following simple identities

$$r(t,n) = -\frac{1}{n}\sum_{i=0}^{n-1} h(t+i,n-i) = -\frac{1}{n}\sum_{i=0}^{n-1} f(t,i), \qquad (8.4)$$

taken together with either (8.1) or (8.3) imply that the yields on longer maturity bonds are equal to the average of expected short yields over the life of the bond:

$$r(t,n) = \mu^*(n) + \frac{1}{n} E_t\left\{\sum_{i=0}^{n-1} r(t+i)\right\}$$

$$\mu^*(n) = \frac{1}{n}\sum_{i=0}^{n-1}\mu(i). \qquad (8.5)$$

It is straightforward to demonstrate, using equation (8.5), that, when formulated in terms of yields, LET and UET are equivalent. Subtracting the short yield from (8.5) leads to the following formulation of the hypothesis:

$$E_t \left\{ \sum_{i=1}^{n-1} \left(1 - \frac{i}{n} \right) \Delta r \left(t + i - 1 \right) \right\} = \mu^* \left(n \right) + \left(r \left(t, n \right) - r \left(t \right) \right). \qquad (8.6)$$

Equation (8.6) provides an alternative interpretation of the expectations hypothesis; high long yields indicate expectation of higher short yields at least for some periods during the life of the long bond.

A number of popular tests based on the implications of the ET are considered in this chapter. The first two are simple regression tests suggested by Fama and Bliss (1987), derived from (8.2) and (8.6), which focus on changes in long yields and short yields respectively. The pertinent equations are

$$r \left(t + 1, n - 1 \right) - r \left(t, n \right) = \alpha + \beta \frac{r \left(t, n \right) - r \left(t \right)}{n - 1} + \varepsilon_1 \left(t + 1 \right) \qquad (8.7)$$

and

$$\sum_{i=1}^{n-1} \left(1 - \frac{i}{n} \right) \Delta r \left(t + i - 1 \right) = \gamma + \delta \left(r \left(t, n \right) - r \left(t \right) \right) + \varepsilon_2 \left(t + n - 1 \right). \qquad (8.8)$$

Two tests of the expectations theory, which will be denoted Tests 1 and 2 respectively, restrict the slope coefficients β, δ in (8.7) and (8.8) to be unity.

The next group of tests was suggested by Campbell and Shiller (1987) and is based on the dynamic of an estimated vector autoregression for the yields. Consider a vector autoregression (VAR) in levels for the yields:

$$y_t = C + \sum_{i=1}^{m} A_i y_{t-i} + \eta_t. \qquad (8.9)$$

Here $y_t = \left[r \left(t \right), r \left(t, 2 \right), ..., r \left(t, n \right) \right]'$ is the vector of n yields. The estimated VAR can be used to construct a 'theoretical' spread as the difference between the average VAR short rate forecast until the maturity of the long bond and the current short rate:

$$S' \left(t, n \right) = \frac{1}{n} \sum_{i=0}^{n-1} r^f \left(t + i \right) - r \left(t \right), \qquad (8.10)$$

where $r_t^f \left(T \right)$ is the time t VAR forecast of the one period yield at T:

$$r^f \left(t + i \right) - E \left(r \right) = \mathbf{1}' \left(\mathbf{A}^c \right)^i \left(y \left(t \right) - E \left(y \right) \right). \qquad (8.11)$$

In (8.11) $\mathbf{A}^c$ is the companion matrix of the VAR and $\mathbf{1}$ is an $n \times m$ vector with 1 in the first position and zeros in all the others.

Campbell and Shiller (1991) suggested that correlations between 'theoretical' or VAR spreads and actual spreads (spread correlation test or Test 3) as well as the ratios of corresponding variances (volatility ratio or Test 4) may provide meaningful tests of economic significance of deviations from the EH.

3. ESTIMATING A MODEL FOR INTEREST RATES

The interest rate data to be used in the estimation comprises one- to twelve-month maturities for the January 1965 to February 1991 sub-sample of the McCulloch and Kwon dataset. The dimensionality of interest-rate cross-sections was reduced to three by exploiting the factor structure in the yields. The first factor is assumed to coincide with the shortest maturity (monthly) yield;[1] the remaining two factors were obtained as the principal components of the sample variance-covariance matrix of the spreads.

By construction the two additional factors are the mutually orthogonal linear combinations of the yields $f_i(t) = w_i' r(t, n)$ with the maximum sample variance normalised to have the unit Euclidean norm:

$$w'\tilde{V}w \to \max_{w}$$
$$s.t. \quad w'w = 1$$

The eigenvectors corresponding to the two largest eigenvalues of the sample variance-covariance matrix of the spreads $\tilde{V}$ determine the factor combinations. To estimate factor loadings observed yields are regressed on the factors.In cross-sectional regressions the three factors capture 97–99% of the sample variation of the spreads with the exception of the spread between the two-month and one-month yields where the amount is a somewhat more modest 90%. Therefore, little information is lost by assuming that the factor structure is exact and conditioning the rest of the analysis on the estimated factor realisations. Figure 8.1 illustrates the dynamics of the estimated factors.

A model is now formulated to describe the joint dynamics of the factors. Empirically, the short rate follows a persistent process very close to the non-stationary region. We follow the contention in Bekaert et al. (1997) and model yields as stationary in levels.

To get an idea of the conditional properties of volatility series, factors were pre-whitened using a second order VAR and the residuals were used to estimate three univariate GARCH(1,1) models. Figure 8.2 illustrates the behaviour of variances based on univariate GARCH estimates. The graph demonstrates the period of elevated volatility during the Federal Reserve monetary experiment (1979–82). Importantly, the series also clearly display the tendency of volatilities to move together, which can be confirmed by looking at the sample correlations between estimated conditional variances (Table 8.1). We model these correlations by introducing a common factor into volatility equations.

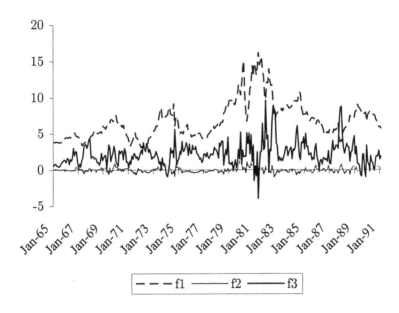

Figure 8.1 Sample factor realisations

Table 8.1 Sample correlations between volatility estimates

	$\hat{\sigma}_{t1}^2$	$\hat{\sigma}_{t2}^2$	$\hat{\sigma}_{t3}^2$
$\hat{\sigma}_{t1}^2$	1		
$\hat{\sigma}_{t2}^2$	0.608	1	
$\hat{\sigma}_{t3}^2$	0.611	0.417	1

The final model used to simulate interest rates is a VAR–GARCH factor model with the mean dynamics of the factors evolving according to a second-order VAR. We also assume that VAR innovations are contemporaneously uncorrelated. While factors are uncorrelated by construction, this assumption is much stronger in that it demands that factors are uncorrelated conditionally as well as unconditionally. The main benefit of such parametrisation is that it leads to a simple model by avoiding the need to model covariance terms. In addition, the common factor in the volatilities is assumed to be completely captured by the conditional variance of the residuals of the short rate equation.

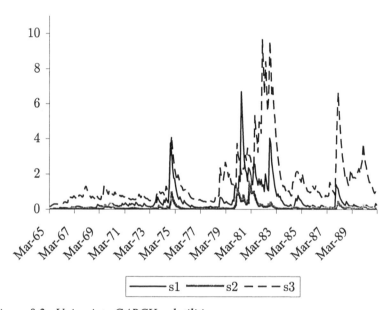

Figure 8.2   Univariate GARCH volatilities

Under these assumptions the model becomes:

$$y_t = C + \sum_{i=1}^{2} A_i y_{t-i} + \eta_t$$
$$\eta_{ti} = \sigma_{ti} \varepsilon_{t,i}$$
$$\sigma_{t1}^2 = \omega_1 + \lambda_1 \varepsilon_{t-1,1}^2 + \theta_1 \sigma_{t-1,1}^2$$
$$\sigma_{ti}^2 = \omega_i + \kappa_i \sigma_{t1}^2 + \lambda_i \varepsilon_{t-1,i}^2 + \theta_i \sigma_{t-1,i}^2, i \in \{1,2\}$$

(8.12)

The parameters of the system (8.12) are estimated by quasi maximum likelihood (QML). Table 8.2 presents selected diagnostics of the scaled residuals. Model parameter estimates, reported in Appendix A, suggest that the process is not covariance-stationary. However, at least if the fundamental innovations are normally distributed, the parameters are in the region of strict stationarity (see e.g. Gourieroux, 1997) and it was decided not to place any further restrictions on the estimated GARCH equations.

Table 8.2   Diagnostics of the standardised shocks (asymptotic p-values in parentheses)

	η_1 / σ_1	η_2 / σ_2	η_3 / σ_3
Skewness	−0.331	0.235	0.524
Kurtosis	5.576	4.361	4.451
JB	91.96	26.94	41.66
	(0.000)	(0.000)	(0.000)
Serial Correlation (5 lags)	0.442	0.242	0.309
	(0.816)	(0.943)	(0.907)
ARCH LM test (5 lags)	0.717	0.336	0.617
	(0.611)	(0.891)	(0.687)

The sample includes the Volcker period from 1979 to 1982 when the Federal Reserve switched from targeting interest rates to targeting money growth, which led to an episode of extremely volatile nominal interest rates (Figure 8.2). This period is usually accommodated by either treating 1979–82 as a structural break or by incorporating a level effect into the volatility equation by scaling it with a power (usually the square root) of the lagged short yield (Gray, 1996) or its affine transformation (Bekaert et al., 1997).

In this set-up, simulating with levels-related volatility created considerable problems. In particular, in a discrete-time model it is impossible to restrict yields from making trips into the negative territory without additional transformations and, with the levels adjustment, volatility is not defined for negative yields. Alternative simple specifications for the volatility effect consistent with the possibility of negative yields were examined (such as scaling with the square root of the absolute value of the yield), but these produced simulations that appeared highly implausible. On the other hand, fitting a simple GARCH process on the selected sub-period produced a reasonable and simple specification (Table 8.2) and simulations without any need for additional adjustments and was judged sufficient for the purposes of this chapter.

4. SIMULATION AND INTERPOLATION

The main part of the experiment involves bootstrapping the standardised residuals of the estimated factor model to produce simulations of the factors, using the bootstrapped factors to reconstruct the yields and then introducing missing observations and re-estimating ET regressions.

Bootstrap samples were constructed by resampling with replacement from the rows of the standardised GARCH shocks. ET-consistent simulations were obtained using the VAR forecasts for the short rate on the bootstrapped sample to construct the theoretical spreads using the ET equation (8.10). The same method was used by Bekaert et al. (1997) to bootstrap small-sample properties of the ET statistics.

Missing observations were introduced through the following mechanism. For each simulated cross-section a draw was taken from the Bernoulli distribution with the number of trials equal to seven. The probability of dropping an observation p_m serves as the parameter modulating the severity of the missing data problem. The results of two sets of simulations are reported, with p_m set equal to 30% and 60% respectively, which corresponds to roughly two and four missing observations in each of the cross-sections of twelve yields on average.

The number of trials parameter reflects the following considerations. First, the twelve-month yield was always left uninterrupted to avoid extrapolation outside the range of available data. Second, at least four observations, in addition to the twelve-month yield, were required in each cross-section. The rationale for this requirement is that simple spline interpolation can be very sensitive to the number of available observations, especially when interpolating over a long block of adjacent points and can occasionally produce extreme spikes in the interpolated cross-sections. In real-life data applications such spikes would be clearly visible and easily eliminated by either judgemental parameter adjustment or by adding a roughness penalty as suggested by Fisher et al. (1995). In simulations, however, interpolating with a roughness penalty is not a feasible solution, as it requires a numerical optimisation for each cross-section. The minimum data requirement was designed as an alternative simple way to control the problem in simulations.

Given the number m_t of missing observations on a cross-section, the missing observations were determined by randomly drawing m_t indices from between maturities of one to eleven months. The yields corresponding to missing observations were then replaced with their interpolated values. The cubic spline was restricted to fit the observed maturities exactly. In addition, the spline curves were constructed to satisfy the requirement that $B(t,0) = 1$.

With the relatively small number of cross-sectional observations, the choice of boundary conditions turned out to be very important. Initially, the natural estimates $\{p(t,1)-1, p(t,12)-p(t,11)\}$ were tried for end-slopes but this led to very poor properties of the ET statistics. The reported results rely on the not-a-knot boundary conditions that demand constant curvature at endpoints of the spline and, surprisingly, appeared to perform best.

It may be noted that the process generating missing observations is greatly oversimplified. In reality, the missing data problem is a lot more severe for longer maturities. For example, according to Gourieroux and Scaillet (1996), to model the money-market maturity spectrum in France one has to rely on the observations of ten to fifteen traded Treasury securities. Real missing data also exhibit deterministic trends as missing points move along the yield curve towards shorter maturities.

5. SIMULATION RESULTS

Simulation results based on 10,000 replications are reported in Tables 8.B.1 to 8.B.3 in Appendix B. The tables detail the average sample bias of the estimates relative to the ET value of unity and standard deviations for all the statistics.

The zero-probability column, $p_m = 0$, in all tables refers to the base case when complete uninterrupted cross-sections are available (no missing observations). All distributions display non-trivial small-sample biases. In terms of the magnitude and direction of these biases the results are roughly consistent with the simulations in Bekaert et al. (1997) with the exception of the correlation test (Test 3). In the present set-up, contrary to what is reported in Bekaert et al. (1997), the VAR correlation test seems to fair quite poorly. It is however doubtful that either of these simulations based on misspecified bivariate VARs enables us to make reliable statements about the magnitude of small-sample distortions in VAR tests.

We define the interpolation bias as the difference between the small-sample bias and the total bias of the statistic. In all tests the one-period yield is the yield on a bond maturing in one month.

The regression test based on the changes in long yields (Table 8.B.1) is the most sensitive to the presence of interpolated data. For $p_m = 60\%$ the contribution of the interpolation bias to the total bias appears to decline with the maturity of the long rate from 24.2% to 5.4% for the regression of long rate changes on the spreads and from 12.1% to 1% for the regression of ex-post spreads on the data spreads. Not surprisingly, interpolation reduces the correlation between the VAR spread and actual spread but the effect is rather small with the maximum interpolation bias equal to 1.4% in absolute value and only the statistics for two- and three-month spreads displaying a bias exceeding 1% in absolute value. In our set-up however, the correlation test is severely affected by the small-sample bias.

The relatively poor performance of the first regression test can be interpreted in light of the criticism levelled at the test by Campbell and Shiller (1987). Namely, because it relies on the relationship between the spread and one-period ahead changes in the long rate, the presence of a small amount of noise can lead to it performing poorly even when the ET is in fact correct.

The effect of interpolation on the standard deviation of ET statistics is consistent with intuition. The loss of information due to the missing data causes all standard deviations to go up. Surprisingly, this effect is rather small and much less pronounced than the bias effect.

6. CONCLUSION

This chapter has examined the sensitivity of a number of expectations theory tests to cubic interpolation of the missing observations in the maturity spectrum of US interest-rate data. The results indicate that, even in the stylised structure used here, a small fraction of missing data can introduce significant biases into some simple regression and VAR tests. Unlike small sample biases documented in the literature, these biases are unlikely to disappear as the sample gets larger. It seems reasonable to hypothesise that these biases can be quite substantial in studies employing interpolated high frequency datasets. Furthermore, it should also be noted that in the studies involving real data the missing maturities problem will probably be a lot more severe than assumed here.

NOTES

1. This assumption is inconsequential; the first principal component extracted from the levels of the yields is almost perfectly correlated with the short rate.

REFERENCES

Bekaert, G., R.J. Hodrick and D.A. Marshall (1997), 'On the Biases of the Expectations Hypothesis of the Term Structure of Interest Rates', *Journal of Financial Economics*, **44**, 309–348.

Bekaert, G. and R.J. Hodrick (2000), 'Expectations Theory Tests', *NBER Working Paper No. 7609*.

Bliss, R.R. (1996), 'Testing Term Structure Estimation Methods', Federal Reserve Bank of Atlanta Working Paper, 96–12a.

Campbell, J.Y. and R.J. Shiller (1987), 'Cointegration and Tests of Present Value Models', *Journal of Political Economy*, **95**, 1062–1088.

Campbell, J.Y. and R.J. Shiller (1991), 'Yield Spreads and Interest Rate Movements: A Bird's Eye View', *Review of Economic Studies*, **58**, 495–514.

Cox, J.C., J.E. Ingersoll and S.A. Ross (1981), 'A Re-examination of Traditional Hypotheses About the Term Structure of Interest Rates', *Journal of Finance*, **36**, 769–799.

Fama, E.F. and R.R. Bliss (1987), 'The Information in Long-Maturity Forward Rates', *American Economic Review*, **77**, 680–692.

Fisher, M., D. Nychka and D. Zervos (1995), 'Fitting the Term Structure of Interest Rates with Smoothing Splines', Working Paper 95-1, Finance and Economics Discussion Series, Federal Reserve Board.

Froot, K.A. (1989), 'New Hope for the Expectations Hypothesis of the Term Structure of Interest Rates', *Journal of Finance*, **44**, 283–305.

Gourieroux, C. (1997), *ARCH Models and Financial Applications*, New York: Springer-Verlag.

Gourieroux, C. and O. Scaillet (1996), 'Estimation of the Term Structure from Bond Data', Working Paper No. 9415, CEPREMAP.

Gray, S. (1996), 'Modelling the Conditional Distribution of Interest Rates as a Regime Switching Model', *Journal of Financial Econometrics*, **42**, 27–62.

Hall, A.D., H.M. Anderson and C.W. Granger (1992), 'A Cointegration Analysis of Treasury Bill Yields', *Review of Economics and Statistics*, **74**, 116–126.

Hurn, A.S., T. Moody and A. Muscatelli (1995), 'The Term Structure of Interest Rates in the London Interbank Market', *Oxford Economic Papers*, **47**, 419–436.

Longstaff, F.A. (2000), 'The Term Structure of Very Short-Term Rates: New Evidence for the Expectations Hypothesis', *Journal of Financial Economics*, **58**, 397–415.

McCulloch, H.J., and H.C. Kwon (1993), 'US Term Structure Data, 1947–1991', Ohio State Working Paper, 93–96.

APPENDIX A

Table 8.A.1   QML model estimates (QML Z-statistics are in parentheses)

	$r(t)$	Z-stat	$f_1(t)$	Z-stat	$f_2(t)$	Z-stat
			Mean equation			
C	0.118	(1.515)	0.001	(0.037)	0.271	(1.378)
$r(t-1)$	1.076	(11.870)	−0.017	(−0.454)	0.014	(0.107)
$f_1(t-1)$	0.273	(2.275)	0.557	(8.269)	−1.218	(−4.722)
$f_2(t-1)$	0.151	(5.911)	−0.077	(−3.797)	0.562	(7.324)
$r(t-2)$	−0.122	(−1.358)	0.032	(0.884)	0.068	(0.525)
$f_1(t-2)$	−0.111	(−1.035)	−0.031	(−0.465)	0.094	(0.351)
$f_2(t-2)$	−0.073	(−2.298)	0.015	(0.891)	0.043	(0.499)
			Volatility equation			
ω_i	0.015	(3.125)	0.004	(1.413)	0.073	(1.760)
λ_i	0.398	(4.763)	0.335	(2.515)	0.157	(2.479)
θ_i	0.650	(12.777)	0.233	(1.593)	0.667	(7.214)
κ_i			0.093	(2.841)	0.427	(2.424)

APPENDIX B

Table 8.B.1   Regression test 1 (long rate changes)

	Bias: $\left(\sum_{i=1}^{N_h} \dfrac{\xi}{n} - 1\right)\%$			Standard deviation		
Long rate	$p_m{=}0.00$	$p_m{=}0.30$	$p_m{=}0.60$	$p_m{=}0.00$	$p_m{=}0.30$	$p_m{=}0.60$
2	2.5%	13.0%	26.7%	0.297	0.330	0.378
3	5.2%	10.2%	18.7%	0.427	0.451	0.484
4	7.8%	12.4%	18.0%	0.530	0.554	0.581
5	10.4%	14.7%	19.2%	0.612	0.635	0.658
6	12.9%	17.0%	20.9%	0.679	0.700	0.720
7	15.4%	19.2%	22.7%	0.734	0.755	0.771
8	17.8%	21.4%	24.6%	0.781	0.801	0.815
9	20.1%	23.6%	26.5%	0.822	0.840	0.852
10	22.4%	25.8%	28.3%	0.858	0.875	0.884
11	24.6%	27.9%	30.2%	0.889	0.905	0.913
12	26.8%	30.0%	32.2%	0.916	0.932	0.938

Table 8.B.2 Regression test 2 (cumulative short rates changes)

Long rate	Bias: $\left(\sum_{i=1}^{N_b}\frac{\xi}{n}-1\right)\%$			Standard deviation		
	$p_m=0.00$	$p_m=0.30$	$p_m=0.60$	$p_m=0.00$	$p_m=0.30$	$p_m=0.60$
2	1.3%	6.6%	13.4%	0.151	0.168	0.191
3	2.6%	4.2%	6.9%	0.160	0.170	0.184
4	3.8%	5.0%	6.3%	0.168	0.177	0.189
5	4.8%	5.9%	6.7%	0.175	0.184	0.196
6	5.8%	6.8%	7.4%	0.183	0.192	0.203
7	6.8%	7.7%	8.1%	0.191	0.199	0.210
8	7.7%	8.5%	8.9%	0.198	0.207	0.216
9	8.6%	9.3%	9.7%	0.205	0.213	0.223
10	9.4%	10.2%	10.5%	0.212	0.220	0.229
11	10.3%	11.0%	11.3%	0.218	0.226	0.235
12	11.1%	11.9%	12.1%	0.225	0.233	0.241

Table 8.B.3 VAR correlation test

Long rate	Bias: $\left(\sum_{i=1}^{N_b}\frac{\xi}{n}-1\right)\%$			Standard deviation		
	$p_m=0.00$	$p_m=0.30$	$p_m=0.60$	$p_m=0.00$	$p_m=0.30$	$p_m=0.60$
2	−6.2%	−6.8%	−7.6%	0.060	0.065	0.074
3	−6.5%	−7.0%	−7.7%	0.062	0.067	0.073
4	−6.6%	−7.1%	−7.6%	0.063	0.066	0.071
5	−6.6%	−7.0%	−7.4%	0.062	0.065	0.069
6	−6.5%	−6.9%	−7.2%	0.061	0.064	0.068
7	−6.5%	−6.8%	−7.1%	0.061	0.063	0.067
8	−6.4%	−6.7%	−6.9%	0.060	0.063	0.067
9	−6.4%	−6.6%	−6.8%	0.060	0.062	0.066
10	−6.3%	−6.5%	−6.7%	0.060	0.062	0.066
11	−6.2%	−6.3%	−6.5%	0.059	0.061	0.065
12	−6.1%	−6.2%	−6.3%	0.059	0.060	0.064

9. Choosing Lag Lengths in Nonlinear Dynamic Models

Heather Anderson

1. INTRODUCTION

There has been considerable interest in nonlinear time series models in recent years, as evidenced by a growing body of studies of asymmetries in business cycles and nonlinearities in asset markets. Models that allow for state-dependent or regime-switching behaviour have been very popular, with well-known examples including the Markov switching (MS) model (Hamilton, 1989), the current depth of recession (CDR) model (Beaudry and Koop, 1993), the smooth transition autoregressive (STAR) model (Teräsvirta, 1994) and the threshold autoregressive (TAR) model (Potter, 1995). At first blush, such models have intuitive appeal and seem relatively easy to work with, although in practice they are often quite difficult to specify and estimate.

One difficulty associated with nonlinear modelling is that the researcher usually needs to determine the lag structure of the data before conducting nonlinearity tests or estimating nonlinear specifications. Researchers often choose this lag length by setting it equal to the lag length chosen for a linear autoregressive model of the data, where the latter choice is based on the partial autocorrelation function, or standard lag selection criteria such as those proposed by Akaike (1974), Hannan–Quinn (1979) or Schwartz (1978). It is recognized that these lag selection techniques will only 'work' if the main features of the linear autocorrelation structure reflect the lag dependencies associated with the underlying nonlinear process, but it is quite impractical to calculate and compare model selection criteria for nonlinear specifications of different lag lengths, when each calculation requires the maximization of a potentially ill-behaved likelihood.

There is a very large literature on lag selection (see the survey article by de Gooijer et al., 1985), but most of this is set in a linear context and there is comparatively little that works within the more general nonlinear framework. There is a small body of research that has used various dependence measures to construct analogues to the autocorrelation and partial autocorrelation functions that are often used in linear settings. Auestad and Tjøstheim (1990) use nonparametric estimates of conditional means and variances for this purpose, while Granger and Lin (1994) suggest the use of Pinsker's (1964) mutual information coefficients and Kendall's (1938) partial correlation coefficients. Granger et al. (2003) have also worked with a dependence metric based on the Bhattacharya–Matuisa–Hellinger measure of entropy. After simulating the distribution of this metric under the null hypothesis of independence, they suggest that it be used for identifying statistically significant lag lengths in potentially nonlinear settings.

The above procedures essentially mimic various aspects of the Box–Jenkins approach for identification, and like the Box–Jenkins methodology, their reliance on the skill and judgement of the researcher invites criticism. Another potential problem with the above procedures is that with the exception of Kendall's coefficient, they require nonparametric estimation of density functions, which is difficult for the novice and often inappropriate when dealing with small samples. The nonparametric final prediction error (FPE) criterion proposed by Tjøstheim and Auestad (1994) offers a less subjective approach to the lag selection problem, but it is nevertheless difficult to implement and impractical, given the size of typical economic data sets.

This chapter looks at the problem of lag selection for nonlinear models from the viewpoint of an applied economist. It focuses on nonlinear autoregressive models because these models are popular in applied work, and the goal is to study simple and practical techniques that might be appropriate for relatively small samples of up to 300 observations. My suggestion is to work with linear approximations to nonlinear forms and then to apply the usual lag selection criteria (for example Akaike– , AIC; Hannan–Quinn– , HQ and Bayes' information criterion, BIC) to discriminate between such approximations. Since these approximations are linear in parameters, the calculation of selection criteria for each lag length is very straightforward. Naturally, the procedure relies on finding reasonable approximations for nonlinear functional forms. I work with second order polynomial expansions and various subsets of these expansions, and although I also experiment with neural network approximations, I find that the former seem to work better for relatively small samples.

I study both linear and nonlinear data generating processes (DGPs), with short, medium and long lag structures. These DGPs are all based on published models of macroeconomic and financial data, so that my conclusions relate to the sorts of series that econometricians actually encounter in practice. I find that when the underlying DGP is nonlinear, standard model selection criteria tend to overestimate the true lag length. This problem is especially pronounced when AIC (which generally favours overfitting) is used, but it is also evident when the Schwartz criterion (which generally favours underfitting) is used. This suggests that when series are potentially nonlinear and the selection criteria use only one parameter to account for each lag, higher parameter penalties are needed to account for the fact that nonlinear DGPs will typically have more than one parameter associated with each lag length. Given that 'counting' parameters in a nonlinear setting can be a problematic concept, because different parameters can affect the data generating process at different points in time, I make no attempt to suggest appropriate parameter penalties here. Instead, I focus on using approximations that have a known number of parameters, and simply report on how well the application of AIC, HQ and BIC to these approximations identifies the true lag length. My simulations suggest that lag selection based on approximations reduces the tendency to overpredict lag length, particularly for nonlinear DGPs. Further, this reduced tendency to overpredict lag length is accompanied by an increased tendency to underpredict lag length.

The organization of this chapter is as follows. Section 2 sets up the lag selection problem and outlines a general framework within which the researcher might tackle this problem. Here, I discuss why standard selection criteria might not work, and suggest a few approaches that might work better. In Section 3, I describe some simulation exercises designed to assess the performance of my procedures within both linear and nonlinear contexts, and then I report the results of the simulations in Section 4. Section 5 summarizes and concludes.

2. LAG SELECTION IN A POTENTIALLY NONLINEAR SETTING

I consider a univariate time series y_t, with history $Y_t = (y_{-2}, y_{-1}, y_0, y_1, \ldots, y_{t-1})$ and that has a DGP given by

$$\mathbf{y}_t = \beta_0 + \beta' Y_{t-1}^{t-p} + \Psi\left(Y_{t-1}^{t-p}, \theta\right) + \varepsilon_t \tag{9.1}$$

where $Y_{t-1}^{t-p} = (y_{t-1}, y_{t-2}, \ldots, y_{t-p})$, β_0, β and θ are parameters, and $\Psi(Y_{t-1}^{t-p}, \theta)$ is a nonlinear function of its first and possibly second arguments. I assume that y_t is essentially stationary and weakly dependent as defined in Wooldridge (1994), and that although the functional form of Ψ might be initially unknown to the researcher, it satisfies conditions that will allow consistent estimation of θ once this functional form has been specified. I further assume that ε_t is a sequence of independent and identically distributed zero mean random variables with $E(\varepsilon_t^2) = \sigma^2$ being a finite constant.

The class of models defined by (9.1) includes the large family of exponential autoregressive (EXPAR) models discussed by Haggan and Ozaki (1981), threshold autoregressive (TAR) models (see Tong, 1990), and closely related models such as smooth transition autoregressive (STAR) models (see Teräsvirta, 1994) and current depth of recession (CDR) models (see Beaudry and Koop, 1993). In the special case given by $\sigma^2 = 0$, model (9.1) also includes chaotic series such as the logistic map series for which $y_t = 4y_{t-1}(1 - y_{t-1})$. This series is especially interesting, because its autocorrelation and partial autocorrelation functions are equal to zero at all lags. Model (9.1) does not allow for autoregressive conditional heteroskedasticity (ARCH) processes, bilinear processes or hidden Markov chains, but given the practical importance of pure autoregressive processes in the applied econometrics literature, it is useful to start with these.

Our problem is to determine the lag length p, possibly prior to determining the dimension of θ and specifying the functional form of Ψ. This situation often arises when the researcher wants to test for nonlinearity, or wants to determine the type of nonlinearity present in Ψ, but the test assumes a knowledge of the lag length p. Alternatively, we might not be able to specify Ψ and estimate β and θ until we have first determined p. Even if we are willing to specify Ψ prior to determining p, we might want to avoid estimating (9.1) using different lags lengths, simply because nonlinear estimation is time consuming and difficult. Furthermore, the difficulty in estimating and comparing nonlinear specifications for a set of different p can be compounded if the true model is actually linear and various parameters in the specification are therefore unidentified. See Davies (1977) or Engle (1984) for further discussion of this identification problem.

Standard lag selection criteria (such as AIC, HQ or BIC) applied to autoregressive time series typically assume a linear process for y_t, and then solve an optimization problem for p that simultaneously rewards the fit of the AR(p) and penalizes its complexity. Higher p will improve the fit, but will also entail more complexity. The assumption that the time series is linear is not innocuous when AR(p) models are being fitted, because it implies that one of the options considered by the researcher will be the true model. The reason why these standard procedures might not work in the nonlinear context given by (9.1) is that by just considering linear AR(p) processes (for $0 \leq p \leq p^{max}$), the researcher does not include the true model in his/her choice set. Tong (1990, p. 288) discusses this issue very briefly, and notes that when the set of models under consideration does not include the true model, the selected model may or may not be adequate, depending on how close the likelihood of the chosen model is to the likelihood of the true model.

Akaike (1985) emphasizes that the researcher's choice set of possible models should reflect his/her particular way of looking at the data, and this suggests that when models such as (9.1) are being considered, the family of AR(p) models might not necessarily provide the most appropriate choice set for determining lag length. This leads to the question of whether there are other families of models which may better account for the nonlinearity in (9.1) and thus provide a more reliable selection of p. Since Ψ is potentially difficult to estimate for different lag lengths p – and its precise functional form is not necessarily known – it seems sensible to focus on families of models that are both simple and capture unspecified nonlinearities.

Tests for unspecified nonlinearity in the conditional mean are often based on simple linear regressions. Various examples are studied and discussed in Granger and Teräsvirta (1993) and Lee et al. (1993), who claim that these tests involve 'specific functions of Y_{t-1}^{t-p}, that are chosen to capture essential features of possible nonlinearities'. Such functions include the duals of Volterra expansions in Y_{t-1}^{t-p} and neural networks in Y_{t-1}^{t-p}, and I discuss these further below. Two important features of each of these functions are that they can be used to approximate Ψ in model (9.1) and that they are linear in parameters. I use these features in the lag selection criteria that I suggest below.

Volterra expansions are discussed in Priestley (1981), and they approximate Ψ using the formula

$$\Psi\left(Y_{t-1}^{t-p},\theta\right) \approx \Psi_0 + \sum_{k=l}^{k=p}\Psi_{1k}y_{t-k} + \sum_{k=1}^{k=p}\sum_{j=1}^{j=k}\Psi_{2jk}y_{t-k}y_{j-j} \qquad (9.2)$$

$$+\sum_{k=1}^{k=p}\sum_{j=1}^{j=k}\sum_{i=1}^{i=j}\Psi_{3kji}y_{t-k}y_{t-j}y_{t-i} + \ldots$$

which includes squares, cross-products, cubic terms and other higher order terms to capture the nonlinearities in Ψ. When Ψ is well-behaved, these polynomial expansions can be justified as Taylor series expansions around $\overline{Y}_{t-1}^{t-p}$, but (9.2) can often provide a good approximation of Ψ even when Ψ is ill-behaved. Such expansions can become unwieldy if p is large and the expansion includes higher order terms, but expansions involving just the squares and cross-products have often proved useful in practice. In the latter case (9.1) is given by

$$y_t \cong \beta_0^* + \beta^{*}Y_{t-1}^{t-p} + \sum_{k=1}^{k=p}\sum_{j=1}^{j=k}\Psi_{2jk}y_{t-k}y_{t-j} + \varepsilon_t \qquad (9.3)$$

which is linear in $(p + 1) + (1/2)p(p + 1)$ parameters.

Neural network approximations of Ψ are based on the intuition that any nonlinear function of Y_{t-1}^{t-p} can be approximated arbitrarily well by a linear combination of elementary nonlinear transformations of q indices of Y_{t-1}^{t-p} (i.e. $\gamma_r' Y_{t-1}^{t-p}, r = 1, \ldots, q$), for q sufficiently large (Hornik et al., 1989). The approximating model of y_t is then given by

$$y_t \cong \beta_0^* + \beta^{*\prime} Y_{t-1}^{t-p} + \sum_{r=1}^{p} \Psi_r \varphi \left(y_r' \left(1, Y_{t-1}^{t-p} \right) \right) + \varepsilon_t \qquad (9.4)$$

where φ is a permissible elementary function,[1] and the γ_r are randomly chosen by the econometrician, independently of y_t and Y_{t-1}^{t-p}. I include a constant in φ because Teräsvirta et al. (1993) found that this helped approximate certain types of nonlinearity. Model (9.4) is linear in $(1 + p + q)$ parameters. Lee et al. (1993) note that elements in φ tend to be collinear with themselves and with Y_{t-1}^{t-p}, but they resolve this difficulty by using $q^* < q$ principal components of the φ functions that are not collinear with Y_{t-1}^{t-p}.

The lag selection procedures that I suggest involve choosing a maximum possible lag length $p^{\max}$, fitting the approximations of the nonlinear forms to the data for each of lags 0 to $p^{\max}$, and then choosing the lag length p^* that minimizes AIC, HQ or BIC. Given the explanator sets used in approximations (9.3) and (9.4), the parameter penalties are $(p + 1) + (1/2)p(p + 1)$ in the calculations based on (9.3), and $(1 + p + q)$ for calculations based on (9.4). These penalties are larger than $(p + 1)$ which is used when fitting linear autoregressions of order p, but we are fitting more highly parameterized models to the data. Since the approximating models can be potentially overparametrized for large p and/or q, I experiment with various subsets of explanators. For instance, when working with (9.3) I consider an approximation that includes just the squares (and not the cross-products) of Y_{t-1}^{t-p}, so that the approximating model contains less parameters and the relevant penalty drops to $(1+2p)$. I also consider using just the first principal component of the set of $(1/2)p(p+1)$ cross-products, so that the approximating models use $(2+p)$ parameters. Table 9.1 contains a list of the various approximating models that I consider, together with a count of how many parameters are used for each approximation.

One could work with many different versions of approximation (9.4). I set $q = 30$ and then use the first 10 principal components of the 30 squashing functions.[2] Although Lee et al. (1993) found that the first two principal components (out of 10 generated) were sufficient to give neural network based nonlinearity tests power against nonlinear AR(1) and AR(2) alternatives, I suspected that more components might be needed to capture nonlinearities that had potentially longer lag structures, and this led to my choice of 10. However, to allow for more frugal approximations, I also used just the first $2p$ principal components. A comparison between these two families of models is potentially interesting, because the first keeps the number of variables in the explanator set for nonlinearity constant while lag length increases, while the second allows the explanator set for the nonlinearity to expand with lag length.

Table 9.1   Families of models used to approximate the DGP

Family (Parameters)	Approximating Equation
AR $1+p$	$y_t \cong \beta_0^* + \beta^{*\prime} Y_{t-1}^{t-p}$
SQ $1+2p$	$y_t \cong \beta_0^* + \beta^{*\prime} Y_{t-1}^{t-p} + \sum_{k=1}^{k=p} \Psi_{2k} y_{t-k}^2$
CR $1+p+p(p+1)/2$	$y_t \cong \beta_0^* + \beta^{*\prime} Y_{t-1}^{t-p} + \sum_{k=1}^{k=p} \sum_{j=1}^{j=k} \Psi_{2kj} y_{t-k} y_{t-j}$
PCC [a] $2+p$	$y_t \cong \beta_0^* + \beta^{*\prime} Y_{t-1}^{t-p} + fpc\{y_{t-k}y_{t-j} \text{ for } 1 \le k, j \le 30\}$
N10 [b] $11+p$	$y_t \cong \beta_0^* + \beta^{*\prime} Y_{t-1}^{t-p} + f10opc\{\phi(\gamma' Y_{t-1}^{t-p}) \text{ for } 1 \le k, j \le 30\}$
NM2 [c] $1+3p$	$y_t \cong \beta_0^* + \beta^{*\prime} Y_{t-1}^{t-p} + f(2p)opc\{\phi(\gamma' Y_{t-1}^{t-p}) \text{ for } 1 \le k, j \le 30\}$

Notes:
a: *fpc* is the first principal component of the bracketed explanator set.
b: *f10opc* takes the first 10 principal components of the bracketed explanator set, orthogonal to the linear explanator set.
c: *f(2p)opc* takes the first 2p principal components of the bracketed explanator set, orthogonal to the linear explanator set.

The ability of these suggested procedures to choose a correct lag depends on whether the approximation to Ψ is 'close' to Ψ, given the data. It is reasonable to expect procedures based on (9.3) and (9.4) to outperform the AR based procedures if the data have 'strong' nonlinear characteristics, but that the AR based procedure might be better if our time series has very subtle nonlinearities. It is also reasonable to expect that the suggested procedures will cloud the choice of lag length when the time series is actually linear, but here one can hope that the parameter penalties that are supposed to correct for the overparameterization that occurs in this case will 'do their job'. These issues are studied by simulation below.

3. SIMULATION DESIGN

The simulation study is based on a set of DGPs that have been chosen from the applied econometrics literature. These DGPs include specifications based on Teräsvirta and Anderson's (1992) models of industrial production, Beaudry and Koop's (1993) model of US output, Rothman's (1998) models of unemployment, Anderson and Vahid's (2001) models of US output, and Martens et al. (1998) data on mispricing errors associated with Standard & Poor's (S&P) stocks and futures contracts. Industrial production indices, unemployment and stock returns all exhibit strong evidence of nonlinearities, whereas the nonlinearities in output are much weaker. Therefore the sample of DGPs includes processes with 'strongly' nonlinear behaviour, as well as processes that are 'almost linear'. I also include some linear DGPs in our study, some of which are published in the above papers, and others which I obtained by estimating linear models for various economic/financial data sets and then setting my DGP parameters equal to my estimated parameters. I chose the DGPs so that they would be representative of the sorts of DGPs that econometricians encounter in practice. Some have short lag structures, others have longer lag structures, and I even include some lag structures with 'holes' or 'near-holes'.[3] Full details of all DGPs are provided in Table 9.A.1, together with references and notes on their properties.

The error terms for our DGPs and neural network random coefficients were generated using Gauss. Error terms are drawn from the standard normal distribution and then scaled according to the standard deviation of the error term of the relevant DGP. For the neural network models I followed Lee et al. (1993), rescaling all variables onto [0,1], and then drawing the hidden weights from the uniform distribution on [−2,2]. I discarded the first 1000 observations of the simulated DGPs to avoid initialization effects, and report results based on 10000 replications of the relevant DGP. I studied samples of size 100, 150, 200, 250, 300, 500, 1000 and 5000, with the last three of these being included so that I could obtain some idea of the asymptotic behaviour of the procedures. I note, however, that the results for these larger samples would also be relevant for studies of financial data, where samples are typically large. I report results on only a subset of the samples to conserve space, but other results are available upon request. In total, I studied five processes of order two, two of order four, two of order five, two of order seven, and two of order nine, and the lag selection procedures considered all possible lag lengths from zero lags to ten.

4. FINITE SAMPLE PROPERTIES OF THE PROPOSED PROCEDURES

Tables 9.A.2, 9.A.3 and 9.A.4 present detailed results of the performance of the Akaike, Hannan–Quinn and Schwartz procedures, and Figures 9.A.1–9.A.4 provide visual summaries of the main patterns that seemed to emerge from these results.

Figure 9.A.1 illustrates how the standard procedures (based on the AR family of models) work for each DGP. The top row relates to linear DGPs, and illustrates with the well-known properties that (i) for small samples AIC usually dominates HQ, which usually dominates BIC; but (ii) HQ and BIC improve with sample size and eventually dominate AIC, because AIC is inconsistent, in contrast to HQ and BIC. For the AR(2) and AR(9) DGPs, the large sample properties are beginning to show for samples of only 250–300, while samples as small as 100 observations on the AR(5) are behaving like large samples. The latter observation is due to the relatively large coefficient on the AR(5) term, which is sufficiently large to be statistically significant in samples of 100.

Similar patterns are observed when the standard procedures are applied to nonlinear DGPs (see the remaining two rows in Figure 9.A.1). However, the latter graphs also suggest that the inconsistency of AIC becomes evident earlier (i.e. for smaller sample sizes) for nonlinear processes relative to linear processes, while the improvement in HQ and BIC with sample size seems to be more rapid.

Figure 9.A.2 illustrates the differences between standard procedures (based on the AR family of models) and approximating procedures (based on other model families), when the true DGP is linear. Since the true DGP is linear, one might expect that the former procedure will dominate, while the other procedures will have lower, but hopefully non-trivial ability to choose lag length. This seems to occur for the AR(2) and AR(9) processes, which are both 'weak' in the sense that they do not generate signals that allow information criteria based on small samples to accurately select lag length. It also occurs for the AR(5), when BIC based procedures are used. However, when AIC or HQ based procedures are applied to the AR(5) process, the SQ, CR and PCC procedures (see Table 9.1 for process details) almost always perform better than the AR based procedures, except when samples are very small. Given that the AR(5) process is 'strong', in the sense that large sample behaviour is already evident for the AR versions of AIC and HQ when samples are relatively small, this latter finding suggests that the better performance of the nonlinear criteria is a large sample phenomenon. Possibly, this phenomenon arises because the nonlinear families of models use more parameters at each lag length than do linear models, and this make it easier to discriminate between different lag lengths. It is noteworthy that for larger samples, the nonlinear procedures also outperform linear procedures for the AR(2) and the AR(9), and the BIC nonlinear procedures also outperform the linear BIC procedures. Differences between the AR and other lines on each graph in Figure 9.A.2 measure the 'cost' of applying nonlinear procedures to linear DGPs. This can be very high, especially if BIC−CR is applied to a 'strong' DGP. However, this cost decreases with sample size and eventually becomes negative. The last panel in Figure 9.A.2 provides an illustration of this.

Figure 9.A.3 illustrates the differences between standard procedures (based on the AR family of models) and approximating procedures (based on other model families), when the true DGP is nonlinear. Since the true DGP is nonlinear, the hope is that the latter procedures will dominate, while the standard procedures based on the AR family will have lower ability to choose lag length. This clearly occurs for the ESTAR(2), TAR(2) and the LSTAR(5) processes illustrated in Figure 9.A.3b, where the SQ, CR and PCC procedures almost always dominate the AR based procedures. It also occurs to a lesser degree for samples of more than 200 of the CDR(2) and LSTAR(2) processes, when AIC based procedures are used. The N10 and NM2 procedures outperform the AR procedures only rarely, and while the CR procedure often dominates all others (especially for 'strong' DGPs and for larger samples (>500 observations)), it is usually the worst for samples of 100. It is interesting to note that there is rarely any substantial difference between the performances of the SQ and PCC procedures.

For samples of 100, there seems to be little advantage for using a nonlinear selection criterion, even when the DGP is nonlinear. The SQ and PCC procedures sometimes work better when the true DGP is truly nonlinear, but this increase in accuracy is never more than 5% in absolute value. Given that the SQ and PCC procedures use fewer parameters to model the nonlinearity while the worst performers in small samples (CR, N10 and NM2 procedure) use many more parameters, it seems that parsimony is essential in small sample settings. Thus, AR based procedures seem best.

The picture starts to change once samples grow to about 200 observations, but this depends on the relative 'strength' of the nonlinear process, and how soon the asymptotic properties of each selection procedure start to set in. Figure 9.A.3 has been roughly arranged in order of 'strength', so that the 'weaker' DGPs appear first in Figure 9.A.3a, and then the 'stronger' DGPs appear later in Figure 9.A.3b.[4]

For weak processes, lag selection based on HQ−AR or BIC−AR dominates selection based on nonlinear versions of AIC, even though the latter dominate AIC−AR. Thus, although the nonlinear versions of AIC are now working better than standard AIC, there is little point in using them, because linear versions of HQ and BIC perform better still. The same is true for the stronger processes illustrated in Figure 9.A.3b, where there can be up to a 20% improvement when AIC–CR is used rather than AIC–AR. Once again, there is little point in 'capitalizing' on these relative benefits when the linear versions HQ and BIC outperform all versions of AIC, but now several of the nonlinear versions of HQ and BIC perform even better. HQ–SQ, HQ–PCC, BIC–SQ and BIC–PCC offer reliable but small improvements over HQ–AR and BIC–AR. The improvements are small, simply because the latter have accuracy rates of well over 80%. The HQ–CR and BIC–CR procedures can have even higher accuracy rates of well over 99%, but the CR criterion seems to be quite unreliable, in that it either works really well, or it doesn't work at all. This is because the CR performance curves are often shaped like a logistic curve with a steep slope (γ), so that essentially one has to pass a certain sample size threshold (c) before good performance is observed. For the weaker processes, this threshold has not yet been reached for samples of 300, so that CR procedures hardly work at all. For the stronger processes, the threshold occurs for samples of less than 100, so that we observe the flat part of the top of the curve, and associated good performance.

The results for samples of 5000 are not reported, but the simulations show the usual inconsistency associated with AIC in large samples. Some of this is already evident in samples of 1000. This is particularly so for the 'stronger' DGPs when AIC–AR is used, but it is also observed for the CDR(2) and ES(9) processes. While the AIC–AR procedure usually shows evidence of inconsistency first (i.e. for relatively smaller samples), the performances of other nonlinear procedures based on AIC also decline after a certain point. This is true for both linear and nonlinear DGPs. I found no evidence that any of the HQ or BIC based procedures were inconsistent when applied to linear DGPs, but the performance of both linear and nonlinear procedures based on HQ or BIC became inconsistent for nonlinear DGPs. Thus, it appears that one cannot rely on standard HQ or BIC when the true DGP is nonlinear. It seems possible that one may be able to maintain consistency of HQ and BIC for nonlinear processes by using higher order approximations as the sample size grows, but this issue is not explored any further here.

Taken together, the accuracy results suggest using AIC or HQ based on AR models for small samples (of less than 150 observations). Nonlinear procedures generally do not work well for small samples, even if the true DGP is nonlinear. HQ and BIC based on the SQ and PCC nonlinear approximations can be useful for moderate samples (of 150–300), especially if the true DGP is nonlinear. Given that typical macroeconomic data sets usually consist of 40 to 45 years of quarterly observations (i.e. 160–180 observations), this finding is potentially useful for applied macroeconomists. Unfortunately the practical question of whether these nonlinear procedures will work in any given situation depends on whether the true DGP is nonlinear, and the practitioner doesn't generally know that in advance. However, if there are good reasons to suspect nonlinearities (because, for instance, one is working with unemployment data which often shows strong evidence of nonlinearity), then it seems sensible to use the procedures based on SQ and PCC approximations. However, if working with a series that is unlikely to have strong nonlinearities (for instance GDP), then it seems best to stay with the standard AR based procedures.

While accuracy is desirable when building time series models, we need to recognize that mistakes will occur and consider whether certain types of mistakes are less costly than others. For instance, overprediction of lag lengths is a problem if we wish to forecast, while underprediction is a problem if we wish to test for and model nonlinearity. Tables 9.A.5 and 9.A.6 contain some statistics that cast light on these considerations. The same general pattern characterizes both AIC and BIC procedures. Relative to procedures based on AR models, the nonlinear criteria tend to underpredict lag length more and overpredict lag length less, although underprediction does not seem to be a problem for many of the nonlinear models we studied. It is interesting to note that a comparison of similar series (say the AR(2) and the LS(2) which were both based on estimates from the same data) shows that underprediction is less likely when the true DGP is nonlinear. This is perhaps comforting when considering nonlinear modelling, because it is relatively easy to reduce a general nonlinear model to a more parsimonious specification, but much harder to design a specific-to-general modelling strategy.

The tables do not include results for the four DGPs based on financial series because all criteria (linear and nonlinear, based on AIC, HQ or BIC) had great difficulty in choosing the correct lag length. AIC based on the AR family performed best in each case, but accuracy ranged from 0.0359 to 0.1568 for the AR(4), 0.0137 to 0.1446 for the AR(7), 0.0355 to 0.1078 for the TAR(4), and 0.0168 to 0.1304 for the TAR(7) (where in each case the first figure relates to samples of 100 and the second relates to samples of 1000). Results for samples of 5000 were considerably better (ranging between 45% and 65% for AIC), but BIC results for this sample size were still small (between 2% and 8%), indicating that much larger samples would be needed before asymptotic properties become evident. In one sense, these findings are not unexpected, given the extremely weak correlation structure that is typically found in financial data. However, the results also illustrate how poorly our standard methods can work, when the true DGP has very weak properties.

5. CONCLUSIONS

This chapter has studied the problem of lag selection for nonlinear models from the viewpoint of an applied economist. Two common approaches include the application of AIC, HQ or BIC to linear autoregressive models, or first specifying the nonlinearity and then applying the same criteria to a sequence of nonlinear models. I argue against the second of these because of its impracticality, but assess the first of these by means of simulation. In general I find that AIC applied to AR models works quite well for small samples even when the true model is nonlinear. In contrast, HQ and BIC perform quite poorly, unless the sample size is large.

I propose and study several lag selection criteria that may be useful in nonlinear settings. Some of these are based on polynomial approximations to the nonlinear DGP, while others are based on neural network approximations. The SQ and PPC procedures seem to improve lag selection performance, when applied to moderately small samples and used in conjunction with HQ and BIC. This offers potential when working with typical macroeconomic data sets. All procedures work well for larger samples of data which follow the sorts of nonlinear processes that are popular in macroeconomic modelling. However, since standard versions of HQ and BIC also work well in this case, the nonlinear procedures improve lag selection only slightly. For large samples of data, both linear and nonlinear procedures are easy to implement, but will be inconsistent. Although harder to implement, nonparametric techniques (such as those suggested by Tjøstheim and Auestad, 1994) might improve accuracy.

The simulations show that the usual lag selection criteria are likely to have difficulty with typical macroeconomic and financial data sets. While the proposed procedures offer some improvement, this improvement is very limited. This leads to the conclusion that more work is needed to develop other techniques that are practical, but more helpful in small sample settings.

NOTES

1. The elementary function, which is called the 'activation function' or the 'squashing function' in the neural network literature, can be any function that satisfies some continuity and denseness conditions discussed in Hornik et al. (1989). The most popular one is the logistic function $\varphi(z)=[1+\exp(z)]^{-1}$.
2. I remove those components in the same basis space as the linear part of the model, prior to calculating the principal components.
3. By 'holes' we mean zero (or very close to zero) coefficients on intermediate lags. It is typically very hard to choose the correct lag structure, given these types of DGPs.
4. Note, from Figure 9.A.1, that for the three processes in Figure 9.A.3a (CDR(2), LSTAR(2) and ESTAR(9)), AIC–AR is still improving with sample size and HQ–AR and BIC–AR have only just started to dominate AIC–AR. For the three processes in Figure 9.A.3b

(LSTAR(5), TAR(2) and ESTAR(2)), Figure 9.A.1 shows that HQ–AR and BIC–AR already dominate AIC–AR, which has already started to decrease with sample size.
5. A logistic function in sample size t is given by $f(t)=(1+\exp\{-\gamma(t-c)\})^{-1}$ for $\gamma > 0$.

REFERENCES

Akaike, H. (1974), 'A New Look at Statistical Model Identification', *IEEE Transactions on Automatic Control*, **AC19**, 716–723.

Akaike, H. (1985), 'Prediction and Entropy', in A.C. Atkinson and S.E. Feinberg (eds.), *A Celebration of Statistics: the ISI Centenary Volume*, New York: Springer, 1–24.

Anderson, H.M. and F. Vahid (2001), 'Predicting the Probability of a Recession with Nonlinear Autoregressive Leading Indicator Models', *Macroeconomic Dynamics*, **5**, 482–505.

Auestad, B. and D. Tjøstheim (1990), 'The Identification of Nonlinear Time Series: First Order Characterization and Order Determination', *Biometrika*, **77**, 669–687.

Beaudry, P. and G. Koop (1993), 'Do Recessions Permanently Change Output?', *Journal of Monetary Economics*, **31**, 149–163.

Davies, R.B. (1977), 'Hypothesis Testing when a Nuisance Parameter is Present only under the Alternative Hypotheses', *Biometrika*, **64**, 247–254.

de Gooijer, J.G., A. Bovas, A. Gould and L. Robinson (1985), 'Methods for Determining the Order of an Autoregressive-moving Average Process: A Survey', *International Statistical Review*, **53**, 301–329.

Engle, R.F. (1984), 'Wald, Likelihood Ratio and Lagrange Multiplier Tests in Econometrics', chapter 24, in Z. Griliches and M. Intriligator (eds.), *Handbook of Econometrics*, volume 2, Amsterdam: North-Holland, pp. 775–826.

Granger, C.W.J. and J. Lin (1994), 'Using the Mutual Information Coefficient to Identify Lags in Nonlinear Models', *Journal of Time Series Analysis*, **15**, 371–384.

Granger, C.W.J., E. Maasoumi and J. Racine (2003), 'A Dependence Metric for Possibly Nonlinear Processes', mimeo, Syracuse University, New York.

Granger, C.W.J. and T. Teräsvirta (1993), *Modelling Nonlinear Economic Relationships*, Oxford: Oxford University Press.

Haggan, V. and T. Ozaki (1981), 'Modelling Nonlinear Random Vibrations using an Amplitude-dependent Autoregressive Time Series Model', *Biometrika*, **68**, 189–196.

Hamilton, J.D. (1989), 'A New Approach to the Economic Analysis of Nonstationary Time Series and the Business Cycle', *Econometrica*, **57**, 357–384.

Hannan, E.J. and B.G. Quinn (1979), 'The Determination of the Order of an Autoregression', *Journal of the Royal Statistical Society*, Series B, **41**, 190–195.

Hornik, K.M., M. Stinchcombe and H.L. White (1989), 'Universal Approximations of an Unknown Mapping and its Derivatives using Multi-layer Feedforward Networks', *Neural Networks*, **3**, 551–360.

Kendall, M. (1938), 'A New Measure of Rank Correlation', *Biometrika*, **30**, 81–89.

Lee, T.-H., H. White and C.W.J. Granger (1993), 'Testing for Neglected Nonlinearity in Time Series Models: A Comparison of Neural Network Methods and Alternative Tests', *Journal of Econometrics*, **56**, 268–290.

Martens, M., P. Kofman and T.C.F. Vorst (1998), 'A Threshold Error Correction Model for Intraday Futures and Index Returns', *Journal of Applied Econometrics*, **13**, 245–264.

Pinsker, M.S. (1964) *Information and Information Stability of Random Variables and Processes,* San Francisco, CA: Holden-Day.

Potter, S.M. (1995), 'A Nonlinear Approach to U.S. GNP', *Journal of Applied Econometrics*, **10**, 109–126.

Priestley, M.B. (1981), *Spectral Analysis and Time Series*, London : Academic Press.

Rothman, P. (1998), 'Forecasting Asymmetric Unemployment Rates', *The Review of Economics and Statistics*, **80**, 164–168.

Schwarz, G. (1978), 'Estimating the Dimension of a Model', *The Annals of Statistics*, **6**, 461–464.

Teräsvirta, T. (1994), 'Specification, Estimation and Evaluation of Smooth Transition Autoregressive Models', *Journal of the American Statistical Association*, **89**, 208–218.

Teräsvirta, T. and H.M. Anderson (1992), 'Characterizing Nonlinearities in Business Cycles Using Smooth Transition Autoregressive Models', *Journal of Applied Econometrics*, **7**, S119–S136.

Teräsvirta, T., C.F. Lin and C.W.J. Granger (1993), 'Power of the Neural Network Linearity Test', *Journal of Time Series Analysis*, **14**, 209–220.

Tjøstheim, D. and B. Auestad (1994), 'Nonparametric Identification of Nonlinear Time Series: Selecting Significant Lags', *Journal of the American Statistical Association*, **89**, 1410–1419.

Tong, H. (1990), *Non-linear Time Series Analysis: A Dynamical System Approach*, Oxford: Oxford University Press.

Wooldridge, J.M. (1994), 'Estimation and Inference for Dependent Processes', in Z. Griliches and M. Intriligator (eds.), *Handbook of Econometrics*, volume 4, Amsterdam: North-Holland, 2640–2738.

APPENDIX

Table 9.A.1 DGPs used in the simulation studies

	DGPs used in the simulation studies
AR(2) [a]	$y_t = 0.49 + 0.25y_{t-1} + 0.13\,y_{t-2} + \varepsilon_t$ with $\varepsilon_t \sim N(0,0.89^2)$
AR(5) [c]	$y_t = 0.005 + 0.935\,y_{t-1} + 0.055y_{t-2} - 0.049y_{t-3} - 0.609y_{t-4} + 0.417y_{t-5} + \varepsilon_t$ with $\varepsilon_t \sim N(0,0.027^2)$
AR(9) [c]	$y_t = 0.008 + 1.423y_{t-1} - 0.7347y_{t-2} + 0.3375y_{t-3} - 0.6423y_{t-4} + 0.5348y_{t-5} - 0.1115y_{t-6} + 0.0409y_{t-7}$ $- 0.2685y_{t-8} + 0.1837y_{t-9} + \varepsilon_t$ with $\varepsilon_t \sim N(0,0.0220155^2)$
CDR2 [a]	$y_t = 0.35 + 0.24y_{t-1} + 0.22y_{t-2} + 0.20CRD_{t-1} + \varepsilon_t$ with $CDR_t = \max\{CDR_{t-1}, y_t\} - y_t$ and $\varepsilon_t \sim N(0,0.89^2)$
ES2 [b]	$y_t = 0.325y_{t-1} - 1.777y_{t-2} + f_t(1.219y_{t-1} + 1.124y_{t-2}) + \varepsilon_t$ with $f_t = (1 - \exp\{-10.230 \cdot 200(y_{t-1})^2\})$ and $\varepsilon_t \sim N(0,0.0576^2)$
TAR2 [b]	$y_t = 0.0529 + 1.349y_{t-1} - 1.665y_{t-2} + f_t(1.646y_{t-1} - 0.733y_{t-2}) + \varepsilon_t$ with $f_t = (1)(y_{t-1} < 0.062)$ and $\varepsilon_t \sim N(0,0.063^2)$
LS2 [a]	$y_t = -1.51 - 1.41y_{t-2} + f_t(2.04 + 0.26y_{t-1} + 1.50y_{t-2}) + \varepsilon_t$ with $f_t = (1 + \exp\{-11(y_{t-2} + 0.55)\})^{-1}$ and $\varepsilon_t \sim N(0,0.89^2)$
LS5 [c]	$y_t = -0.030 + 0.64y_{t-1} - 0.29y_{t-2} - 0.64y_{t-4} + f_t(0.044 + 0.49y_{t-2} + 0.45y_{t-5}) + \varepsilon_t$ with $f_t = (1 + \exp\{-7.3 \times 21.6(y_{t-1} + 0.015)\})^{-1}$ and $\varepsilon_t \sim N(0,0.0231^2)$
ES9 [c]	$y_t = 0.0075 + 3.03y_{t-1} - 1.31y_{t-2} - \Delta 0.49y_{t-4} + f_t(-1.68y_{t-1} + 0.87y_{t-2} - \Delta 0.30y_{t-8}) + \varepsilon_t$ with $f_t = (1 - \exp\{-1.54 \times 196(y_{t-1} + 0.082)^2\})$ and $\varepsilon_t \sim N(0,0.0185^2)$
AR(4) [d]	$y_t = 0.0033 + 0.8679y_{t-1} + 0.0429y_{t-2} + 0.0228y_{t-3} + 0.0348y_{t-4} + \varepsilon_t$ with $\varepsilon_t \sim N(0,0.02856^2)$

Table 9.A.1 DGPs used in the simulation studies (... continued)

AR(4)[d] $y_t = 0.0033 + 0.8679y_{t-1} + 0.0429y_{t-2} + 0.0228y_{t-3} + 0.0348y_{t-4} + \varepsilon_t$ with $\varepsilon_t \sim N(0, 0.02856^2)$

AR(7)[d] $y_t = 0.00085 + 0.8976y_{t-1} - 0.0142y_{t-2} - 0.0073y_{t-3} - 0.0002y_{t-4} + 0.0121y_{t-5} + 0.0011y_{t-6}$
$+ 0.0372y_{t-7} + \varepsilon_t$ with $\varepsilon_t \sim N(0, 0.0296240^2)$

TAR4[d] $y_t = I(y_{t-1} < -0.090)(0.0031 + 0.6098y_{t-1} + 0.3577y_{t-2} - 0.1996y_{t-3} + 0.1682y_{t-4})$
$+ I(-0.090 \le y_{t-1} < 0.062)(0.0025 + 0.8916y_{t-1} + 0.0124y_{t-2} - 0.0061y_{t-3} + 0.0220y_{t-4})$
$+ I(0.062 \le y_{t-1})(0.008 + 0.8547y_{t-1} + 0.0142y_{t-2} - 0.0048y_{t-3} + 0.0251y_{t-4}) + \varepsilon_t$
with $\varepsilon_t \sim N(0, 0.0248^2)$

TAR7[d] $y_t = I(y_{t-1} < -0.073)(-0.0161 + 0.6748y_{t-1} - 0.0578y_{t-2} + 0.0362y_{t-3} + 0.10321y_{t-4} - 0.0244y_{t-5}$
$+ 0.0182y_{t-6} + 0.1147y_{t-7}) + I(-0.073 \le y_{t-1} < 0.072)(0.0002 + 0.9311y_{t-1} - 0.0048y_{t-2} - 0.0154y_{t-3}$
$+ 0.02119y_{t-4} + 0.0003y_{t-5} + 0.0016y_{t-6} + 0.0164y_{t-7}) + I(0.072 \le y_{t-1})(0.0159 + 0.8185y_{t-1}$
$- 0.0292y_{t-2} - 0.004275y_{t-3} - 0.0695y_{t-4} + 0.0803y_{t-5} - 0.0222y_{t-6} + 0.060y_{t-7}) + \varepsilon_t$
with $\varepsilon_t \sim N(0, 0.0294^2)$

Notes and sources:

a: The AR(2), CDR(2) and LS(2) are based on ΔlnGDP for the USA (see Anderson and Vahid, 2001). These DGPs are 'weak' in that coefficients and/or evidence of nonlinearity do not become statistically significant until the sample is large.

b: The TAR(2) and ES(2) are based on log linear detrended unemployment for the USA (Rothman, 1998). These DGPs are 'strong', in that coefficients and evidence of nonlinearity are statistically significant, regardless of sample size.

c: The AR(5) and LS(5) are based on fourth differences of the logarithms of industrial production for Belgium (see Teräsvirta and Anderson, 1992). Both are 'strong' DGPs, although LS(5) has a 'hole' at lag 3. The AR(9) and ES(9) are based on similarly transformed data for the USA and Japan. Both are moderately 'strong' DGPs, but the ES(9) process for Japan has 'holes' (no structure for lags 6 and 7, and restrictions for lags 5 and 9).

d: The AR(4), AR(7), TAR(4) and TAR(7) are based on data for mispricing errors associated with the S&P 500 index and matching futures contracts. See Martens et al. (1998). As is typical for financial data, the lag structure is 'weak'. Evidence of nonlinearity is strong, but the corresponding threshold models contain many 'holes'.

Table 9.A.2 *Performance of AIC based criteria (proportion of times correct lag is picked)*

	AR(2)	AR(5)	AR(9)	CDR(2)	ES(2)	TAR(2)	LS(2)	LS(5)	ES(9)
Data Generating Process (samples of 100)									
Model Family									
AR[a]	**0.230**[b]	**0.701**	**0.246**	**0.329**	0.705	0.698	**0.401**	0.653	**0.503**
SQ	0.174	0.693	0.146	0.251	0.743	0.743	0.352	**0.677**	0.291
CR	0.105	0.273	0.053	0.147	0.539	0.522	0.221	0.272	0.072
PCC	0.174	0.696	0.149	0.251	**0.757**	**0.744**	0.345	0.672	0.304
N10	0.139	0.444	0.171	0.187	0.672	0.623	0.300	0.420	0.269
NM2	0.136	0.439	0.148	0.177	0.607	0.674	0.320	0.330	0.252
Data Generating Process (samples of 150)									
Model Family									
AR	**0.341**	0.722	**0.422**	**0.472**	0.709	0.694	**0.531**	0.643	**0.706**
SQ	0.275	0.767	0.267	0.414	0.771	0.753	0.509	0.725	0.509
CR	0.242	**0.772**	0.055	0.375	**0.836**	**0.829**	0.488	**0.748**	0.147
PCC	0.276	0.764	0.269	0.414	0.773	0.758	0.505	0.704	0.545
N10	0.217	0.513	0.259	0.320	0.693	0.610	0.447	0.486	0.383
NM2	0.218	0.567	0.192	0.317	0.671	0.759	0.488	0.354	0.400
Data Generating Process (samples of 200)									
Model Family									
AR	**0.419**	0.726	**0.556**	**0.561**	0.711	0.689	0.616	0.628	**0.775**
SQ	0.357	0.782	0.388	0.522	0.777	0.755	0.612	0.727	0.652
CR	0.320	**0.867**	0.060	0.511	**0.855**	**0.848**	**0.620**	**0.825**	0.232
PCC	0.354	0.781	0.387	0.525	0.781	0.756	0.606	0.709	0.686
N10	0.275	0.526	0.355	0.419	0.700	0.596	0.551	0.539	0.437
NM2	0.282	0.605	0.252	0.413	0.676	0.796	0.592	0.322	0.540

Table 9.A.2 Performance of AIC based criteria (proportion of times correct lag is picked) (... continued)

Data Generating Process (samples of 250)								
Model Family	AR(2)	AR(5)	AR(9)	CDR(2)	ES(2)	TAR(2)	LS(2)	LS(5)	ES(9)
AR	**0.490**	0.724	**0.664**	0.602	0.713	0.680	0.661	0.616	**0.786**
SQ	0.430	0.782	0.506	0.593	0.785	0.765	0.672	0.729	0.714
CR	0.392	**0.901**	0.076	**0.615**	**0.864**	**0.854**	**0.694**	**0.851**	0.353
PCC	0.432	0.780	0.510	0.593	0.785	0.754	0.671	0.699	0.745
N10	0.341	0.535	0.408	0.504	0.705	0.578	0.618	0.578	0.475
NM2	0.340	0.622	0.323	0.494	0.685	0.821	0.664	0.280	0.648

Data Generating Process (samples of 300)								
Model Family	AR(2)	AR(5)	AR(9)	CDR(2)	ES(2)	TAR(2)	LS(2)	LS(5)	ES(9)
AR	**0.541**	0.733	0.725	0.629	0.711	0.673	0.683	0.598	**0.789**
SQ	0.493	0.783	**0.795**	0.645	0.784	0.765	0.716	0.726	0.735
CR	0.468	**0.913**	0.101	**0.694**	**0.870**	**0.846**	**0.750**	**0.860**	0.473
PCC	0.494	0.787	0.607	0.645	0.785	0.758	0.709	0.692	0.758
N10	0.403	0.535	0.486	0.564	0.698	0.569	0.669	0.606	0.475
NM2	0.402	0.635	0.393	0.554	0.676	0.833	0.721	0.243	0.717

Data Generating Process (samples of 1000)								
Model Family	AR(2)	AR(5)	AR(9)	CDR(2)	ES(2)	TAR(2)	LS(2)	LS(5)	ES(9)
AR	0.714	0.730	0.849	0.608	0.708	0.529	0.710	0.390	0.705
SQ	0.783	0.796	0.864	0.618	0.792	0.692	0.784	0.666	0.510
CR	**0.858**	**0.937**	0.810	**0.757**	**0.881**	0.782	0.857	**0.811**	**0.773**
PCC	0.788	0.792	**0.867**	0.386	0.794	0.666	0.772	0.508	0.696
N10	0.734	0.526	0.697	0.580	0.617	0.553	0.741	0.722	0.327
NM2	0.712	0.667	0.692	0.563	0.550	**0.926**	**0.870**	0.052	0.916

Notes:
a: See Table 9.1 for a description of model families and Table 9.A.1 for the DGPs.
b: Bold numbers indicate the maximum in the column.

Table 9.A.3 Performance of HQ based criteria (proportion of times correct lag is picked)

	Data Generating Process (samples of 100)								
Model Family	AR(2)	AR(5)	AR(9)	CDR(2)	ES(2)	TAR(2)	LS(2)	LS(5)	ES(9)
AR[a]	**0.186**[b]	**0.831**	**0.112**	**0.289**	0.876	0.868	**0.368**	**0.801**	**0.329**
SQ	0.087	0.773	0.024	0.146	0.924	0.923	0.239	0.790	0.091
CR	0.053	0.320	0.002	0.090	**0.963**	**0.964**	0.178	0.442	0.009
PCC	0.087	0.774	0.026	0.147	0.930	0.924	0.232	0.790	0.107
N10	0.063	0.608	0.047	0.100	0.882	0.848	0.191	0.540	0.113
NM2	0.053	0.558	0.015	0.078	0.905	0.926	0.198	0.445	0.059

	Data Generating Process (samples of 150)								
Model Family	AR(2)	AR(5)	AR(9)	CDR(2)	ES(2)	TAR(2)	LS(2)	LS(5)	ES(9)
AR	**0.291**	0.886	**0.236**	**0.470**	0.892	0.877	**0.542**	0.840	**0.615**
SQ	0.149	0.917	0.056	0.281	0.950	0.940	0.410	**0.912**	0.246
CR	0.084	0.687	0.000	0.185	**0.980**	**0.981**	0.313	0.803	0.004
PCC	0.146	**0.918**	0.056	0.281	0.947	0.938	0.398	0.902	0.280
N10	0.096	0.776	0.095	0.185	0.910	0.859	0.334	0.667	0.226
NM2	0.086	0.819	0.018	0.156	0.928	0.958	0.352	0.559	0.121

	Data Generating Process (samples of 200)								
Model Family	AR(2)	AR(5)	AR(9)	CDR(2)	ES(2)	TAR(2)	LS(2)	LS(5)	ES(9)
AR	**0.385**	0.905	**0.369**	**0.601**	0.905	0.883	**0.674**	0.847	**0.789**
SQ	0.212	0.949	0.111	0.417	0.956	0.947	0.543	0.932	0.453
CR	0.125	0.900	0.000	0.299	**0.986**	**0.982**	0.437	**0.950**	0.005
PCC	0.212	**0.950**	0.110	0.425	0.956	0.944	0.535	0.919	0.495
N10	0.129	0.821	0.156	0.286	0.920	0.849	0.457	0.713	0.332
NM2	0.129	0.902	0.035	0.256	0.941	0.970	0.500	0.567	0.246

Table 9.A.3   Performance of HQ based criteria (proportion of times correct lag is picked) (...continued)

Model Family	Data Generating Process (samples of 250)								
	AR(2)	AR(5)	AR(9)	CDR(2)	ES(2)	TAR(2)	LS(2)	LS(5)	ES(9)
AR	**0.469**	0.907	**0.490**	**0.700**	0.908	0.881	**0.762**	0.845	**0.860**
SQ	0.277	0.959	0.185	0.544	0.960	0.951	0.660	0.940	0.633
CR	0.168	**0.974**	0.000	0.407	**0.989**	**0.985**	0.547	**0.985**	0.010
PCC	0.276	0.957	0.184	0.550	0.959	0.947	0.651	0.919	0.680
N10	0.171	0.837	0.225	0.387	0.929	0.841	0.572	0.732	0.404
NM2	0.177	0.922	0.055	0.365	0.945	0.973	0.619	0.532	0.409

Model Family	Data Generating Process (samples of 300)								
	AR(2)	AR(5)	AR(9)	CDR(2)	ES(2)	TAR(2)	LS(2)	LS(5)	ES(9)
AR	**0.546**	0.911	0.604	**0.773**	0.913	0.877	**0.815**	0.844	**0.884**
SQ	0.353	0.960	**0.612**	0.655	0.963	0.951	0.742	0.944	0.756
CR	0.221	**0.994**	0.000	0.524	**0.991**	**0.986**	0.647	**0.994**	0.023
PCC	0.351	0.961	0.270	0.656	0.966	0.949	0.737	0.918	0.801
N10	0.218	0.846	0.323	0.502	0.933	0.823	0.667	0.749	0.465
NM2	0.223	0.930	0.097	0.479	0.947	0.977	0.714	0.489	0.552

Model Family	Data Generating Process (samples of 1000)								
	AR(2)	AR(5)	AR(9)	CDR(2)	ES(2)	TAR(2)	LS(2)	LS(5)	ES(9)
AR	**0.917**	0.938	0.953	0.869	0.933	0.802	0.936	0.756	0.863
SQ	0.898	0.975	0.958	0.912	0.978	0.935	0.973	0.943	0.788
CR	0.811	**1.00**	0.022	**0.977**	**0.996**	0.982	**0.990**	**0.995**	**0.927**
PCC	0.900	0.975	**0.960**	0.898	0.974	0.922	0.970	0.822	0.906
N10	0.800	0.857	0.830	0.961	0.928	0.774	0.968	0.799	0.389
NM2	0.793	0.965	0.796	0.930	0.929	**0.994**	0.979	0.127	0.950

Notes:
a: See Table 9.1 for a description of model families and Table 9.A.1 for the DGPs.
b: Bold numbers indicate the maximum in the column.

Table 9.A.4   Performance of BIC based criteria (proportion of times correct lag is picked)

Model Family	Data Generating Process (samples of 100)								
	AR(2)	AR(5)	AR(9)	CDR(2)	ES(2)	TAR(2)	LS(2)	LS(5)	ES(9)
AR[a]	**0.102**[b]	**0.847**	**0.022**	**0.179**	0.958	0.953	**0.247**	**0.830**	**0.111**
SQ	0.022	0.558	0.001	0.043	0.986	0.986	0.089	0.633	0.006
CR	0.007	0.025	0.000	0.017	**0.997**	**0.997**	0.044	0.075	0.000
PCC	0.022	0.556	0.001	0.043	0.987	0.985	0.088	0.639	0.001
N10	0.013	0.446	0.002	0.023	0.967	0.958	0.060	0.475	0.018
NM2	0.006	0.241	0.000	0.011	0.985	0.989	0.047	0.271	0.001

Model Family	Data Generating Process (samples of 150)								
	AR(2)	AR(5)	AR(9)	CDR(2)	ES(2)	TAR(2)	LS(2)	LS(5)	ES(9)
AR	**0.170**	**0.952**	**0.059**	**0.322**	0.966	0.962	**0.422**	**0.938**	**0.336**
SQ	0.041	0.867	0.001	0.094	0.992	0.989	0.187	0.903	0.032
CR	0.013	0.123	0.000	0.037	**0.999**	**0.999**	0.095	0.268	0.000
PCC	0.040	0.866	0.001	0.096	0.993	0.988	0.179	0.906	0.039
N10	0.018	0.774	0.006	0.043	0.977	0.965	0.120	0.720	0.052
NM2	0.011	0.589	0.000	0.025	0.993	0.995	0.113	0.524	0.003

Model Family	Data Generating Process (samples of 200)								
	AR(2)	AR(5)	AR(9)	CDR(2)	ES(2)	TAR(2)	LS(2)	LS(5)	ES(9)
AR	**0.236**	0.972	**0.121**	**0.467**	0.972	0.963	**0.562**	0.952	**0.592**
SQ	0.065	0.972	0.004	0.167	0.994	0.992	0.295	**0.977**	0.103
CR	0.019	0.341	0.000	0.067	**0.999**	**1.000**	0.158	0.559	0.000
PCC	0.065	**0.973**	0.003	0.168	0.995	0.991	0.285	0.974	0.121
N10	0.024	0.919	0.013	0.072	0.980	0.964	0.180	0.824	0.117
NM2	0.018	0.844	0.000	0.051	0.994	0.997	0.186	0.671	0.012

Table 9.A.4   Performance of BIC based criteria, (proportion of times
correct lag is picked) (...continued)

Model Family	AR(2)	AR(5)	AR(9)	CDR(2)	ES(2)	TAR(2)	LS(2)	LS(5)	ES(9)
Data Generating Process (samples of 250)									
AR	**0.307**	0.976	**0.203**	**0.586**	0.976	0.966	**0.678**	0.955	**0.772**
SQ	0.091	**0.993**	0.007	0.260	0.996	0.993	0.402	**0.989**	0.226
CR	0.028	0.610	0.000	0.117	**1.000**	**1.000**	0.231	0.807	0.000
PCC	0.091	0.991	0.007	0.263	0.996	0.992	0.395	0.984	0.254
N10	0.034	0.957	0.024	0.115	0.986	0.963	0.257	0.859	0.219
NM2	0.027	0.956	0.000	0.089	0.997	0.999	0.288	0.737	0.039
Data Generating Process (samples of 300)									
AR	**0.381**	0.981	**0.292**	**0.695**	0.980	0.965	**0.764**	0.955	**0.875**
SQ	0.128	0.995	0.137	0.359	0.997	0.993	0.503	**0.992**	0.378
CR	0.039	0.828	0.000	0.175	**1.000**	**1.000**	0.308	0.938	0.000
PCC	0.127	**0.996**	0.017	0.364	0.997	0.993	0.494	0.987	0.417
N10	0.043	0.964	0.050	0.170	0.988	0.960	0.339	0.864	0.300
NM2	0.038	0.989	0.000	0.143	0.997	0.999	0.390	0.753	0.103
Data Generating Process (samples of 1000)									
AR	**0.913**	0.992	**0.969**	0.969	0.988	0.939	**0.989**	0.952	**0.955**
SQ	0.665	0.999	0.687	**0.980**	0.999	0.993	0.987	0.995	0.953
CR	0.384	**1.000**	0.000	0.935	**1.000**	**1.000**	0.958	**1.000**	0.051
PCC	0.666	0.999	0.689	0.978	0.999	0.992	0.988	0.964	0.986
N10	0.371	0.975	0.767	0.917	0.992	0.945	0.962	0.882	0.479
NM2	0.385	1.000	0.247	0.923	0.998	1.000	0.983	0.363	0.971

Notes:
a: See Table 9.1 for a description of model families and Table 9.A.1 for the DGPs.
b: Bold numbers indicate the maximum in the column.

Table 9.A.5 Under– and overprediction when AIC procedures are used (proportion of times under (U), correctly (C) or over (O) predicted)

Model Family		AR(2)	AR(5)	AR(9)	CDR(2)	ES(2)	TAR(2)	LS(2)	LS(5)	ES(9)
		Data Generating Process (samples of 100)								
	U	0.562	0.016	0.674	0.414	0.000	0.000	0.370	0.015	0.351
AR	C	**0.230**	**0.701**	**0.246**	**0.329**	**0.705**	**0.698**	**0.401**	**0.653**	**0.503**
	O	0.208	0.283	0.080	0.258	0.295	0.302	0.229	0.332	0.146
	U	0.688	0.043	0.789	0.572	0.000	0.000	0.478	0.034	0.412
SQ	C	**0.174**	**0.693**	**0.146**	**0.251**	**0.743**	**0.743**	**0.352**	**0.677**	**0.291**
	O	0.138	0.264	0.066	0.177	0.257	0.257	0.170	0.289	0.121
	U	0.553	0.100	0.440	0.483	0.000	0.000	0.381	0.062	0.320
CR	C	**0.105**	**0.273**	**0.053**	**0.147**	**0.539**	**0.522**	**0.221**	**0.272**	**0.065**
	O	0.342	0.628	0.507	0.370	0.461	0.479	0.399	0.666	0.615

Model Family		AR(2)	AR(5)	AR(9)	CDR(2)	ES(2)	TAR(2)	LS(2)	LS(5)	ES(9)
		Data Generating Process (samples of 200)								
	U	0.340	0.000	0.315	0.134	0.000	0.000	0.118	0.000	0.028
AR	C	**0.419**	**0.726**	**0.556**	**0.561**	**0.711**	**0.689**	**0.616**	**0.628**	**0.775**
	O	0.240	0.274	0.129	0.306	0.289	0.311	0.266	0.329	0.197
	U	0.482	0.000	0.509	0.252	0.000	0.000	0.190	0.000	0.140
SQ	C	**0.357**	**0.782**	**0.388**	**0.522**	**0.777**	**0.755**	**0.612**	**0.727**	**0.652**
	O	0.161	0.218	0.103	0.226	0.223	0.245	0.198	0.273	0.208
	U	0.592	0.004	0.911	0.350	0.000	0.000	0.251	0.002	0.615
CR	C	**0.320**	**0.867**	**0.060**	**0.511**	**0.855**	**0.848**	**0.612**	**0.825**	**0.237**
	O	0.088	0.129	0.029	0.139	0.145	0.152	0.137	0.173	0.148

Model Family		AR(2)	AR(5)	AR(9)	CDR(2)	ES(2)	TAR(2)	LS(2)	LS(5)	ES(9)
		Data Generating Process (samples of 300)								
	U	0.202	0.000	0.137	0.042	0.000	0.000	0.038	0.000	0.002
AR	C	**0.541**	**0.733**	**0.725**	**0.629**	**0.711**	**0.673**	**0.683**	**0.598**	**0.789**
	O	0.257	0.267	0.138	0.329	0.289	0.327	0.279	0.402	0.209
	U	0.332	0.000	0.278	0.093	0.000	0.000	0.070	0.000	0.018
SQ	C	**0.493**	**0.783**	**0.600**	**0.645**	**0.784**	**0.765**	**0.717**	**0.726**	**0.735**
	O	0.175	0.217	0.122	0.262	0.216	0.235	0.213	0.274	0.248
	U	0.438	0.000	0.884	0.155	0.000	0.000	0.109	0.000	0.375
CR	C	**0.468**	**0.913**	**0.101**	**0.694**	**0.870**	**0.846**	**0.750**	**0.860**	**0.479**
	O	0.094	0.087	0.018	0.175	0.130	0.154	0.141	0.140	0.146

Table 9.A.6   Under− and overprediction when BIC procedures are used (proportion of times under (U), correctly (C) or over (O) predicted)

Model Family		Data Generating Process (samples of 100)								
		AR(2)	AR(5)	AR(9)	CDR(2)	ES(2)	TAR(2)	LS(2)	LS(5)	ES(9)
AR	U	0.884	0.110	0.976	0.801	0.000	0.000	0.734	0.113	0.891
	C	**0.102**	**0.847**	**0.022**	**0.179**	**0.958**	**0.953**	**0.247**	**0.830**	**0.111**
	O	0.014	0.043	0.003	0.020	0.042	0.047	0.020	0.058	0.008
SQ	U	0.976	0.429	0.999	0.955	0.000	0.000	0.908	0.351	0.992
	C	**0.022**	**0.558**	**0.001**	**0.043**	**0.986**	**0.986**	**0.089**	**0.633**	**0.006**
	O	0.002	0.013	0.000	0.002	0.014	0.014	0.003	0.017	0.001
CR	U	0.993	0.975	1.000	0.984	0.000	0.000	0.956	0.925	1.000
	C	**0.007**	**0.025**	**0.000**	**0.017**	**0.997**	**0.997**	**0.044**	**0.075**	**0.000**
	O	0.000	0.000	0.000	0.000	0.003	0.003	0.000	0.001	0.000

Model Family		Data Generating Process (samples of 200)								
		AR(2)	AR(5)	AR(9)	CDR(2)	ES(2)	TAR(2)	LS(2)	LS(5)	ES(9)
AR	U	0.751	0.001	0.874	0.508	0.000	0.000	0.419	0.001	0.381
	C	**0.236**	**0.972**	**0.121**	**0.467**	**0.972**	**0.963**	**0.562**	**0.952**	**0.592**
	O	0.013	0.027	0.005	0.026	0.028	0.037	0.019	0.046	0.027
SQ	U	0.934	0.021	0.996	0.831	0.000	0.000	0.702	0.013	0.891
	C	**0.065**	**0.972**	**0.004**	**0.167**	**0.994**	**0.992**	**0.295**	**0.977**	**0.103**
	O	0.001	0.007	0.000	0.003	0.006	0.008	0.002	0.010	0.006
CR	U	0.981	0.659	1.000	0.932	0.000	0.000	0.842	0.441	1.000
	C	**0.019**	**0.341**	**0.000**	**0.067**	**0.999**	**1.000**	**0.158**	**0.559**	**0.000**
	O	0.000	0.000	0.000	0.000	0.001	0.000	0.000	0.000	0.000

Model Family		Data Generating Process (samples of 300)								
		AR(2)	AR(5)	AR(9)	CDR(2)	ES(2)	TAR(2)	LS(2)	LS(5)	ES(9)
AR	U	0.608	0.000	0.702	0.278	0.000	0.000	0.217	0.000	0.086
	C	**0.381**	**0.981**	**0.292**	**0.695**	**0.980**	**0.965**	**0.764**	**0.955**	**0.875**
	O	0.011	0.019	0.007	0.028	0.020	0.045	0.019	0.045	0.039
SQ	U	0.871	0.000	0.983	0.637	0.000	0.000	0.494	0.000	0.609
	C	**0.128**	**0.995**	**0.017**	**0.359**	**0.997**	**0.993**	**0.503**	**0.992**	**0.378**
	O	0.001	0.004	0.000	0.000	0.003	0.007	0.003	0.008	0.013
CR	U	0.961	0.173	1.000	0.825	0.000	0.000	0.691	0.062	1.000
	C	**0.039**	**0.828**	**0.000**	**0.175**	**1.000**	**1.000**	**0.308**	**0.938**	**0.000**
	O	0.000	0.000	0.000	0.000	0.000	0.001	0.000	0.000	0.000

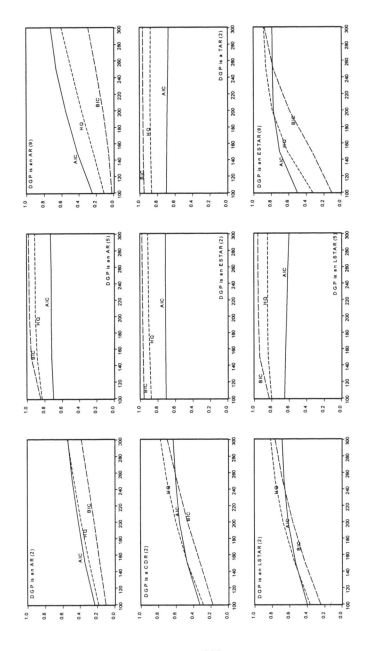

Figure 9.A.1 Performance of standard model selection criteria (proportion of correct picks vs sample size)

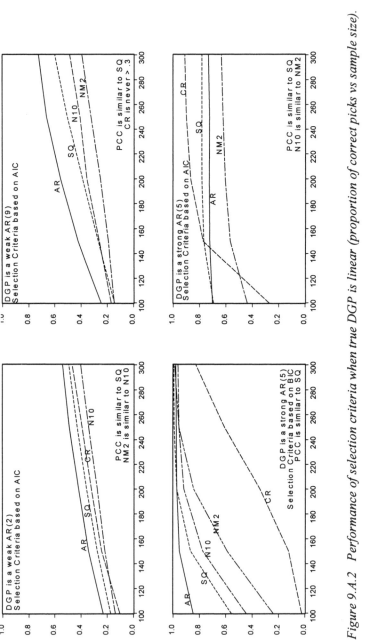

Figure 9.A.2 Performance of selection criteria when true DGP is linear (proportion of correct picks vs sample size).

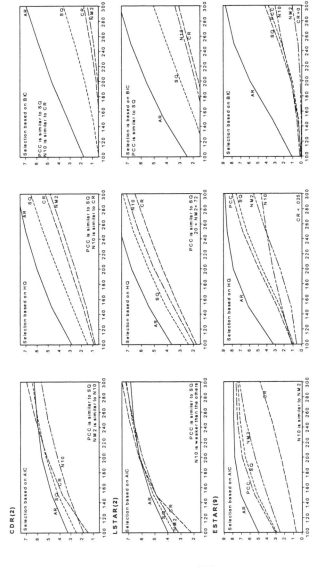

Figure 9.A.3a Performance of model selection criteria when true DGP is nonlinear (proportion of correct picks vs sample size)

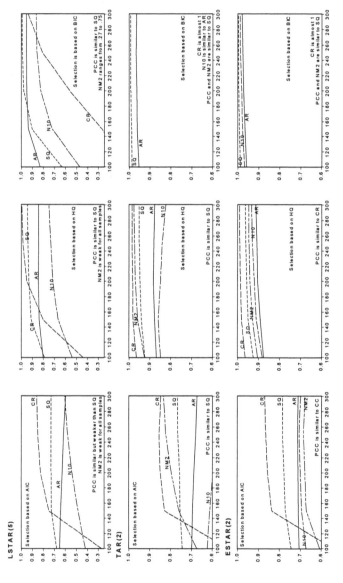

Figure 9.A.3b Performance of model selection criteria when true DGP is nonlinear (proportion of correct picks vs sample size)

10. D-TAR versus C-TAR Models? Modelling the Dynamics of Inflation

Walter Enders and Pierre Siklos

1. INTRODUCTION

Threshold models are widely used to model a variety of economic phenomena. Such models arise naturally from economic analysis because shifts in macroeconomic policies often have permanent effects on macroeconomic time series such as inflation, interest rates, unemployment rates or output, to give just a few examples. Nevertheless, problems of testing and inference arise because economists ordinarily do not know the exact location of the threshold that separates one 'regime' from another. Moreover, while a unique long-run equilibrium relationship drives movements in a particular time series over time, inference in threshold models will be dependent on whether the model is continuous at the threshold. Currently, there is a well-defined literature dealing with inference on the coefficients of a continuous threshold model. In this case there is a single attractor.

This chapter develops the mathematical relationship among the parameter values of a threshold autoregressive (TAR) model that determines whether it is continuous at the threshold. There are several reasons to be interested in the relationship between the magnitudes of the intercepts, autoregressive coefficients and the threshold and in a two-regime TAR model. The value of the threshold is generally unknown so that there are two plausible tests for continuity. The first test determines whether there is continuity at a given value of the threshold. The second test simply seeks to determine whether the process is continuous. Consequently, we consider two modelling strategies, namely the continuous TAR, or C-TAR, versus the discontinuous TAR, or D-TAR approach. It is shown that the appropriate tests for continuity are not pivotal. It is tempting then to suggest that a supremum test be used. It is shown that this type of test will not have attractive properties under most circumstances.

Our application consists in modelling the time series behaviour of inflation. There is considerable evidence to suggest that inflation rates are highly persistent, and that they have been subject to important shifts over time due to changing monetary policy strategies. In the USA, the Bretton Woods period and the era since Alan Greenspan became Chair of the Board of Governors of the Federal Reserve (Fed) stand out as low inflation rate regimes. In contrast, a sample covering the two oil price shocks of the 1970s, culminating with the appointment to of Paul Volcker to head the Fed in the early 1980s, constitutes a regime of high inflation followed by a significant disinflation. We argue that it is appealing to model the behaviour of US inflation in the TAR framework but that there are significant differences in the interpretation of the behaviour of inflation depending on whether the C-TAR or D-TAR modelling strategy is employed.

The chapter is organized as follows. In the following section we contrast D-TAR versus C-TAR models. Section 3 considers the problems of inference when the threshold is unknown and why bootstrapping is appropriate under the circumstances. Section 4 considers the behaviour of inflation in the United States as an illustration of the usefulness of our modelling strategy. Section 5 concludes.

2. DISCONTINUOUS (D-) VERSUS CONTINUOUS (C-) TAR MODELS

Consider the basic threshold model:

$$y_t = \begin{cases} \alpha_1 + \rho_1 y_{t-1} + \varepsilon_t & \text{if } y_{t-1} > \tau \\ \alpha_2 + \rho_2 y_{t-1} + \varepsilon_t & \text{if } y_{t-1} \leq \tau \end{cases} \tag{10.1}$$

where: $\rho_1 < 1$, $\rho_2 < 1$, and $\rho_1\rho_2 < 1$. An explicit role for the intercept is developed below.

Notice that the standard AR(1) model is the special case in which $\alpha_1 = \alpha_2$ and $\rho_1 = \rho_2$. The nature of the model is such that the degree of autoregressive decay equals $(1 - \rho_1)$ if the value of y_{t-1} exceeds the threshold τ, and equals $(1 - \rho_2)$ otherwise. It seems reasonable then to use (10.1) if the degree of autoregressive decay is deemed to be asymmetric. However, the role of the intercept terms (α_1 and α_2) is not innocuous for two important reasons.

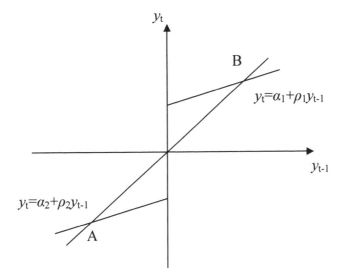

Figure 10.1 Two stable equilibrium points

It is well known (see Hansen, 1999 and Enders and Falk, 2001), that coefficient estimates in a TAR model have poor finite sample performance. Also, inference concerning the estimated values of the α_i, ρ_i and τ become problematic if the likelihood function is not continuous at the threshold. It is the relationship between the intercepts, autoregressive coefficients and the threshold that determine whether the model is continuous. Another problem arising out of concern over the intercepts relates to the nature of the potential attractor(s). Most economic models contain a single stable equilibrium. Those with multiple equilibria typically contain an unstable equilibrium bounded above and below by a stable equilibrium. But this is not the case with a discontinuous TAR model. To see why, suppose that the threshold is $\tau = 0$. In Figure 10.1, the 45-degree guideline passing through points A and B indicates all points such that $y_t = y_{t-1}$; clearly, any attractor must lie on this line. Figure 10.1 depicts a situation such that $\alpha_1 > 0$ and $\alpha_2 < 0$. Notice that the skeleton of the discontinuous TAR model in (10.1) passes through AB twice. Hence, both A and B are attractors. If the initial condition is such that $y_0 \leq 0$, the successive values of $\{y_t\}$ will tend to approach A; if $y_0 > 0$, the successive values of $\{y_t\}$ will tend to approach B. Notice that these two stable equilibria do not bound an unstable equilibrium. Consider now the situation in Figure 10.2 where $\alpha_1 < 0$ and $\alpha_2 > 0$. Now it should be clear that there is no attractor whatsoever; in fact, there is no attractor even though ρ_1 and ρ_2 are both positive and less than unity.

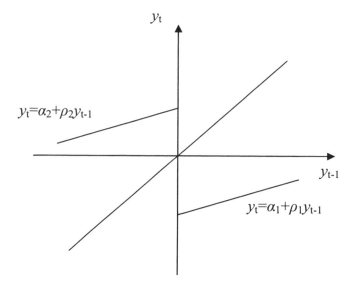

Figure 10.2   No stable equilibrium points

For $0 < (\rho_1, \rho_2) < 1$, the relationship between the intercepts and the threshold is straightforward: if $\alpha_1 > \tau$, there will be a stable equilibrium above τ and if $\alpha_2 < \tau$, there will be a stable equilibrium below τ. Hence, a single attractor is possible if α_1 and α_2 both exceed τ or are both less than τ. Implicitly, if (10.1) is constrained to be continuous at τ, there must be a unique stable equilibrium.

For (10.1) to be continuous at the threshold, it is necessary that the two segments of (10.1) be equal to each other when $y_{t-1} = \tau$. For this equality to hold it must be the case that:

$$\alpha_1 + \rho_1 y_{t-1} = \alpha_2 + \rho_2 y_{t-1} \text{ when } y_{t-1} = \tau \qquad (10.2)$$

Hence, the relationship between α_1, ρ_1, α_2, ρ_2 and τ that guarantees continuity at the threshold is:

$$\alpha_1 + \rho_1 \tau = \alpha_2 + \rho_2 \tau \qquad (10.3)$$

Combining (10.1) and (10.3), we can write the C-TAR model as:

$$y_t = \tau + I_t \rho_1 (y_{t-1} - \tau) + (1 - I_t) \rho_2 (y_{t-1} - \tau) + \varepsilon_t \qquad (10.4)$$

where I_t is the Heavyside indicator such that:

$$I_t = \begin{cases} 1 \text{ if } y_{t-1} > \tau \\ 0 \text{ if } y_{t-1} \leq \tau \end{cases} \qquad (10.5)$$

The point is that the C-TAR model contains a single attractor at $y_{t-1} = \tau$. The degree of autoregressive decay is $(1 - \rho_1)$ when $y_{t-1} > \tau$ and $(1 - \rho_2)$ otherwise.

The difficulty in estimating (10.1) and/or (10.4) is that the value of τ is unknown to the researcher; hence, its magnitude must be estimated along with the other parameters of the model. Fortunately, Chan (1993) shows that it is possible to obtain a super-consistent estimate of the threshold by ordering the $\{y_t\}$ sequence such that $y_1^0 < y_2^0 < y_3^0 ... < y_T^0$. For each value of y_j^0, set $\tau = y_j^0$ and estimate an equation in the form of (10.1) or (10.4). The regression equation with the smallest residual sum of squares contains the consistent estimate of the threshold.

Properties of the Coefficient Estimates

Monte Carlo simulations by Hansen (1999), and Enders and Falk (2001), illustrate the poor finite sample performance of normal confidence intervals, bootstrap-t, and bootstrap-percentile confidence intervals for the TAR model (10.1) when the specification is correct. We differ from their work in that we focus on estimates of a D-TAR model when the true data generating process is continuous. Clearly, in a general-to-specific modelling strategy, the applied researcher will begin with the unrestricted D-TAR specification.

To illustrate the properties of the parameter estimates when a continuous process is estimated in the form of (10.1), we generated 25,000 TAR series in the form of (10.4) and (10.5). Since the selection of the appropriate initial condition is particularly acute for a TAR model, we performed the following procedure. For sample sizes $T = 100$, a simulated $\{\varepsilon_t\}$ sequence of length $T + 50$ was generated from a set of normally distributed and uncorrelated pseudo-random numbers. Randomizing the initial value of y_1 and selecting specific values for ρ_1 and ρ_2, a total of $T + 50$ values of $\{y_t\}$ were generated using $\tau = 0$. To avoid the initial condition problem, the first 50 realizations were discarded so that we used only the last T observations of the series. Each series was then sorted in ascending order and the upper and lower 15% of the $\{y_j^0\}$ values were discarded. For each of the remaining $\{y_j^0\}$ values, we estimated an equation in the form of (10.1). The equation yielding the lowest residual sum of squares was deemed to be the appropriate estimate of the threshold. Using this threshold value, we obtained the estimates of the α_i, ρ_i, τ and F-statistic for restriction given by (10.3). This process was repeated 25,000 times and the distribution of the resulting summary statistics are shown in Table 10.1 for various choices of the ρ_i. Table 10.A.1 reports summary statistics of the estimated parameter values using a sample size of 100 and a standard deviation of the simulated error process equal to unity.[1] For example, when the true value of $\rho_1 = \rho_2 = 0.3$, the mean values of the estimates of α_1, ρ_1, α_2, ρ_2 and τ were 0.0283, 0.2603, –0.0365, 0.2569 and –0.0240, respectively. When the model was estimated as a continuous process (i.e., when the appropriately restricted model was estimated), the mean values of the estimates ρ_1, ρ_2 and τ were 0.2494, 0.2514 and –0.0010, respectively. Note the following points.

The autoregressive coefficients (i.e., ρ_1 and ρ_2)

When the true data generating process is symmetric (i.e., $\rho_1 = \rho_2$), estimates of the ρ_i are biased downward. This should not be surprising since OLS estimates of a linear AR(1) process are known to be downward biased. However, when $\rho_1 \neq \rho_2$, the estimated values of the autoregressive coefficients are *not* necessarily biased downward. The reason is that increasing ρ_2 tends to increase the estimated value of ρ_1. For example, when $\rho_1 = 0.3$ and $\rho_2 = 0.95$, the estimated values of the parameters averaged 0.3820 and 0.7587, respectively. In essence, the coefficients appear to be more symmetric than the true parameters in the data generating process. When the C-TAR model is estimated, the pattern is not so pronounced. Moreover, the standard errors of the coefficient estimates from the continuous model are far smaller than those from the discontinuous model. Thus, the presence of the intercepts in the regression equation makes inference on the autoregressive coefficients more difficult.

The intercept terms (i.e., α_1 and α_2)

Consider the case where $\rho_1 = \rho_2 = 0.3$; the estimated values of α_1 and α_2 have mean values of 0.0283 and –0.0365, respectively and the respective standard errors are 0.7910 and 0.9007. In this case the estimated values of the α_i lie on opposite sides of the threshold (since the true value of $\tau = 0$). However, in a number of other instances, the estimates lie on the same side of the threshold. As such, it appears that there are two attractors when there is only a single attractor in the data generating process. The pattern is such that increasing ρ_2 (for a given value of ρ_1) decreases the estimated value of α_1 and α_2. It should be noted that changes in the variance of the error term in the data generating process change the properties of the estimated α_i.

The estimated threshold

Increasing the degree of asymmetry increases the bias of the threshold. The estimated value of the threshold is drawn towards the regime with the larger value of ρ. Thus, increasing ρ_2 (for a given value of ρ_1) decreases the estimated value of the threshold. The bias of the estimated threshold for the D-TAR is larger than that for the continuous estimate. For example, when $\rho_1 = \rho_2 = 0.3$, the mean of the threshold estimates is -0.0240 for the discontinuous model and 0.0010 for the C-TAR model. Respectively, the standard errors are 0.6840 and 0.2577. When $\rho_1 = 0.3$ and $\rho_2 = 0.9$, the mean of the threshold estimates is -0.9521 for the D-TAR model and -0.2697 for the C-TAR model.

We also generated the distribution of the sample F-statistics for the restriction given by (10.3). These are not shown here to conserve space. We do find, for example, that for $T = 100$, $\rho_1 = 0.3$ and $\rho_2 = 0.6$, 90% of the sample F-statistics were less than 8.80883 and 95% of the F-statistics were less than 10.53756. (The critical values are symmetric in the values of ρ_i, $i = 1,2$.) The magnitudes of these F-statistics increase with the degree of asymmetry and decrease with the individual ρ_i. Although other sample sizes are not reported, the critical values decrease with the sample size. If the true values of the ρ_i are known, these values can serve as critical values in order to determine if a TAR model can be restricted so as to be continuous. Suppose that in a sample of 100 observations with $\rho_1 = 0.3$ and $\rho_2 = 0.6$, the F-statistic for joint restriction in (10.3) equals 10.0. If the model were truly continuous, such an occurrence would occur more than 90% of the time but less than 95% of the time. As such, it would be possible to reject the null hypothesis of continuity at the 95%, but not the 90%, significance level.

The experiment above constrains the value of the threshold to remain unchanged. In essence, the experiment asks: Given the threshold value estimated by Chan's method, is (10.3) a binding restriction? An alternative methodology is to estimate $\{y_t\}$ in the form of (10.1) and call the residual sum of squares $RSSu$. Next, re-estimate $\{y_t\}$ in the form of (10.4) and (10.5) – allowing for the possibility of finding a new estimate of τ – and call the residual sum of squares $RSSr$. The difference between the restricted and unrestricted sum of squares can be tested as in a conventional F-test. We repeated the Monte Carlo experiment using this alternative methodology – the results are shown in Table 10.A.2. In contrast, the magnitudes of these F-statistics do not necessarily increase with the degree of asymmetry.

The more important point is that the F-statistic for each test depends on the actual values of ρ_1 and ρ_2 in the data generating process. As such, it is necessary to know these values in order to perform the F-test. However, since the true values of ρ_1 and ρ_2 are unknown, there is no way of knowing which critical values should be used. (Note that the critical values do not depend on the variance of the error process.)

In such circumstances, it is standard to use the supremum test statistic. Since the desired F-statistic is a function of ρ_1 and ρ_2, we could follow Davies (1987) and use the supremum $F^*(\rho_1, \rho_2) = \sup \{F^*(\rho_1, \rho_2)\}$ where: ρ_1 and ρ_2 range from 0 to unity. Notice that the largest critical values for the first test occur when the degree of asymmetry is at a maximum (e.g., $\rho_1 = 0$ and $\rho_2 = 1$). If we impose this restriction on equation (10.4), it should be clear that the null hypothesis of the supremum test requires that $\{y_t\}$ behave like a random walk on one side of the attractor and exhibit no persistence on the other side of the attractor. However, we found that such a test has very little power when the values of ρ_i are nearly symmetric. Moreover, the second test (allowing the threshold to be re-estimated) seems more attractive. Typically, there is no particular reason to test for continuity at the fixed value of τ found from the OLS estimate of the D-TAR model. However, the supremum values for this test display no obvious pattern. As there appears to be no sensible way to implement a supremum test, any plausible test statistic for the continuity of a TAR model should be bootstrapped.

3. APPLICATION: THE BEHAVIOUR OF US INFLATION

Figure 10.A.1 shows the quarterly values of the US inflation rate as measured by the Consumer Price Index (CPI) and by the core inflation rate since 1958. Both measures are expressed in annualized form.[2] Core inflation is the measure that in recent years central banks such as the Fed are most concerned about when setting the instruments of monetary policy, since this proxy for inflation excludes the most volatile components of prices such as food and energy.

If we assume that central banks have a tolerance zone for inflation of, say, 1–3% then we can, as a first approximation, sub-divide the US inflationary experience into two distinct regimes.[3] The period from the late 1950s until the early 1970s overlaps with the Bretton Woods system of pegged but adjustable exchange rates. The sample that begins approximately in the late 1980s until the present day essentially covers the period during which Alan Greenspan has been serving as Chair of the Federal Reserve's Board of Governors. The middle of the plot then represents the era of the 'Great Inflation', one that appears to have been exceptional by historical standards (DeLong, 2000). One can also think of the early 1970s and late 1980s, respectively, as episodes of accelerating and disinflationary periods, so that the transition between one inflationary 'regime' to another may have been continuous, or at least the long-run equilibrium level of inflation in the USA was interrupted only temporarily. Finally, if we interpret the Fed as attempting to aim for the mid-point of the inflation target range then there appears to be asymmetric behaviour around the desired target. Explanations include the inability to control inflation perfectly, uncertainty about the impact of monetary policy decisions on inflation and lags in the effect of monetary policies, and the belief that there are asymmetries in the economic costs of tight versus loose monetary policies.

The behaviour of inflation suggests the possibility of modelling inflation in a target-zone-type framework for regimes such as Bretton Woods or the implicit 'inflation targeting' era that characterizes Fed behaviour since the early 1990s. Nevertheless, unlike the target zone literature that assumes the 1–3% barrier cannot be crossed, this is clearly not true of the US inflationary experience. Therefore, a more flexible model for inflation would seem to be more desirable.

It has been popular in recent years to model inflation as an AR(1) process since the resulting fit for the data seems good. Indeed, an AR(1) model of core inflation for the full sample yields an adjusted R^2 of 0.77. Nevertheless, examination of the residuals reveals that the model fails to track inflation well during the regime of the 'Great Inflation'. Moreover, economic theory gives good reasons why inflation persistence may be influenced by the monetary policy strategy in place, such as the type of exchange rate regime or whether there is a form of inflation targeting, not to mention other institutional factors that might give rise to changing inflation persistence. A number of recent papers have made this point. An important question is whether the AR(1) model is adequate since there is the possibility that the residuals display serial correlation (see below).

Alogoskoufis and Smith (1991) suggest that inflation persistence in the USA increased following the end of the Gold Standard and Bretton Woods. Burdekin and Siklos (1999) use recent advances in testing for unit roots with endogenously estimated breakpoints to demonstrate that shifts in inflation persistence are better associated with institutional factors (such as greater or reduced central bank autonomy), wars and changes in monetary policy strategy as opposed to just a change in the exchange rate regime. Siklos (1999) makes the same point but for more recent data and focuses on the impact of the adoption of explicit inflation targets to demonstrate how these can lead to statistically significant shifts in inflation persistence. Bleany (2001) finds that, while inflation persistence is higher after the end of Bretton Woods, there is no significant difference in inflation persistence across exchange rate regimes.

Cogley and Sargent (2002a, 2002b; also see Sargent 1999) take a different approach to modelling the inflation process but with similar implications for the degree of inflation persistence over time in the USA. The uniqueness of the high inflation era of the 1970s and 1980s is due to adherence to faulty economic analysis by the monetary authorities. This led to the misinterpretation of the position of the economy in the business cycle with negative consequences for inflation. Once the Fed 'learned' from its mistakes, inflation rates and persistence fell to long-run historical levels. DeLong (1997) and Taylor (1997) also point to gradual learning in what drives the inflation process. Ireland (1999) also investigates the changing inflation persistence in the USA and attributes such changes to the time-inconsistency in monetary policy, that is, a failure of the Fed to permanently commit to low and stable inflation by being tempted to exploit the short-run inflation-unemployment trade-off. Finally, Benati (2002) not only concludes that inflation need not be intrinsically persistent but that the sample beginning with the ending of Bretton Woods in August 1971 until the end of the Volcker disinflation era in the mid-1980s marks a clear regime shift that is a distinct one in postwar US economic history. Indeed, his findings are robust to a large number of econometric considerations including whether conditional heteroscedasticity is permitted or the particular sample, price index or econometric technique employed. He also concludes that the AR(1) model works best in most circumstances.

We can write an AR(1) model of inflation as follows:

$$\pi_t = \alpha + \rho \pi_{t-1} + \varepsilon_t \tag{10.6}$$

where: π_t is inflation and ρ measures the degree of inflation persistence.

The preceding discussion implies that inflation persistence is likely to be time varying. As such, a TAR specification is likely to be more informative than persistence estimated from a linear model such as (10.6). Nevertheless, to provide baseline comparisons, Table 10.A.2 provides linear estimates of CPI and core inflation for various sub-samples identified earlier with US inflation history since 1958. There is considerable variation in both α and ρ though we do not know, of course, a priori whether the timing and size of shifts in inflation persistence have been correctly estimated.

Table 10.A.3, therefore, considers the case where the two inflation rates are modelled as D-TAR models while Table 10.A.4 reports the results for the C-TAR model. The thresholds are estimated consistently using Chan's method described above. The data are again analysed for a variety of sub-samples to ascertain the impact on both the intercept and slope terms. It is apparent that there is both asymmetry between periods of rising and falling inflation while there is a range of thresholds depending on the chosen sample and inflation measure. Except for the 1958.1–1972.2 period, thresholds are very similar for CPI and core inflation. However, the estimates for the various sub-samples can be substantially different and the discontinuous and continuous estimates tell very different stories.

To get a better sense of the most appropriate form of the TAR model (i.e., C-TAR versus D-TAR), we resorted to the bootstrap. We first estimated the annual logarithmic change in the CPI as a linear AR(1) for the full sample shown in Table 10.A.2 and saved the residuals as $\{\hat{\varepsilon}_t\}$. We then constructed 2500 bootstrap series $\{y_t^b\}$ of length 177, corresponding to the sample size used in estimation, as follows:

$$y_t^b = \hat{\alpha} + \hat{\rho} y_{t-1}^b + \hat{\varepsilon}_t^b \qquad (10.7)$$

where $\{\hat{\varepsilon}_t^b\}$ are the sampled values of the $\{\hat{\varepsilon}_t\}$ sequence and $\hat{\alpha}$ and $\hat{\rho}$ are the OLS estimates of α and ρ. Each bootstrap series was estimated as a D-TAR model in the form of (10.1) and the following three tests were performed: (*i*) $\rho_1 = \rho_2$, (*ii*) $\alpha_1 + \rho_1\tau = \alpha_2 + \rho_2\tau$ and (*iii*) $\alpha_1 = \alpha_2$ and $\rho_1 = \rho_2$. The first tests for identical inflation persistence over the two periods, the second tests for continuity at the threshold and the third tests for linearity. We found that 90% of the *F*-values for the first restriction were less than 8.57 (and 7.50 for the 1982.1–2002.1 sample). Since the sample value for the model reported in Table 10.A.2 was only 3.75, we cannot reject the null hypothesis of equal persistence. Similarly, 90% of the *F*-values for the second restriction were less than 10.17 (and 10.11 for the 1982.1–2002.1 sample). Since the sample value for the model reported in Table 10.A.2 was only 5.10, we cannot reject the null hypothesis that the model is continuous. Also, 90% of the *F*-values for the third restriction were less than 6.17 and 95% were less than 7.40. Since the sample value was 6.79, we can reject the linearity hypothesis at the 10% (but not the 5%) significance level.

Given that the model appears to be nonlinear, we bootstrapped the residuals from a D-TAR model. We used the residuals and coefficient estimates of the CPI inflation rate reported in Table 10.A.3 over the entire sample period. We reconstructed 2500 bootstrapped series of the estimated D-TAR model and estimated each as a D-TAR model. For each of the 2500 replications, we also performed the three tests: (*i*) $\rho_1 = \rho_2$, (*ii*) $\alpha_1 + \rho_1\tau = \alpha_2 + \rho_2\tau$ and (*iii*) $\alpha_1 = \alpha_2$ and $\rho_1 = \rho_2$. Now it was not possible to reject any null hypothesis at any conventional significance level. Thus, the results are contradictory – the null hypothesis of linearity cannot be rejected.

One potential difficulty is the possibility of serial correlation in the residuals for some of the samples. While the threshold was estimated consistently, the samples were chosen according to the 'official' dating of certain events such as the appointment of Alan Greenspan as Chair of the Board of Governors of the Fed (1987) or the oil price shock of 1972. It is possible that a technique that permits the data to select the timing of the 'break' in inflation persistence might have produced sub-sample estimates for an AR(1) without serial correlation.[4]

4. APPROXIMATING NONLINEAR COEFFICIENTS WITH A FOURIER SERIES

The TAR estimates suggest that inflation persistence rose for some time and then began to decline following the end of the era of the 'Great Inflation'. Yet serial correlation found in some of the samples suggests that we obtain additional estimates using a different approach to measuring inflation persistence. A simple modification of the standard AR(1) model is to allow the autoregressive coefficient to be a time-dependent function denoted by $\rho(t)$:

$$y_t = \alpha + \rho(t) y_{t-1} + \varepsilon_t \tag{10.8}$$

where: ε_t is white noise with variance σ^2 and $\rho(t)$ is a function of t.

Although (10.8) is linear in $\{y_t\}$, the specification is reasonably general in that $\rho(t)$ can be a deterministic polynomial expression in time, a p-th order difference equation, a threshold function, or a switching function. Under very weak conditions, the behaviour of $\rho(t)$ can be exactly represented by a sufficiently long Fourier series:

$$\rho(t) = a_0 + \sum_{k=1}^{n} \left[a_k \sin \frac{2\pi k}{T} \cdot t + b_k \cos \frac{2\pi k}{T} \cdot t \right] + e_n(t) \tag{10.9}$$

where: n refers to the number of summands contained in the approximation of $\rho(t)$ and $e_n(t)$ is the approximation error such that: $\lim_{n \to \infty} e_n(t) = 0$.

Note that the AR(1) specification emerges as the special case in which all values of a_k and b_k are set equal to zero. The key point to stress is that if a_k and/or b_k differ from zero, the speed of adjustment is not constant − instead, it can be represented by the time-dependent function $\rho(t)$. Thus, instead of positing a specific nonlinear model, the specification problem becomes one of selecting the most appropriate frequencies to include.

One difficulty in developing a test statistic is that the frequency k is a nuisance parameter that is unidentified under the null hypothesis of linearity. Nevertheless, Ludlow and Enders (2000) and Becker, Enders and Hurn (2004) show that it is appropriate to use the following methodology. First, for each integer frequency in the interval $1 \le k \le T/2$, estimate:

$$y_t = \alpha + \left[\alpha_0 + \alpha_k \sin(2\pi kt / T) + b_k \cos(2\pi kt / T) \right] y_{t-1} + \varepsilon_t$$

Call the frequency yielding the best fit k^* and the associated coefficients a^* and b^*.

Obtain the sample value of F for the null $a^* = b^* = 0$. Compare these to the critical values reported in Ludlow and Enders (2000). If the sample value of F exceeds the critical value, reject the null hypothesis of linearity. Hence, the test is a 'supremum' test in that it uses the regression with the largest value of F. Next, it is possible to test if a second frequency is present. Incorporating each significant frequency yields an approximation of the time-varying autoregressive coefficient; in this way you can 'back-out' the form of the autoregressive coefficient.

Interpolating for our sample size of 177, the 10%, 5% and 1% critical values reported in Ludlow and Enders (2000) are 6.77, 7.57 and 9.40, respectively. We applied the procedure and found three frequencies. For the frequencies $k_1 = 58$ (one-third of the number of observations), $k_2 = 1$ and $k_3 = 8$, the sample values of F are 15.48, 9.33 and 8.65, respectively. The plot of the time path for the estimated autoregressive coefficient is shown in Figure 10.A.2. The clear impression is that inflation persistence rose steadily through the sample period until the late 1970s. In fact, the autoregressive coefficient is estimated to be in the neighbourhood of unity in 1978. Thereafter, inflation persistence falls fairly steadily. After 1996, the autoregressive coefficient has an average value of approximately 0.3.[5] The Fourier model seems to capture changes in the persistence of the Great Inflation that were also picked up by the TAR models estimated earlier. Moreover, it seems to explain the problematic estimates for the TAR models in all of the various samples reported in Tables 10.A.3 and 10.A.4. The TAR models imply a constant rate of inflation persistence in each of the two regimes. While this may be a convenient simplification depending on the problem at hand, instead it appears that inflation persistence can also be characterized as having steadily increased until the late 1970s and then steadily decreased until the middle to late 1990s.

5. CONCLUSIONS

It is well known that inference in a TAR model is difficult when the likelihood function is discontinuous. It was shown that the poor performance of TAR models is exacerbated when a continuous threshold process is estimated as a discontinuous process. However, application of the general-to-specific modelling strategy requires the estimation of a discontinuous model. The presence of the intercept terms in the estimating equation acts to make a TAR model appear symmetric. Moreover, the estimate of the threshold is biased towards the regime with the greatest amount of persistence.

Unfortunately, there is no plausible way to test for continuity at the threshold. To illustrate the issues, the dynamics of the US inflation rate were examined, and it was shown that we can reject the null hypothesis of linearity and simultaneously reject the null hypothesis of TAR adjustment. Put differently, we could not reject outright either the C-TAR or D-TAR specifications. An alternative model of inflation persistence was estimated using a Fourier approximation. The Fourier model shows that inflation persistence steadily increased until the late 1970s and then steadily decreased until the mid-1990s. From then on, inflation persistence has remained steady.

NOTES

1. The 1–3% figure has historical significance and roughly summarizes the inflation target ranges presently in place in many countries. See, for example, Bernanke et al. (1999) and Siklos (2002).
2. In other words, the plot shows 100 (log P_t – log P_{t-4}), where P_t is the price level. We also generated all econometric estimates based on inflation evaluated as 400 times (log P_t – log P_{t-1}) but the conclusions of this chapter are unaffected by this change.
3. The 1–3% figure has historical significance and roughly summarizes the inflation target ranges presently in place in many countries. See, for example, Bernanke et al. (1999) and Siklos (2002).
4. If there is a permanent change in inflation persistence at time T^* then an estimate over the full sample will suffer from serial correlation while individual estimates for each of the two sub-samples would not. As shown by Cukierman and Meltzer (1982), if agents cannot identify a permanent change when it occurs, this will show up as serial correlation in the data. The problem then is not the AR(1) model but the difficulty of distinguishing permanent from transitory shocks to the inflation process. Since it is important to model both types of shocks, the procedure outlined in this chapter may be useful. This will be especially true following 'violent' changes in a series due to some large shock. This possibility is clearly evident in the behaviour of US inflation since the late 1950s.
5. We repeated the method using the core inflation rate. However, no low frequency was found to be associated with an F value that was statistically significant.

REFERENCES

Alogoskoufis, G. and R. Smith (1991), 'The Phillips Curve, the Persistence of Inflation, and the Lucas Critique: Evidence from Exchange Rate Regimes', *American Economic Review*, **81**, 1254–1275.

Becker, R., W. Enders and S. Hurn (2004), 'Testing for Time Dependence in Parameters', *Journal of Applied Econometrics*, forthcoming.

Benati, L. (2002), 'Investigating Inflation Persistence Across Monetary Regimes', Working Paper, Monetary Assessment and Strategy Division, Bank of England.

Bernanke, B., T. Laubach, F. Mishkin, and A. Posen (1999), *Inflation Targeting: Lessons from the International Experience*, Princeton: Princeton University Press.

Bleany, M. (2001), 'Exchange Rate Regimes and Inflation Persistence', *IMF Staff Papers*, **47**, 387–402.

Burdekin, R.C.K. and P.L Siklos (1999), 'Exchange Rate Regimes and Shifts in Inflation Persistence: Does Nothing Else Matter?', *Journal of Money, Credit and Banking*, **31**, 235–247.

Chan K.S. (1993) 'Consistency and Limiting Distribution of the Least Squares Estimator of a Threshold Autoregressive Model', *Annals of Statistics*, **21**, 520–533.

Cogley, T., and T.J. Sargent (2002a), 'Evolving Post-WWII Inflation Dynamics', in B. Bernanke and K. Rogoff (eds.), *NBER Macroeconomics Annual 2001,* Cambridge, MA.: The MIT Press.

Cogley, T. and T.J. Sargent (2002b), 'Second Thoughts on the Evolution of US Inflation Dynamics: Drifting Parameters and Stochastic Volatility', Working Paper, Stanford University.

Cukierman, A., and A.H. Meltzer (1982), 'What do Tests of Market Efficiency Show?', mimeo, August.

Davies R.B. (1987), 'Hypothesis Testing when a Nuisance Parameter is only Identified Under the Alternative', *Biometrika*, **47**, 33–43.

DeLong, J.B. (1997), 'America's Peacetime Inflation: The 1970s', in C.D. Romer and D. Romer (eds.), *Reducing Inflation: Motivation and Strategy,* Chicago: University of Chicago Press, pp.247–276.

DeLong, J.B. (2000), 'America's Historical Experience with Low Inflation', *Journal of Money, Credit and Banking*, **32**, 973–993.

Enders, W. and B. Falk (2001), 'Confidence Intervals in TAR Models with an Example Using Real US GDP', mimeo.

Hansen, B.E. (1999), 'The Grid Bootstrap and the Autoregressive Model', *The Review of Economics and Statistics*, **81**, 594–607.

Ireland, P.N. (1999), 'Does the Time-consistency Problem Explain the Behaviour of Inflation in the United States?', *Journal of Monetary Economics*, **44**(October), 279–292.

Ludlow, J. and W. Enders (2000), 'Estimating Non-linear ARMA Models Using Fourier Coefficients', *International Journal of Forecasting*, **16**, 333–347.

Sargent, T.J. (1999), *The Conquest of American Inflation,* Princeton, NJ: Princeton University Press.

Siklos, P.L. (1999), 'Inflation Target Design: Changing Inflation Performance and Persistence in Industrial Countries', *Review of the Federal Reserve Bank of St. Louis*, **81**, 47–58.

Siklos, P I. (2002), *The Changing Face of Central Banking: Evolutionary Trends Since World War II,* Cambridge: Cambridge University Press.

Taylor, J.B. (1997), 'Comment', in C.D. Romer and D. Romer (eds.), *Reducing Inflation: Motivation and Strategy*, Chicago: University of Chicago Press, pp.276–280.

APPENDIX

Table 10.A.1 Properties of the coefficient estimates

$\hat{\alpha}_1$		$\hat{\rho}_1$		$\hat{\alpha}_2$		$\hat{\rho}_2$		$\hat{\tau}$	
mean	s.e.	mean	s.e.	mean	s.e.	mean	s.e.	mean	s.e.
$\rho_1 = 0.3, \rho_2 = 0.3$									
0.0283	0.7901	0.2603	0.5025	−0.0365	0.9007	0.2569	0.5514	−0.0240	0.6840
		0.2494	0.2151			0.2514	0.2143	0.0010	0.2577
$\rho_1 = 0.3, \rho_2 = 0.6$									
−0.0281	0.6821	0.2893	0.4731	−0.2307	0.9334	0.4586	0.4629	−0.2531	0.7380
		0.2314	0.2769			0.5437	0.1737	−0.0208	0.3498
$\rho_1 = 0.3, \rho_2 = 0.9$									
−0.0772	0.4986	0.3235	0.4314	−0.5699	1.030	0.7049	0.2909	−0.9521	1.062
		0.2513	0.3593			0.8351	0.1421	−0.2697	0.8007
$\rho_1 = 0.3, \rho_2 = 0.95$									
−0.1390	0.4566	0.3820	0.4234	−0.7525	1.305	0.7587	0.2626	−1.543	1.502
		0.3430	0.3707			0.8700	0.1616	−0.7490	1.457
$\rho_1 = 0.6, \rho_2 = 0.6$									
0.1124	0.7894	0.5043	0.4253	−0.1289	0.8914	0.4979	0.4613	−0.0265	0.8229
		0.5200	0.2277			0.5216	0.2265	0.0011	0.4796
$\rho_1 = 0.6, \rho_2 = 0.9$									
0.0048	0.5918	0.5404	0.3774	−0.5743	1.137	0.6983	0.3212	−0.8817	1.198
		0.4998	0.3030			0.8104	0.1821	−0.2923	1.037
$\rho_1 = 0.6, \rho_2 = 0.95$									
−0.0557	0.5334	0.5679	0.3617	−0.7963	1.390	0.7439	0.2869	−1.524	1.628
		0.5388	0.3091			0.8489	0.1853	−0.7916	1.689
$\rho_1 = 0.90, \rho_2 = 0.90$									
0.3446	0.9656	0.7350	0.3028	−0.4076	1.096	0.7174	0.3321	−0.0519	1.682
		0.7652	0.2254			0.7590	0.2395	0.0136	1.757
$\rho_1 = 0.90, \rho_2 = 0.95$									
0.2521	0.9014	0.7429	0.2922	−0.6690	1.418	0.7472	0.3090	0.7769	2.118
		0.7621	0.2320			0.8040	0.2214	−0.5455	2.354
$\rho_1 = 0.95, \rho_2 = 0.95$									
0.4689	1.215	0.7720	0.2784	−0.5375	1.355	0.7563	0.3050	−0.0419	2.555
		0.8022	0.2154			0.7956	0.2267	−0.0292	2.898

Notes: For each (ρ_1, ρ_2) pair, the first row reports values when the series were estimated as a discontinuous process (D–TAR) and the second row reports values when the series were estimated as a continuous process (C–TAR).

Table 10.A.2 Changing inflation persistence in the USA

| | Coefficient estimates | | | | | |
| | α | | β | | R^2 | |
	CPI	Core	CPI	Core	CPI	Core
1958.2–2002.1	3.70	4.20	0.978	0.979	0.95	0.96
	(2.80)	(2.84)	(0.033)	(0.031)		
1958.2–1972.2	2.75	3.20	0.966	0.980	0.93	0.96
	(2.08)	(3.90)	(0.039)	(0.041)		
1972.4–1987.2	6.86	6.88	0.959	0.945	0.92	0.91
	(4.46)	(3.06)	(0.045)	(.045)		
1987.3–2002.1	2.33	1.69	0.960	0.987	0.87	0.97
	(1.88)	(3.87)	(0.067)	(0.041)		
1991.1–2002.1	2.30	2.35	0.815	0.903	0.85	0.97
	(0.42)	(0.28)	(0.053)	(0.034)		
1958.2–1982.2	8.11	9.98	0.985	0.988	0.96	0.96
	(12.42)	(19.57)	(0.033)	(0.033)		
1982.2–2002.1	2.85	3.11	0.853	0.859	0.78	0.91
	(0.50)	(0.284)	(0.064)	(0.069)		

Notes: CPI and core inflation defined in Figure 10.A.1. Estimates are based on least squares estimates of (10.1) with standard errors in parentheses. All coefficients are statistically significant at least at the 5% level of significance. Inflation in the CPI and core is measured on a quarterly basis (i.e., 100 ($\log P_t - \log P_{t-4}$)). 1972.2 marks the end of Bretton Woods, 1987.2 marks the end of Paul Volcker's chairmanship at the Board of Governors of the US Federal Reserve, 1991.1 marks the unofficial beginning of 'inflation targeting'. The last two estimates are based on a finding of an endogenous break in the inflation process at 1982.2 using the Perron–Vogelsang test.

*Table 10.A.3 Discontinuous threshold effects and asymmetric inflation
persistence in the United States*

(A) CPI – Coefficient estimates				
	α_1	α_2	ρ_1	ρ_2	τ
1958.1–2002.1	0.0002	0.002	0.979	0.571	0.0053
	(0.0003)	(0.001)	(0.020)	(0.276)	
1958.1–1972.2	0.0008	0.0019	0.916	0.416	0.0053
	(0.0007)	(0.0007)	(0.066)	(0.219)	
1972.4–1987.2	−0.0004	0.0007	1.001	1.085	0.009
	(0.0009)	(0.0002)	(0.046)	(0.351)	
1987.4–2002.1	0.0080	0.0003	0.352	0.934	0.0110
	(0.003)	(0.0005)	(0.242)	(0.075)	
1991.1–2002.1	0.0017	0.0025	0.745	0.423	0.0060
	(0.0005)	(0.016)	(0.064)	(0.339)	
1958.1–1982.2	0.0008	0.0019	0.960	0.416	0.00527
	(0.0003)	(0.001)	(0.027)	(0.360)	
1982.3–2002.1	0.0084	0.0010	0.283	0.840	0.01104
	(0.0030)	(0.0006)	(0.241)	(0.082)	

(B) Core – Coefficient estimates				
	α_1	α_2	ρ_1	ρ_2	τ
1958.1–2002.1	0.0025	0.0002	0.882	0.982	0.0154
	(0.0011)	(0.0003)	(0.049)	(0.031)	
1958.1–1972.2	0.0128	0.0002	0.117	0.969	0.0126
	(0.0049)	(0.0003)	(0.336)	(0.041)	
1972.4–1987.2	−0.0118	−0.00005	1.371	1.026	0.0254
	(0.0115)	(0.0009)	(0.415)	(0.056)	
1987.4–2002.1	0.0015	0.0007	0.863	0.881	0.0097
	(0.001)	(0.0004)	(0.091)	(0.058)	
1991.1–2002.1	−0.0008	0.0006	1.015	0.901	0.0090
	(0.0008)	(0.0004)	(0.071)	(0.054)	
1958.1–1982.2	0.0070	0.00005	0.714	1.016	0.0174
	(0.002)	(0.0003)	(0.100)	(0.036)	
1982.3–2002.1	0.0095	0.0003	0.224	0.958	0.0117
	(0.0140)	(0.0003)	(0.106)	(0.039)	

Notes: CPI and core inflation defined in Figure 10.A.1. Estimates are based on a version of
(10.1) with allowance for positive and negative deviations from the thresholds estimated as
explained in the text. Standard errors are in parentheses.

Table 10.A.4 Continuous threshold effects and asymmetric inflation persistence

(A) CPI

Samples	ρ_1	ρ_2	Threshold
1958.1–2002.1	0.987	0.608	0.00381
	(0.012)	(0.291)	
1958.1–1972.2	0.985	0.387	0.00331
	(0.027)	(0.286)	
1972.4–1987.2	0.984	0.720	0.00903
	(0.027)	(0.213)	
1987.4–2002.1	0.672	1.017	0.01150
	(0.172)	(0.031)	
1991.1–2002.1	0.653	0.999	0.00696
	(0.075)	(0.095)	
1958.1–1982.2	0.907	0.989	0.02773
	(0.074)	(0.013)	
1982.3–2002.1	0.933	0.410	0.00511
	(0.037)	(0.359)	

(B) Core

Samples	ρ_1	ρ_2	Threshold
1958.1–2002.1	0.945	0.995	0.01593
	(0.031)	(0.013)	
1958.1–1972.2	0.863	0.992	0.01258
	(0.135)	(0.016)	
1972.4–1987.2	0.710	0.978	0.02433
	(0.188)	(0.027)	
1987.4–2002.1	0.980	0.639	0.00570
	(0.016)	(0.316)	
1991.1–2002.1	0.883	0.593	0.00565
	(0.016)	(0.230)	
1958.1–1982.2	0.907	0.990	0.02273
	(0.074)	(0.013)	
1982.3–2002.1	0.529	1.000	0.01153
	(0.160)	(0.021)	

Notes: CPI and core inflation defined in Figure 10.A.1. Estimates are based on a version of (10.1) with allowance for positive and negative deviations from the thresholds estimated as explained in the text. Standard errors are in parentheses.

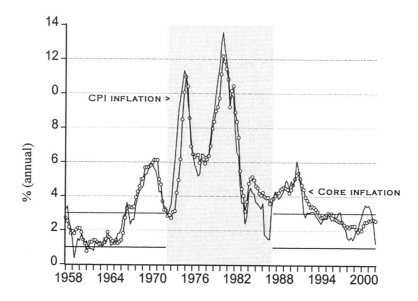

Source: FRED (www.stls.frb.org/fred/data/cpi.html)

Notes: CPI is the monthly consumer price index for all urban consumers (series *CPIAUCSL*), core is the monthly consumer price index excluding food and energy prices (series CPILFESL). All data were converted into annualized quarterly figures via application of the following transformation: 100 (log P_t – log P_{t-4}), where P_t is the level for the relevant price index at time t. The horizontal lines depict a possible zone of inflation 'tolerance' around 1–3% inflation. The shaded area highlights the era of the 'Great Inflation'.

Figure 10.A.1   Inflation in the USA, 1958–2002

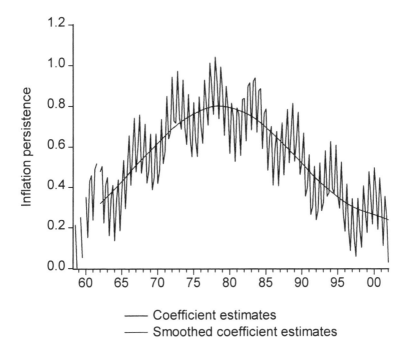

—— Coefficient estimates
—— Smoothed coefficient estimates

Notes: The 'rough' line represents the estimate of persistence based on the Fourier model (an AR(3) model) as described in the text. A 'smoothed' estimate is based on applying a Hodrick–Prescott filter with a smoothing parameter of 9600.

Figure 10.A.2   The time path of inflation persistence: the Fourier model

11. Predicting Incomplete Observations in Unbalanced Panels: A Kalman Filtering-Smoothing Approach

Alicia Rambaldi, R. Carter Hill and Howard Doran

1. INTRODUCTION

Unbalanced panels are frequently found in empirical settings. Common occurrences are data in which some countries can be tracked back longer than others for some variables of interest, or consumer panels on households. In this chapter we concentrate on the case where a particular variable of interest is only observed sporadically for the members of the panel, but a set of possible explanatory variables exist for the complete panel. We propose a methodology that optimally interpolates the incomplete observations and ensures that when an observation exists the prediction will equal the actual observation. We start by defining an econometric model for the variable of interest, which is written in state-space representation as a function of the observed data at each time period. The predictions gain information from other cross-sectional units in the panel through a contemporaneously correlated covariance matrix. The method produces a prediction (and prediction error) for each incomplete observation, estimates of the parameters of the original econometric model and one-step-ahead forecasts for each cross-section in the panel. The estimation and prediction are carried out using the Kalman filtering-smoothing algorithms. The method can handle both stationary and integrated cases. An empirical application is presented for the prediction of (log) sale prices for houses based on a hedonic price function.

   Earlier attempts at the problem of incomplete observations and measurement errors in panel data have been made. Schmid (1996) used a state-space specification within an expectation-maximisation (EM) algorithm to fit an autoregressive model of order one (AR(1)).[1] Our approach differs in that we use a prediction error decomposition method and maximise the likelihood function using a constrained maximisation algorithm. Other differences are that our measurement equations effectively set a constraint to ensure time-space consistency between observed and unobserved data (discussed in detail in Section 2) and our specification encompasses both the stationary and non-stationary cases. From a Bayesian approach to estimation, incomplete data can be handled through the use of data-augmentation algorithms (Tanner and Wong, 1987; Liu and Wu, 1999). The argument is that when the problem cannot be approximated closely to the normal likelihood, computation of a posterior distribution may provide more valid estimates of parameters and standard errors.

This chapter is concerned with obtaining a complete data set that is time-space consistent. Section 2 introduces the state-space representation of the problem from models that are widely used in the econometrics literature. The state-space representation of these models shows how the actual observations can be related to the full panel and the specific features of the state-space representation proposed in this chapter. Section 3 discusses the estimation of the parameters. Section 4 presents an empirical example of the estimation of a hedonic price function using the proposed procedure. Section 5 concludes.

2. A STATE-SPACE REPRESENTATION

We will assume a panel which is 'reasonably long' in the time dimension. Cross-sectional units are indexed by i ($i = 1, \ldots, N$) and the time periods by t ($t = 1, \ldots, T$).

Consider the linear regression model with autocorrelated error term:

$$y_{it} = \sum_{j=1}^{K} X_{it,j} \beta_j + \alpha_{it} \qquad (11.1)$$

where

$$\alpha_{it} = \rho \alpha_{i,t-1} + \varepsilon_{it} \qquad (11.2)$$

Grouping the observations in time periods, we have, in obvious notation,

$$\mathbf{y}_t = \mathbf{X}_t \boldsymbol{\beta} + \boldsymbol{\alpha}_t \qquad (11.3)^2$$

$$\boldsymbol{\alpha}_t = \mathbf{D} \boldsymbol{\alpha}_{t-1} + \boldsymbol{\varepsilon} \qquad (11.4)$$

where $\mathbf{D} = \rho \mathbf{I}_N$ and $\mathbf{I}_N$ is the identity. We denote $\text{cov}(\varepsilon_t)$ by $\mathbf{Q}_t$ and will assume a form for $\mathbf{Q}_t$ which is flexible enough to capture heteroscedasticity and contemporaneous correlation across cross-sectional units.

The prediction of $\mathbf{y}_t$ is defined from (11.3) as

$$\hat{\mathbf{y}}_t = \mathbf{X}_t \hat{\boldsymbol{\beta}} + \hat{\boldsymbol{\alpha}}_t \tag{11.5}$$

where $\hat{\boldsymbol{\beta}}$ is the generalised least squares (GLS) estimate of $\boldsymbol{\beta}$ and $\hat{\boldsymbol{\alpha}}_t$ an optimal predictor of $\boldsymbol{\alpha}_t$, $\hat{\boldsymbol{\alpha}}_t \sim (\boldsymbol{\alpha}_t, \mathbf{P}_t)$.

We are assuming that in each period t a subset of $\mathbf{y}_t$ is observed. We denote this subset by $\mathbf{y}_t^*$, where the dimension of $\mathbf{y}_t^*$ is N_t.

$$\mathbf{y}_t^* = \mathbf{Z}_t \mathbf{y}_t \tag{11.6}$$

where $\mathbf{Z}_t$ is a known $N_t \times N$ selection matrix.

Substituting (11.3) into (11.6), we obtain

$$\mathbf{y}_t^* = \mathbf{X}_t^* \boldsymbol{\beta} + \mathbf{Z}_t \boldsymbol{\alpha}_t \tag{11.7}$$

where $\mathbf{X}_t^* = \mathbf{Z}_t \mathbf{X}_t$, and is known.

Equations (11.4) and (11.7) are, respectively, the 'transition' and 'observation' equations of a state-space system in the unobservable 'state vector' $\boldsymbol{\alpha}_t$.

It is well known that the Kalman filter (KF) can be used to estimate (or predict) $\boldsymbol{\alpha}_t$ optimally from the observations $\mathbf{y}_1^*, \mathbf{y}_2^*, ..., \mathbf{y}_t^*$. In addition, the KF produces as outputs the one-step-ahead prediction error, $\boldsymbol{\upsilon}_t$ and its covariance matrix $\mathbf{F}_t$ (required to evaluate the likelihood function) and can be used to simultaneously obtain GLS estimates of $\boldsymbol{\beta}$. A full discussion of the KF algorithm and GLS estimation can be found in Harvey (1990, pp.100–110 and 130–133).

A crucial, and non-standard, feature of the observation equation (11.7) is that there is no error term. Thus, (11.7) can be viewed as imposing N_t linear constraints on $\boldsymbol{\alpha}_t$, of the form

$$\mathbf{Z}_t \boldsymbol{\alpha}_t = \mathbf{y}_t^* - \mathbf{X}_t^* \boldsymbol{\beta} \tag{11.8}$$

Doran (1992) has shown that the KF estimates $\hat{\boldsymbol{\alpha}}_t$ always satisfy the constraints, and so,

$$\mathbf{Z}_t \hat{\boldsymbol{\alpha}}_t = \mathbf{y}_t^* - \mathbf{X}_t^* \hat{\boldsymbol{\beta}}. \tag{11.9}$$

or,

$$\mathbf{y}_t^* = \mathbf{X}_t^*\hat{\boldsymbol{\beta}} + \mathbf{Z}_t\hat{\boldsymbol{\alpha}}_t \qquad (11.10)$$

It follows from (11.10) and (11.5) that

$$\mathbf{Z}_t\hat{\mathbf{y}}_t = \mathbf{X}_t^*\hat{\boldsymbol{\beta}} + \mathbf{Z}_t\hat{\boldsymbol{\alpha}}_t = \mathbf{y}_t^* . \qquad (11.11)$$

Thus from (11.6) and (11.11) it follows that

$$\mathbf{Z}_t\hat{\mathbf{y}}_t = \mathbf{Z}_t\mathbf{y}_t , \qquad (11.12)$$

which implies that if an element of $\mathbf{y}_t$, say y_{jt} is observed, then $\hat{y}_{jt} = y_{jt}$. This is an important feature of our prediction methodology.

3. ESTIMATION OF THE PARAMETERS OF THE STATE-SPACE REPRESENTATION

Let θ be a vector that includes all the unknown parameters in $\mathbf{D}$ and $\mathbf{Q}_t$. The KF operates under the assumption that $\boldsymbol{\beta}$ and θ are known. In practice this is not the case, requiring the parameter vectors $\boldsymbol{\beta}$ and θ to be estimated. An important feature of the KF is that it enables us to formulate the likelihood function in terms of the *prediction error* (this is discussed by Harvey, 1990, chapter 3):

$$\ell n L(\boldsymbol{\beta},\theta;\mathbf{y}) = -\frac{1}{2}\ell n(2\pi)\sum_{t=1}^{T}N_t - \frac{1}{2}\sum_{t=1}^{T}\ell n\,|\,\mathbf{F}_t\,| - \frac{1}{2}\sum_{t=1}^{T}\mathbf{v}_t'\mathbf{F}_t^{-1}\mathbf{v}_t \quad (11.13)$$

where $\mathbf{v}_t$, and $\mathbf{F}_t$ were defined in the previous section. Harvey (1993) shows that the decomposition that gives rise to (11.13) is *unconditional* on the initial observation. The decomposition is such that the initial observation is not assumed *fixed* but it has a defined density (i.e. $y_1 \sim N(\mu_1, F_1)$). This is of particular importance in the fixed effects model for example, where it is well known that the maximum likelihood estimator of the dynamic fixed effects panel model *conditional* on a fixed initial observation is biased (see Nerlove, 1999, section 3.5).

In most applications of this methodology, the dimension of $\boldsymbol{\beta}$ is likely to be large, as it might involve dummy variables as well as other explanatory regressors. It is then advantageous to implement an estimation method that does not involve a numerical optimisation of (11.13) over $\boldsymbol{\beta}$. This can be achieved by using a GLS maximum likelihood estimation (MLE) procedure such as that described in Harvey (1990, pp.130–133). For an initial value θ_0, of θ, the KF can be used to obtain $\hat{\beta}$.[3] This estimate is then used in the observation equations (11.3):

$$\mathbf{y}_t^* - \mathbf{X}_t^* \hat{\beta} = \mathbf{Z}_t \alpha_t$$

or

$$\mathbf{y}_t^{**} = \mathbf{Z}_t \alpha_t \qquad (11.14)$$

and the likelihood function that is numerically maximised is based on the observation equation (11.14). Using constrained numerical optimisation methods successive values of $\hat{\theta}$ are obtained, and at each step, the corresponding estimates $\hat{\beta}$ are also obtained.[4] The process is repeated until convergence.

The KF filtering-smoothing sequence (a detailed description can be found in Harvey, 1993, pp.85–89) is now used to obtain optimal predictions of the state vector, α_t and its covariance matrix, $\hat{\mathbf{P}}_t$.

The next section presents an empirical example dealing with the estimation and prediction of a hedonic price function.

4. A HEDONIC PRICE FUNCTION: AN EMPIRICAL EXAMPLE

Case and Quigley (1991, hereafter CQ) and Hill, Knight and Sirmans (1997, hereafter HKS) have suggested the combination of a hedonic model and a repeat sales model to estimate price indexes for durable assets. CQ introduced the idea and suggested a GLS estimation of the combined equations, while HKS proposed a maximum likelihood estimation procedure that accounts for the serial correlation in the hedonic data.

We show that the hedonic model with serially correlated errors and the repeat sales data can be written in the state-space form and estimated with the filtering-smoothing technique explained in previous sections. The technique provides a prediction for each time period within the sample and a one-step-ahead prediction for the full panel. As mentioned in the previous section, the in-sample predictions (both non-smooth and smooth) for the periods when the assets were actually sold coincide with the actual sales values through the constraint in (11.8).

The sample used for this application is of real estate sales in Stockton, California. The authors are grateful to Professor John Knight for providing the data set. The sample contains 243 houses for the period 1991 to 1996. The selling day, month and year are recorded for each house in the sample.

Most houses were sold twice during the sample period, while five houses were sold three times during the sample period. This illustration is intended to demonstrate the time-space-consistent results obtained through the proposed technique. Houses that were sold only once during the sample period were not included in this empirical example, although there is no technical impediment to doing so. The time period, t, was defined as a month. Therefore, the panel contains $N = 243$ houses and $T = 72$ months. A vector of housing character-istics including square feet of living area, number of bedrooms, number of bathrooms, number of storeys, and a dummy variable (equal to 1, if vacant at the time of sale), the age of the house and dummy variables for the year the house was sold (six dummies), was defined as X_{it} (1×12) in the hedonic model:

$$y_{it} = \sum_{j=1}^{K} X_{it}\beta_j + u_{it} \qquad (11.15)$$

and y_{it} is the natural log of the selling price for house i and month t. At any time period, t, N_t houses are sold. Following HKS, the u_{it} are assumed to follow a first-order autocorrelation scheme.

$$u_{it} = \rho u_{i,t-1} + \varepsilon_{it} \qquad (11.16)$$

and the ε_{it} are assumed to have zero mean and variance, σ_i^2. That is, the errors ε_{it} are heteroscedastic.[5]

The econometric model in (11.15) and (11.16) can be written in state-space form as follows:

$$\mathbf{y}_t^* = \mathbf{Z}_t\boldsymbol{\alpha}_t + \mathbf{X}_t^*\boldsymbol{\beta} \quad \text{(observation equations)}$$

$$\boldsymbol{\alpha}_t = \mathbf{D}\boldsymbol{\alpha}_{t-1} + \boldsymbol{\varepsilon}_t \quad \text{(transition equations)}$$

where

    $\boldsymbol{\alpha}_t$, the state vector of size $N = 243$,
    $\mathbf{y}_t^*$, the vector of (log) observed prices of size N_t,
    $\mathbf{Z}_t$ is an $N_t \times 243$ selection matrix,
    $\mathbf{X}_t^* = \mathbf{Z}_t\mathbf{X}_t$, is $N_t \times 12$,
    $\mathbf{X}_t$ is the matrix of explanatory variables for the full panel, 243×12,
    $\boldsymbol{\beta}$ is a vector of unknown parameters, 12×1,
    $\mathbf{D} = \rho\mathbf{I}_N$.
    $E(\boldsymbol{\varepsilon}_t) = \mathbf{0}$
    $E(\boldsymbol{\varepsilon}_t\boldsymbol{\varepsilon}_t') = \mathbf{Q}_t$

Table 11.1   GLS-MLE estimates of the parameters of the state-space model

Explanatory variable/parameter	GLS–ML estimates	Standard errors	Slope at mean price ($) $(\hat{\beta}_k \cdot price)$
Intercept	0.73[a]	0.1577	
Ft² of living area	0.00061 [a]	8.48e−5	76.14
Number of bedrooms	−0.00186	0.03469	
Number of bathrooms	0.12477 [a]	0.05015	15574.17
Number of storeys	8.56e−6	0.00023	
Age of the house	−0.11547[c]	0.07144	−14413.3
Dummies: $(100\hat{\beta}_k)$			
Vacant	−0.07426[c]	0.04144	−7.40
Sale year 92	−0.01537	0.19124	
Sale year 93	−0.09705	0.19403	
Sale year 94	−0.17851	0.19535	
Sale year 95	−0.07713	0.19594	
Sale year 96	−0.41528[b]	0.18002	−41.5
Parameters associated with the error structure:			
$\hat{\rho}$	0.215 [a]	0.03315	
$\hat{\sigma}$	2.2e−6 [a]	4.614e−7	
$\hat{c}$	0.8205 [a]	0.02315	
$\hat{\phi}$	0.6118 [a]	0.0805	

Notes:
a: Significant at the 1% level. b: Significant at the 5% level. c: Significant at the 10% level.

As mentioned in Section 2, $\mathbf{Q}_t$ should capture the heteroscedasticity and contemporaneous correlation across cross-sectional units. We will assume a form of $\mathbf{Q}_t$ that is constant over time, and denoted by $\mathbf{Q}$. Starting with the specification of the heteroscedasticity, we propose a form proportional to the square of the size of the house as follows:

$$\mathbf{Q}_{ii} = \sigma^2 \mathbf{A}_{ii}^2, \qquad (11.17)$$

where $\mathbf{A}$ is a diagonal matrix with elements equal to the size of the living area of house i in square feet; $\mathbf{A}_{ii}^2$ is the ith diagonal element of $\mathbf{AA}'$; σ^2 is a constant of proportionality; and $\mathbf{Q}_{ii}$ is the ith diagonal element of $\mathbf{Q}$.

We now introduce contemporaneous correlation across cross-sectional units by assuming

$$\mathbf{Q}_{ij} = \sigma^2 \phi \mathbf{A}_{ij}, \tag{11.18}$$

where ϕ is the cross-sectional correlation coefficient ($0 < \phi < 1$) and $\mathbf{A}_{ij}$ is the (i,j)th element of $\mathbf{AA}'$.

It is important to note that without the specification of the contemporaneous correlation, the model would treat each house as an island. It is easily verified algebraically that the optimal estimator of $\mathbf{\alpha}_{it}$ would only change when house i is sold. As a consequence, a more realistic model is to assume that general economic conditions affect all houses in a similar way.

To add flexibility to the specification we add one more parameter, c, with

$$\mathbf{Q} = \sigma^2 \mathbf{A}^c [\phi \, \mathbf{j}_N \mathbf{j}'_N + (1-\phi) \mathbf{I}_N] (\mathbf{A}^c)'. \tag{11.19}$$

Estimates of $\boldsymbol{\beta}$ were obtained following the GLS–MLE approach as explained in Section 3. A range of starting values were used for $\theta = (\sigma, c, \phi, \rho)'$ and the maximum likelihood estimates are presented in Table 11.1.

As expected, the size of the living area and number of bathrooms are positively related to the selling price, while the age of the house is negatively related to the selling price (significant at the 10% level with a t-ratio of -1.899). The number of bedrooms and number of storeys are not statistically significant in this sample. The 'vacant' dummy is significant at the 10% level (t-ratio of -1.73). All the year dummies are significant.

To appropriately interpret the results from a log-linear model, the parameter estimates of non-dummy variables have been multiplied by the average sale price to obtain a conventional slope, while dummies have a percentage interpretation. These results appear in the last column of Table 11.1. Thus, for example, an extra bathroom is expected to increase the average sale price by $15,574, an additional year of age is expected to decrease the average price by $14,413, and a vacant house will reduce the average sale price by 7.4%. The estimated model included an intercept and five dummies for the year of sale. The dummies for 1992 to 1995 were not significant. It appears that there is not enough information in this sample to accurately estimate the effect of the year on selling price.

The remaining parameters of the state-space model are all highly significant. The estimate of the cross-sectional correlation parameter, ϕ, is 0.61. This parameter measures the degree of correlation across (log) selling prices once basic characteristics have been taken into account. The transition equation's autocorrelation parameter, $\hat{\rho}$, is 0.215. This is the estimate of the autocorrelation coefficient of the AR(1) error term in the original econometric model (11.16). Finally the flexibility parameter, c, defined earlier has an estimate of 0.82.[6]

Table 11.2   Data of the houses displayed in the figures

Selling price	Ft² living area	Bed- rooms	Bath- rooms	Age	Storeys	Vacant	Sale month	Sale year	ID
118,500	1586	3	2	17	1	0	11	93	6
108,650	1586	3	2	20	1	1	9	96	6
135,000	1885	3	2	43	1	0	6	93	10
125,000	1885	3	2	45	1	0	11	95	10
292,500	2505	4	2.5	18	1	0	8	91	110
250,000	2505	4	2.5	20	1	0	3	94	110
247,000	2505	4	2	22	1	0	12	96	110

Using these estimates, the Kalman filtering-smoothing sequence is run one more time to obtain the complete series of the state vector and predicted house sale prices. Three houses were selected from the 243 in the sample to illustrate the non-smooth and smoothed predictions of sales price obtained by this method. The data for the three houses are presented in Table 11.2. Figures 11.A.1 to 11.A.3 plot the smoothed predictions of the sales price. In all cases note that the monthly predictions and actual sales price coincide with each other when the house was sold. These points have been marked with a circle in the figures.

5. CONCLUSIONS

In this chapter we propose a methodology that optimally interpolates the incomplete observations of a variable of interest in an unbalanced panel. The method ensures that when an actual observation exists the prediction will equal the actual observation. We start by defining an econometric model for the variable of interest. The econometric model is written in state-space representation as a function of the *observed* data at each time period. The predictions gain information from other cross-sectional units in the panel through a contemporaneously correlated error. The method produces a prediction (and prediction error) for each incomplete observation, estimates of the parameters of the original econometric model and one-step-ahead forecasts for each cross-section in the panel. The estimation and prediction are carried out using Kalman filtering-smoothing algorithms. The method can handle both stationary and integrated cases. An empirical application is presented for the prediction of (log) sale prices for houses based on a hedonic price model.

NOTES

1. The seminal work in this literature is by Dempster, Laird and Rubin (1976).
2. We note here that an alternative to (11.1) is the dynamic fixed effects model. This model can also be written in standard state-space representation and this is presented in Appendix B.
3. The same Kalman filter is applied separately to the observations, y^{**}_j and each of the explanatory variables in X_t, to produce transformed $\ddot{y}$ and $\ddot{X}$. A WLS estimate $\beta(\theta_0)$ is obtained by regressing $\ddot{y}$ on $\ddot{X}$.
4. Fully tested *GAUSS* procedures are available from the authors.
5. HKS assumed a multiplicative model.
6. The authors are currently working on concentrating the factor of proportionality, σ^2, out of the likelihood function. This should considerably simplify the numerical optimisation as the remaining parameters are either bounded, ρ and ϕ, or are expected within a known range, c.

REFERENCES

Case, B. and J.M. Quigley (1991), 'The Dynamics of Real Estate Prices', *The Review of Economics and Statistics*, **73**, 50–58.

Dempster, A.P., N.M. Laird and D.B. Rubin (1977), 'Maximum Likelihood from Incomplete Data via the EM Algorithm', *Journal of the Royal Statistical Society*, Series B (Methodological), **39**, 1–38.

Doran, H.E. (1992), 'Constraining Kalman Filter and Smoothing Estimates to Satisfy Time-varying Restrictions', *The Review of Economics and Statistics*, **74**, 568–572.

Harvey, A.C. (1990), *Forecasting, Structural Time Series Models and the Kalman Filter*, Cambridge: Cambridge University Press.

Harvey, A.C. (1993), *Time Series Models*, 2nd edition, Cambridge, MA: The MIT Press.

Hill, R.C., J.R. Knight and C.F. Sirmans (1997), 'Estimating Capital Asset Price Indexes', *The Review of Economics and Statistics*, **79**, 226–233.

Liu, J.S. and Y.N. Wu (1999), 'Parameter Expansion for Data Augmentation', *Journal of the American Statistical Association*, **94**, 1264–1274.

Nerlove, M. (1999), 'Properties of Alternative Estimators of Dynamic Panel Models: An Empirical Analysis of Cross-country Data for the Study of Economic Growth', in C. Hsiao, M.H. Pesaran and K. Lahiri (eds.) *Analysis of Panels and Limited Dependent Variable Models*, Cambridge: Cambridge University Press.

Schmid, C.H. (1996), 'An EM Algorithm Fitting First-order Conditional Autoregressive Models to Longitudinal Data', *Journal of the American Statistical Association*, **91**, 1322–1330.

Tanner, M.A. and W.H. Wong (1987), 'The Calculation of Posterior Distributions by Data Augmentation', *Journal of the American Statistical Association*, **82**, 528–540.

APPENDIX A

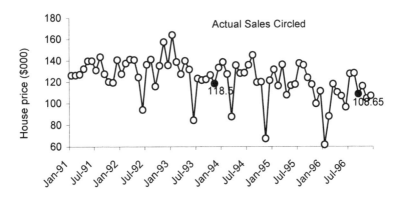

Figure 11.A.1 Complete data of house value and actual selling prices. house no.6

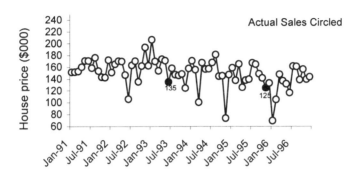

Figure 11.A.2 Complete data of house value and actual selling prices. house no.10

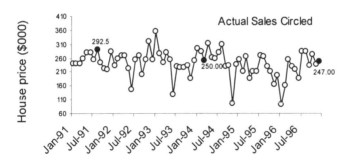

Figure 11.A.3 Complete data of house value and actual selling prices. house no.110

APPENDIX B

State-Space Representation of the Dynamic Fixed Effects Model for An Unbalanced Panel

We start with the model

$$y_{it} = \delta y_{i,t-1} + \sum_{j=1}^{K} X_{it,j}\beta_j + \varepsilon_{it}.$$

Let $y_t = (y_{1t}, y_{2t}, \ldots, y_{Nt})'$ and write it as

$$y_t = \delta y_{t-1} + X_t\beta + \varepsilon_t$$

For an unbalanced panel, at any time period t, the observations are given by

$$y_t^* = Z_t y_t$$

where Z_t is a known selection matrix. Setting $\beta_t = \beta_{t-1}$, and defining the state vector as

$$\alpha_t = (y_t', \beta_t')'$$

we can write a transition equation

$$\alpha_t = \begin{bmatrix} \delta I & X_t \\ 0 & I \end{bmatrix} \alpha_{t-1} + \begin{bmatrix} \varepsilon_t \\ 0 \end{bmatrix}$$

or

$$\alpha_t = D\alpha_{t-1} + \upsilon_t \qquad (11.B.1)$$

where

$$\mathbf{D} = \begin{bmatrix} \delta\mathbf{I} & \mathbf{X}_t \\ \mathbf{0} & \mathbf{I} \end{bmatrix} \text{ and } \boldsymbol{v}_t = \begin{bmatrix} \boldsymbol{\varepsilon}_t \\ \mathbf{0} \end{bmatrix},$$

and an observation equation

$$\begin{aligned} \mathbf{y}_t^* &= [\mathbf{S}_t, \mathbf{0}]\boldsymbol{\alpha}_t \\ \mathbf{y}_t^* &= \mathbf{Z}_t\boldsymbol{\alpha}_t \end{aligned} \tag{11.B.2}$$

where

$$\mathbf{Z}_t = [\mathbf{S}_t, \mathbf{0}].$$

Then, the state-space representation of the model is given by (11.B.1) and (11.B.2). When the panel is unbalanced, estimation of the state-space form, for both the stationary and non-stationary cases, can be handled by the methodology presented in this chapter.

Index